Greek Religion and Society

Greek Religion and Society

Edited by

P. E. EASTERLING

Fellow of Newnham College, Cambridge

and

J. V. MUIR

King's College London

With a Foreword by

SIR MOSES FINLEY

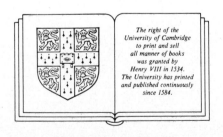

The right of the
University of Cambridge
to print and sell
all manner of books
was granted by
Henry VIII in 1534.
The University has printed
and published continuously
since 1584.

CAMBRIDGE UNIVERSITY PRESS
Cambridge
London   New York   New Rochelle
Melbourne   Sydney

Published by the Press Syndicate of the University of Cambridge
The Pitt Building, Trumpington Street, Cambridge CB2 1RP
32 East 57th Street, New York, NY 10022, USA
10 Stamford Road, Oakleigh, Melbourne 3166, Australia

First published 1985
Reprinted 1986

Printed in Great Britain
at the University Press, Cambridge

Library of Congress catalogue card number: 84-19964

British Library Cataloguing in Publication Data

Greek religion and society.
1. Greece – Religious life and customs
I. Easterling, P. E.   II. Muir, J. V.
306'.6'0938   DF 121

ISBN 0 521 24552 4 hard covers
ISBN 0 521 28785 5 paperback

FOR
JOHN SHARWOOD SMITH

Contents

List of illustrations   viii
Preface   xi
Foreword by Sir Moses Finley   xiii

1 *On making sense of Greek religion*   1
JOHN GOULD University of Bristol

2 *Greek poetry and Greek religion*   34
P. E. EASTERLING Newnham College, Cambridge

3 *Early Greek views about life after death*   50
N. J. RICHARDSON Merton College, Oxford

4 *Greek temples: Why and where?*   67
J. N. COLDSTREAM University College London

5 *The Greek religious festivals*   98
PAUL CARTLEDGE Clare College, Cambridge

6 *Delphi and divination*   128
SIMON PRICE Lady Margaret Hall, Oxford

7 *Greek art and religion*   155
MARTIN ROBERTSON, Cambridge

8 *Religion and the new education: the challenge of the Sophists*   191
J. V. MUIR King's College London

Notes   219
Notes for further reading   231
Index   235

Illustrations

1   Perachora, clay model of a temple, restored. From H. Payne, *Perachora* I (1940) pl. 9b   70

2   Samos, early temples of Hera, plans. (a) From *Ath.Mitt.* 58 (1933) 162 fig. 14 (b) From H. Berve and G. Gruben, *Greek Temples, Theatres and Shrines* (1963) 450 fig. 117 (hereafter *GTTS*)   71

3   Olympia, temple of Hera, plan. After *Olympia* II (1892).   74

4   Kerkyra, temple of Artemis, plan and restored elevation. After *Korkyra* I (1940) fig. 56, p. 26   75

5   Priene, temple of Athena Polias, plan. From A. W. Lawrence, *Greek Architecture* (1968) fig. 105   76

6   Priene, model reconstruction of the town. Berlin (E). Photo: Antikensammlung, Staatliche Museen zu Berlin   77

7   Olympia, temple of Zeus, restored elevation with east pediment, and cross-section with view of metopes. After *Olympia* II (1892)   79

8   Olympia, temple of Zeus, plan. After *Olympia* II (1892)   80

9   Olympia, temple of Zeus, cross-section through *cella* showing position of cult-statue. After *Olympia* I (1892)   81

10 Bassae, temple of Apollo. Photo: J. N. Coldstream   82

11 Bassae, temple of Apollo. (a) *GTTS* 43. (b) E. Kirsten, 1938   83

12 Segesta, the temple. Photo: J. N. Coldstream   85

13 Selinus, temple F, plan and restored elevation. J. Hulot and G. Fougères, 1910   86

14 Eleusis, model reconstruction by J. Travlos. Eleusis Museum. Photo: J. Travlos   87

15 Eleusis, *Telesterion*, successive temples. After J. Travlos, 1950   89

16   Eleusis, *Anaktoron*, imaginative reconstruction of the Mysteries. After J. Travlos, 1950/1   91

17   Kos, sanctuary of Asclepius, restoration. From Lawrence, pl. 109a   92

18   Kos, sanctuary of Asclepius. Photo: J. N. Coldstream   93

19   Didyma, temple of Apollo, restored elevation and plan. After H. Knackfuss, *Didyma* I.3 (1940)   94

20   Didyma, temple of Apollo, interior court, or *adyton*. Photo: J. N. Coldstream   95

21   The world of the competitors at Delphi. Redrawn from J. Swaddling, *The Ancient Olympic Games* (1980) p. 8   104

22   The site of Olympia. Redrawn from Swaddling p. 36   105

23   The development of the Olympic programme. From Swaddling p. 38   108

24   The sanctuary of Zeus at Olympia. Redrawn from M. I. Finley and H. W. Pleket, *The Olympic Games: The First Thousand Years* (1976) fig. 8   109

25   The theatre of Dionysus at Athens. Redrawn from R. E. Wycherley *The stones of Athens* (1978) fig. 60   122

26   View of Delphi. Photo: Editions 'Hannibal', Greece   128

27   Plan of the Sanctuary of Apollo. *GTTS* 328 fig. 19. After P. de la Coste-Messelière, *Au Musée de Delphes* (1936) pl. 50   130

28   Plan of the Temple of Apollo. Redrawn from G. Roux, *Delphes* (1976) figs. 4 and 7   135

29   Dionysus greets Apollo. Scene on a red-figure krater. Leningrad, Hermitage 0.28. Photo: Hermitage   136

30   Hypothetical reconstruction of the *adyton*. From G. Roux, *Delphes* fig. 8   137

31   Themis seated on a tripod. From a drawing in A. Furtwängler and K. Reichhold, *Griechische Vasenmalerei* (1904–32) pl. 140, 3   138

32   Orestes flees for protection to the *omphalos*. Scene on an early Apulian volute-krater. Naples 3249. From a drawing in Furtwängler and Reichhold, pl. 179   145

33   Free copy of Pheidias's Parthenos from Pergamon. Berlin (E). Photo: Museum   156

34   The Parthenon. Photo: Alison Frantz   161

35   Kleobis and Biton. Delphi 467, 1524. Photo: Alison Frantz   163

36   Piraeus Apollo. Athens, National Museum. Photo: Museum   166
37   Geneleos group. Samos. Photo: Deutsches Archäologisches Institut, Athens   167
38   Archaic Attic grave-relief. Athens, National Museum 4472. Photo: Museum   170
39   Classical Attic grave-relief. Athens, National Museum 833. Photo: Museum   172
40   Attic votive relief, fourth century. Athens, National Museum 3369. Photo: Museum   173
41   Relief from Eleusis. Athens, National Museum 126. Photo: Alison Frantz   183
42   Attic funeral *lekythos*. Munich Antikensammlung 2797. Photo: Museum   186
43   Bronze krater from Derveni. Thessaloniki Museum. Photo: Museum   188
44   Bronze statuette copying Tyche of Antioch. Florence, Museo Archeologico 2341. Photo: Museum   189

Preface

This book has two purposes. First, it is intended for students in the upper forms of schools, undergraduates, and others who may be studying aspects of Greek society and Greek civilization and who need access to a useful range of modern scholarly views on Greek religion. Second, it is intended by the editors and by all who have contributed to it as a small token of gratitude from the world of scholarship to a modest and remarkable man who has devoted a great part of his life to maintaining the vigour of the Classics in education and for whom Greek religion has been a perennial subject of fascination.

The editors would like to express their thanks to the contributors for their ready co-operation, to Sir Moses Finley for writing the Foreword, and to Cambridge University Press for their help in producing the book.

Cambridge   P. E. EASTERLING
London   J. V. MUIR
October 1984

Foreword

M. I. FINLEY

As is stressed by Cartledge later in this volume, religion was one area of human behaviour in which the archaic and classical Greeks left no legacy, in any strict sense, to the modern world. That role was taken over by Christianity, and, however much Christianity in its early period was formulated in language and concepts borrowed from Greek philosophy, it nonetheless created an unbridgeable divide from the pagan religions that came before. That divide and the absence of a legacy are responsible for the desperately alien quality of much of ancient Greek religious belief and practice.

It follows that the effort to comprehend is an extremely difficult one. There is a familiar, traditional approach that really can no longer be tolerated, what Gould calls 'decoding'. It has two facets. One is to draw lines between the superstitions of the untutored masses and the rational beliefs of the intellectual (and social) élite. That requires us either to forget or to explain away Socrates' last words: 'I owe a cock to Asclepius, Crito. You pay it and do not neglect it' (Plato, *Phaedo* 118). The other is to hunt for similarities and then to play them up far beyond anything they can bear. The Greeks – more correctly, the educated élite among them – were thereby converted into good chaps basically like us. A case in point is the equation heroes = saints, which I find worse than unhelpful. No doubt one appealed to Heracles when in trouble as some today appeal to Santa Lucia, and no doubt the Greeks were faced like us with tensions and uncertainties, with unanswered and unanswerable questions. But that no more justifies confusing the quality of the attempted solutions in religion than it warrants confusing modern physicians and surgeons with witch-doctors because they both try to grapple with disease and death.

A new way of looking at Greek religion is therefore required, and in recent decades that has been one of the central efforts in the study of antiquity. This volume reflects that effort. And one important point that immediately emerges (from the enterprise as a whole, not necessarily from each chapter in this book) is that for parallels and comparative insights, one must turn to such people as the Dinka or Azande of Africa. In doing so, it is immediately essential to add, one is not conjuring up the spirit of James Frazer and Jane Harrison at the turn of the present century. Value-judgements, based on our own value-systems, are taboo. The current approach, which draws on a new generation of anthropologists, such as Evans-Pritchard, Geertz and Lienhardt, rejects the very notion of 'primitive' or of a 'rational' as against a 'non-rational' (or even 'irrational') approach to the questions to which religion addresses itself. However, at least one difference between the ancient Greeks and their modern parallels strikes me, for one, as important: we know about Greek spirits and Greek possession from Pindar and Herodotus and Euripides, themselves Greeks, whereas about the Dinka we must rely on Professor Lienhardt of Oxford. The Dinka have produced no poets, no scientists, no philosophers. They are not even literate. To that extent, a difference in cultural levels is hardly deniable.

How fundamentally alien Greek religion was (to our eyes) is most easily shown by a simple listing, in which I shall try to stress aspects of religion that have been widespread since antiquity and not to consider phenomena that may be thought to be a peculiarity of the twentieth century. (Exceptions are known to every point that follows, but they do not invalidate the generalizations.)

(1) Greek religion had no sacred books (until the late appearance of such anomalies as Orphic texts or the so-called Sibylline books), no revelation, no creed. It also lacked any central ecclesiastical organization or the support of a central political organization. The Greek world was a cultural concept, an abstrac-

tion. Individual city-states had virtually unlimited authority in religious affairs as in everything else. However, there was no body with the power or the authority either to lay down rules for the whole Greek world or to enforce any. Hence there could, strictly speaking, be neither Greek orthodoxy nor Greek heresy. When Herodotus wrote that it was Homer and Hesiod who 'first fixed for the Greeks the genealogy of the gods, gave the gods their titles, divided among them then their honours and functions, and defined their images' (2.53), he was pointing to the essential truth that it was only the cultural authority of the poets that preserved a measure of unity and coherence among the religious ideas and practices of Greek communities that in his day extended from the eastern end of the Black Sea almost to the Straits of Gibraltar. That unity is remarkable under the circumstances, but the extreme diversity, at least in details, magnifies by many times the burden of the modern student. The tradition had it that when Anaxagoras fled from Athens because of a charge of blasphemy under a law of about 433 B.C., he was welcomed in Lampsacus, where he was buried with honours a few years later. And Plato has Socrates informed in prison that if he would flee he would receive a warm welcome from Crito's friends in Thessaly.

(2) Although large numbers of men and women were involved in the administration of religion, in the care of temples and altars or sacred sites, in the conduct of festivals and sacrifices, and so forth, and though we call them 'priests' in modern languages, a priesthood as that vocation is understood in many post-ancient religions did not exist. The great majority of so-called priests were simply public officials whose duties in whole or in part, usually the latter, included responsibility for some portion of the religious activity of the community. More often than not, they were selected by lot and they held office for only a year or even six months (as at Delphi), though some exceptional priesthoods were hereditary and, eventually, quite a number became life offices available for purchase (openly and legally). There was no special training, no sense of a vocation.

Greek 'priests', in sum, were customarily not holy men; they were also not particularly expert or qualified in matters pertaining to their duties in office. Yet someone had to settle disagreements over the rules of sacrifice or matters of pollution and purification or of blasphemy, and it is remarkable how ill-informed we are as to who these people were and as to their activity. Athens had a small number of such official experts, called *exēgētai*, but so far as we know not before about 400 B.C.; so did some other cities, and others may have relied on unofficial experts. Against that apparently small number there were countless unofficial 'holy men', like the oracle-mongers and soothsayers about whom Thucydides was so contemptuous, and against whom, he says (8.1.1), the Athenians turned in anger when their predictions of a successful invasion of Sicily in 415 B.C. were falsified by the disaster of 413. The contrast with Rome is striking: there divination was a state matter, though also in the hands of laymen, resorted to with staggering frequency and according to recognized rules, whereas private diviners and soothsayers were almost, though not entirely, unknown. The latter, it need hardly be said, led an uncertain existence everywhere, for their prosperity and sometimes their safety depended on their 'success'.

(3) It follows as a matter of simple logic that places of worship were also radically different from anything known in later ages – despite the fact that the temple was the most expensive and imposing building of the Greek city. To begin with, the temple was hardly ever 'a place for congregational worship' (Coldstream): the exceptions, such as the *Telestērion* at Eleusis or the temple of Asclepius in Epidaurus, were rare and in fact help 'prove the rule'. The temple was the house of the god, where his or her cult-image and often his or her treasure were stored; where, therefore, public access was severely restricted as to both numbers and times. The treasure was, after all, often very considerable (including costly decorations of the statue) and a temptation to robbery. Furthermore, wherever very large statues existed, most spectacularly in

the temple of Zeus at Olympia, little space was left for anyone else.

The siting of Greek temples was extraordinarily varied, and today we often fail to grasp the reasons behind a particular choice. It would be neat if the main temples of a city were regularly on its acropolis, but that was not the case. Apart from the fact that not all cities had an acropolis, there appears to have been a tendency in the early years of stone-temple construction to locate them on frontiers rather than at the centre. The ridge of temples in Sicilian Agrigentum is an extreme illustration. Sometimes there was an obvious functional reason for the location, as in temples of Poseidon, god of the sea, on headlands and promontories (such as Cape Sunium in Attica). But again that was not always the case: the temple of Poseidon in Corinth was in the city centre. And there were great numbers of shrines, for example at springs, that were neither temples nor in a sense structures at all. The one indispensable mark of a sacred shrine was an altar.

The centrality of the altar had two fundamental implications. The first is that most public worship and much private worship as well took place out of doors. In so far as an Olympian divinity was involved, the image was taken out of its temple-home for the occasion and 'presided' over the festivities, whatever they were, whether processions, games, dances or sacrifices. The second implication is that the sacrifice was the central act in worship, if one may be singled out. It is hard to think of a public action in which some god or gods were not sacrificed to as a preliminary step in seeking divine favour and support.

Vegetable and animal matter were both frequently employed (and a number of different liquids were poured out as libations), and the burning of parts of animals was of itself a sufficient excuse for out-of-doors worship. It is necessary to stress 'parts of animals' because the sacrifice was not only a way of offering the gods food and drink, it was also a way of establishing a table fellowship in which human beings shared with the divine. The feast commonly followed the sacrifice, and the edible parts of the sacrificial animals were largely reserved for the feast. Many meanings can be read into the burnt offering, not all of them logically compatible. One is the idea of a continuum that held together all living parts of the universe; men shared in the feast with each other as they did with the gods.

(4) Given the political fragmentation of the Greek world, with the corresponding autonomy of hundreds of city-states, given the fact that the administration of public religion was within the province of the state, and given the large number of divine and semi-divine beings to be honoured, it is hardly surprising that the total number of festivals was 'extraordinarily high, both absolutely and as a proportion of the days in the year given over' to them (Cartledge). In Athens, which appears to have been somewhat exceptional, one third or perhaps slightly more of the days in each year were marked by one festival or another (though of course not all of them were celebrated by everyone).

The range of rituals at these festivals was no less extraordinary, many of them having originated in the early archaic period (or even before) and having therefore become more or less unintelligible to the participants in classical times (and to us). But in general they comprised sacrifices, 'hymns', dances and processions, which are intelligible enough in essence if not in the details. There was, however, one feature of a number of festivals that was peculiarly, perhaps uniquely, Greek. That was the practice of competition in athletics, music, dance and theatre (but never in the plastic arts).

The most striking aspect of this competitive ritual was the way in which it dominated some of the major panhellenic festivals, including the 'Big Four', the games at Olympia (for Zeus), Delphi (for Apollo), Nemea, about two-thirds of the way from Corinth to Mycenae (also for Zeus), and at the Isthmus of Corinth (for Poseidon). All four were in places that were politically insignificant, whereas the efforts of Athens to elevate its own Panathenaic festival to comparable standing were unsuccessful: there was too much danger to the rest of the Greek world in allowing an already powerful state to acquire the added halo of a major religious festival. Tragedy and comedy were written for a similar (annual) competition in Athens, but the Greater Dionysia, at which the new plays were performed each year, made no claim to panhellenic religious status. Some idea of the place of these particular festivals in Greek culture may be gained from the fact that the Olympic Games, the greatest of all and the only one that remained exclusively an athletic competition, were repeated every four years for more than a thousand years from their foundation, traditionally in 776 B.C.. An estimated 40,000 men attended, many coming from considerable distance – the largest number of people assembled in one place on a particular occasion (other than a few major battles) in all Greek history.

It would be absurd to imagine that they all came to Olympia from the same motives and had the same reactions, or even that their motives and reactions were somehow consistent with each other. Ambiguity was inherent in Greek religious thinking and practice: the gods, after all, could be forces for disorder as well as for order, their shrines were 'holy but dangerous places' (Easterling). All this was abundantly manifest in their myths, their accounts of what lay behind the sacred places and practices.

A myth is a story, but it is not only a story: it was the standard Greek device of explanation in the sphere of the divine and the religious. Like everything else we have been concerned with, myth was open-ended: the myth-making process went on throughout Greek history. We can see it at work only in the restricted sphere of imaginative literature, where we can watch, so to speak, while Aeschylus or Euripides shapes or re-shapes myths. In a way, that leaves us with a distorted picture, for the 'original' myth-making process was a non-literary one in inception and for most of the centuries thereafter. I do not underestimate the contribution of the poets: Herodotus' remark about Homer and Hesiod which I have already quoted sums up their role in tidying up an inherently untidy, indeed chaotic, accumulation of tales. But one wonders how much of this process, this conversion of myth into an art-form, affected the day-to-day life of ordinary Greeks, with which religion was enmeshed in every crevice. In a fundamentally non-literate world, myth performed a variety of roles and functions. It gave shape and meaning to the past, to history, for one thing. Our concern here, however, is with myth in its particular role as the vehicle for religious explanation, and the danger must be recognized of 'rationalizing' it by over-stressing its most artistic, most intellectual manifestations.

That brings us back to the question I touched upon at the beginning, the significance of differences in social status and education. That there was no simple correlation should be obvious: one need only think of Nicias or Xenophon, men of wealth and education, whose almost oppressive conventional piety was abundantly displayed, or of the quite vicious sneering at Socrates in the *Clouds* of Aristophanes (the impact of which is clearly noticed by Plato, *Apology* 19c–d). But there were the famous sceptics whom Muir discusses, Xenophanes in the sixth century B.C., Protagoras and Thucydides in the fifth, and others. How much impact did they have, and on whom? That kind of question is hard enough to grapple with in a world we can observe directly; it is much worse in a world that is long since dead.

These are the kinds of questions this book is concerned with. The effort to make sense of ancient Greek religion is, as Gould says in his closing words, not of merely antiquarian concern; it 'may perhaps tell us as much about our world and our society'. It is fitting, finally, that such an enterprise should be dedicated to the presiding genius over the renewal in our time of classical studies in this country, John Sharwood Smith.

1

On making sense of Greek religion

JOHN GOULD*

> The notion is that life involves maintaining oneself between
> contradictions that can't be solved by analysis.
>   William Empson, note to *Bacchus* (*The Gathering Storm*, 1940)

To talk meaningfully about the religion of another culture is not
easy, and requires of us some degree of tact and imagination. We
need to be aware of the pitfalls. To begin with, it will seem all too
clear that what we are dealing with is a human invention, a 'fiction' constructed by men for their own purposes – an interpretation which we can never quite give to the religion of our own
culture, even if we have rejected it. To make that assumption will
not help us to understand though it may boost our sense of
superiority. And secondly, there is the difficulty, if not the
impossibility, of avoiding thinking about someone else's religion
as a kind of exercise in 'decoding', in translating myth and ritual
into a 'natural' language (our own, of course) in which these things
can be made to yield their true sense, which may be hidden from
those who carry out the rituals and who recount the myths.

   Moreover, to propose to 'make sense' of Greek religion is to
lay oneself at once open to objections. Why should we suppose
that Greek religion does 'make sense', when to many it seems
obvious that it does not and cannot? There are two different sorts
of objections that can be made. One, that the whole undertaking is
unsound in method, because there is no such single *thing* as 'Greek
religion' and there can be no 'making sense' in any unified way of
so vast and disparate a body of data as the data which *we* put

1

together and call 'Greek religion': the best we can hope for will be
no more than piecemeal explanations of a particular ritual or a
particular myth. The second objection is more insidious: it is that
what we are dealing with is itself without sense, a rag-bag without
significance, an agglomeration of literary 'devices' and mere
'superstitious' survivals that did not 'make sense' to any ancient
Greek whom we can take seriously; to the backwoodsmen
(perhaps) among the Attic peasantry, but not (surely) to Homer,
nor (evidently) to Xenophanes or Heraclitus or Euripides or
Thucydides or Plato . . . That is a view which seems to be held as
self-evident by a large number of undergraduates, and, I suspect,
sixth-formers, and is not unknown among scholars.

I want in this essay to argue the contrary, in the belief that not
only does this approach enable us to understand more, but also
that it is consistent with more of what we know both about ancient
Greeks and about other societies in the way they understand the
world about us. I want to put forward a description of Greek
religion which sees it as constituting a complex and quite subtle
statement about what the world is like and a set of responses for
dealing with that world, and in doing so I shall make use of one or
two analogies and assumptions which I had better begin by
making clear.

My first point is negative: it will not be helpful, I think, to start
any enquiry into Greek religious ideas by drawing a distinction
(whether implicit or explicit) between valid or correct ways of
thinking about the world, on the one hand, and invalid ones, on
the other; between 'mystical', 'magical' or 'superstitious' thinking
(which is mistaken) and 'scientific' or 'common-sense' (which is
true). By 'ways of thinking about the world', I mean the ways in
which we approach such questions as questions of cause and effect
('Why/How do things happen?') and of effective action in and on
the world around us ('How can we cause this or that to happen?'). I
am suggesting that we should not simply rule out religious answers
to such questions as 'unscientific', proved wrong by observation
and common-sense: the analogy which approaches religion as a

sort of pseudo-science outmoded by the progress of true science is one that, in one form or another, has dogged and hampered the study of primitive religion from Frazer to Evans-Pritchard and beyond. Evans-Pritchard's classic study, *Witchcraft, Oracles and Magic among the Azande* – an account of his field-work among a southern Sudanese tribal people – is a brilliant, subtle and sophisticated analysis of a culture's complex religious thinking, but Evans-Pritchard is still sufficiently under the influence of the pseudo-science analogy to treat the thought-processes of the Azande as characterized by error and illogicality. He speaks of their displaying 'patterns of thought that attribute to phenomena supra-sensible qualities which . . . are not derived from observation or cannot be logically inferred from it, *and which they do not possess*' (my italics), as opposed to 'common-sense notions . . . that attribute to phenomena only what men observe in them or what can logically be inferred from observation'. That is to say, Evans-Pritchard assumes that the evidence of our senses and the application of an objective 'common-sense' are enough to show that Zande assumptions about the operation of oracles, magic and witchcraft in the way things happen are simply wrong, and 'pseudo-scientific' in the sense that science is merely a methodologically more demanding development of 'common-sense notions', one which 'has better techniques of observation and reasoning'.[1] On this view Zande thought-processes are unscientific and therefore simply mistaken, not 'in accord with objective reality': 'witches, as the Azande conceive them, cannot exist',[2] and therefore their magical rituals are, to quote a distinguished philosopher of religion, 'a pseudo-technique, an effort to make up for poor practical skills with an imaginary technology'.[3]

Evans-Pritchard would presumably have said much the same about ancient Greek religious notions and thought-processes. The trouble about this is that not only is the thesis vulnerable to philosophical argument about the nature of 'objective reality',[4] but also that Evans-Pritchard's own experiences of the Azande during his field-work demonstrated how absolutely fundamental these 'unscientific notions' were in their daily life and with what unassailable seriousness they were regarded. He himself found it all too easy, while among them, to think in terms of Zande notions; indeed all too hard to 'check', as he disarmingly puts it, 'this lapse into unreason'.[5]

For the truth is that systems of religious belief, in any culture in which they are living things, are not only self-justifying[6] (and thus impossible to disprove by empirical observation, as Evans-Pritchard found in talking to the Azande), but also all-pervasive within the culture, so that there is no corner of life that is not lived in their terms: it is not possible to be a member of the society and think in wholly different categories. If we want an analogy to help us understand religion, one that will direct our attention positively to what is important in religious systems, we should turn not to the concept of a pseudo-science and a pseudo-technology but to language. Like language, religion is a cultural phenomenon, a phenomenon of the group (there are no 'private' religions, any more than there are 'private' languages, except by some metaphorical devaluation of the two terms), and like language, any religion is a system of signs enabling communication both between members of the group in interpreting and responding to experience of the external world and in the individual's inner discourse with himself as to his own behaviour, emotional and private. We do not need to go all the way in the direction of cultural relativism to see the relevance to our thinking about Greek religion of Edward Sapir's words about language:

The fact of the matter is that the 'real world' is to a large extent unconsciously built up on the language habits of the group. No two languages are ever sufficiently similar to be considered as representing the same social reality. The worlds in which different societies live are distinct worlds, not merely the same world with different labels attached.[7]

For 'language' here, we could read 'religion' and 'religious'.

If Greek religion, then, is among other things a way of representing and interpreting (even, at the limit, of constructing) the external world and man's experience of himself, we can best approach it as a mode of experience, a response to life as lived by ancient Greeks. In particular, as a system of responses to those aspects of experience which threatened to overturn the sense of an intelligible order in terms of which men lived. Here I would like to quote once more, this time from a splendidly illuminating essay by the American anthropologist Clifford Geertz. Geertz himself quotes with approval the philosopher Suzanne Langer '[Man] can adapt himself somehow to anything his imagination can cope with; but he cannot deal with Chaos', and goes on:

There are at least three points where chaos – a tumult of events which lack not just interpretations but interpretability – threatens to break in upon man: at the limits of his analytic capacities, at the limits of his powers of endurance, and at the limits of his moral insight. Bafflement, suffering, and a sense of intractable ethical paradox are all, if they become intense enough or are sustained long enough, radical challenges to the proposition that life is comprehensible and that we can, by taking thought, orient ourselves effectively within it – challenges with which any religion, however 'primitive', which hopes to persist must attempt somehow to cope.[8]

With the help of this remark, let us assume that what Greek religion offered to those brought up within its field of efficacy was both a framework of explanation for human experience and a system of responses to all that is wayward, uncanny and a threat to the perception of order in that experience – a language for dealing with the world. In which case, to make sense of it, to see what Greek religion is a response to and what kind of response it is, we need first of all to take account of differences of two kinds: firstly, differences of 'world', that is between our experience of the external world and that of ancient Greeks, and secondly, institutional differences in the response, differences between two traditions and conventions in the organization of religious thought and behaviour.

To start with the first kind of difference, we need to acknowledge the precariousness of life in the ancient world and to take stock of the real poverty of its technological resources. The support of life, even in a prosperous and 'advanced' community like that of fifth-century Attica, was based almost wholly on subsistence farming, carried on with minimal agricultural technology and in a world in which the onset of disease attacking crops, animals and men was subject to no effective control. The result was a world constantly vulnerable to crop failure and sickness and far closer to present-day village India than to anything in our own immediate experience, a world in which the expectation of life was appallingly low and in which medicine (the most articulate and sophisticated of ancient sciences) was all too often an unavailing witness of human suffering, disease and death; not merely, as Thucydides notes, in major epidemics such as the famous plague at Athens in the 420s but in the ordinary run of human sickness during the average year. The Hippocratic doctor who worked for four years on the island of Thasos and the mainland opposite, and whose case-notes we have in the collection of writings attributed to Hippocrates as *Epidemics* 1 and 3 (a misleading title), records 25 fatalities out of 42 cases that he attended and recorded.[9] To encounter anything similar in our experience we have to go back to the nineteenth century or earlier, to a world in which a tombstone in the Tewkesbury Abbey precinct can record the twelve children of a marriage who died aged 58, 57, 52, 18, 17 and 'seven in infancy', before we confront an experience of which 'natural death' was so pervasive and ordinary a part. To this we can, of course, add such 'extras' as earthquakes and the violent deaths among the male population brought about by endemic warfare and the recurrent political confrontations which Greeks called *stasis*.

In such a world the threat of chaos, in Geertz's sense, is never far away. Yet the religious institutions and systems of belief of ancient Greeks were equally different, less structured, less 'worked out' than those we tend to take for granted. For if the differences in experience are fundamental, so too are the differences in religious tradition, which reach into every aspect of consciousness. Greek religion is not 'revealed' as Christianity is; there is no sacred text claiming the status of the 'word of God', nor even of His prophets; no Ten Commandments, no creed, no doctrinal councils, no heresies, no wars of religion in which 'true believers' confront the 'infidel' or the heretic. Central terms of our religious experience such as 'grace', 'sin', and 'faith' cannot be rendered without disfigurement into the ancient Greek of the classical period: the central *Greek* term, *theous nomizein*, means not 'believe in the gods', but 'acknowledge' them, that is, pray to them, sacrifice to them, build them temples, make them the object of cult and ritual. There is never an assumption of divine omnipotence, nor of a divine creation of the universe, except in philosophical 'theology', nor any consistent belief in divine omnipresence. There is no church, no organized body persisting through time comprising those with dogmatic authority, able to *define* divinity and rule on what is correct or incorrect in religious belief. Men of religion in ancient Greece are of two kinds, those with ritual functions (*hiereis*, meaning primarily 'sacrificers') and custodians of religious tradition and customary law on the one hand (that is men such as the Athenian *exēgētai* and the *hierophants* of the Eleusinian mysteries), and, on the other, men with a god-given and peculiar closeness to divinity, with a special insight into or power to communicate with the divine, that is *manteis*, dream-interpreters and such figures as the Pythia (Apollo's prophetess) at Delphi. All these are indeed essential parts of the fabric of Greek religion (no army took the field in fifth-century Greece without a *mantis* to accompany its dangerous enterprise[10]), but they do not constitute a church; there is no system of relationships joining them together and making them conscious of a common stance or a common ideology; there is no 'training for the priesthood'.

All this means that, for all its weight of tradition (not less evident in ancient Greek religion than in other religions), Greek religion remains fundamentally improvisatory. By which I mean that though the response to experience crystallizes, on the one hand as ritual, on the other as myth, and both involve repetition and transmission from generation to generation, there is always room for new improvisation, for the introduction of new cults and new observances: Greek religion is not theologically fixed and stable, and it has no tradition of exclusion or finality: it is an open, not a closed system. There are no true gods and false, merely powers known and acknowledged since time immemorial, and new powers, newly experienced as active among men and newly acknowledged in worship (as were Bendis and Asclepius in the last decades of the fifth century at Athens).

The same absence of finality is characteristic of Greek myth. If there is one reason beyond all others why we have no tradition of religious myth in our culture, it is that the Christian 'myth' of the Old and New Testament is once for all an unchanging and unchangeable revelation of divine truth in its entirety; all that is left for improvisation in the face of new experience is hagiography and martyrology, the creation of new intermediaries, new saints and new martyrs in the Christian tradition. By contrast, Greek myth is open-ended; a traditional story can be re-told, told with new meanings, new incidents, new persons, even with a for-mal reversal of old meanings, as in the myth of Helen (seduced to Troy as the *casus belli* of the Trojan war, the 'woman of many men', or in Egypt as a wronged and virtuous wife), or in the myth of Orestes (example of filial duty to Telemachus in the *Odyssey*, or paradigm of moral dilemma, of the inextricability of good and evil in fifth-century tragedy). The improvisatory character of Greek myth is not just a literary fact, not only the source of its perennial vitality in literature, but also the guarantee of its centrality in Greek religion. It is not bound to forms hardened and stiffened by canonical authority, but mobile, fluent and free to respond to a changing experience of the world.

Ritual and myth, I am arguing, are both modes of religious re-sponse to experience in a world in which 'chaos', the threat posed by events which seem to be unintelligible or which outrage moral feeling, is always close. But if we are to make sense of Greek religion as response to experience, we have to ask: What aspects of experience? What kinds of event are taken to be signs of divine activity and stimulate a religious response? How did an ancient Greek *know* that a divine power was at work in the world of his experience? The answer, of course, is that he didn't – outside, say, the fictional worlds of the *Iliad* and *Odyssey*. He had to guess, to wrestle with uncertainty and disagreement, both in discerning the active power of divinity at work in events and, more particularly, in determining what divinity and for what reason. And until these questions could be answered, response was premature and might be misguided and misdirected; it was inhibited by thoughts of the consequences; it might involve irreparable loss in the effective destruction of foodstuffs, in the slaughter of scarce animal resources (or in myth even of sons or daughters), and might even result in an outcome counter to the intentions of the respondent. So these are questions that matter, and our sources (particularly Herodotus) reflect the doubts and anxieties that attend their answering.

Before I turn to Herodotus, let me cite an example that he would have understood, an example of 'the signs of ultra-human activity', of the putative effect of divine activity, from another culture. It comes from the world of the Dinka, another tribal people of the southern Sudan, reported by Godfrey Lienhardt in his outstanding book *Divinity and Experience*, a work to which I owe much in the writing of this essay; I quote the Dinka case because it offers a wealth of recorded detail that is hardly ever available in the Greek evidence. Its relevance to Greek religion will, I hope, become clear. The case concerns Lienhardt's 'boy', Ajak, who had left home to find work in town and in doing so had broken with his father, who died before the breach was healed. Ajak had been drinking and was subsequently said to be possessed. Lienhardt's account goes on:

Ajak was running round and round outside the hut, breathing heavily and panting and groaning. He did not appear to hear when addressed. It was said that this outburst had been preceded by a period of sitting alone, during which he chanted and muttered to himself. This is often a sign of impending possession. [Compare the beginning of the Cassandra scene in Aeschylus' *Agamemnon*.] Nobody knew the songs he had been singing: they were said to be hymns to Divinity . . . Ajak ran about for some twenty minutes, apparently quite unaware of spectators. As he gradually tired, his movements became clumsier and less vigorous, and his breathing was deeper and quicker. Although he seemed to be gazing straight ahead, without care for where he was going, he avoided bushes and stumps of wood in his path. Eventually his legs began to give way beneath him and he staggered and eventually fell sprawling on the ground, where he stayed, rolling about and lashing out with his arms and legs. [Cf. some of the symptoms of epilepsy, widely regarded as the 'sacred disease' in ancient Greece.]

He lay there for some time. Bursts of frenzied movement were interspersed with quieter periods, when he sang snatches of songs which nobody could understand. By this time a few spectators from the village had gathered round . . . 'It is a Power . . . of his home', one of the spectators said, while another said, 'he has a ghost . . . in his body'. Then a minor master of the fishing-spear [hereditary priests of the Dinka] came and, addressing what he said to the threshing form of Ajak, asked whatever it was which troubled him to tell its name and say what it wanted.

The spear-master addresses the disturbing power by various possible names, and, getting no reply, takes the power to task for wantonly seizing a man far from home, in a foreign place. The spectators listen eagerly to Ajak's unintelligible mumblings, saying that in due course 'it' would leave him; to Lienhardt's question, what 'it' was, they answer variously 'that it would be his [clan] divinity . . . or the ghost of his father, or the free-divinity Deng, or "just a power" '. Ajak, dazed and exhausted, goes to bed and the next day is unable to remember anything. The seizure is repeated twice more: on the second occasion when Ajak becomes quieter, Lienhardt tries to speak to him by name. 'Someone said: "It is no use speaking to Ajak; it is *not* Ajak." ' Spectators argue about the source of possession (was it Garang or Macardit or 'just a power of the forest'?) and characteristically use arguments from the circumstances of the attack to support or rebut attempts to diagnose the power at work.[11]

For all the elements of this series of incidents that are specific to Dinka religion (such as the categorization of divine powers and the significance of 'being away from home'), the greater part of this story, and in particular the way in which it evokes a religious response by threatening 'chaos', could be rendered without distortion into Greek terms. Indeed, an example, strikingly close to the case of Ajak, can be found in the behaviour of Phaedra in the early scenes of Euripides' *Hippolytus*, with its wayward, contradictory fluctuations of mood and state of mind: Phaedra's failure to reply to the nurse's anxious questions and her apparently senseless words addressed to no one in particular of those present – all this leads the women of the chorus, like the spectators of Ajak's possession, to attempt diagnosis. They too are inclined to discern a supernatural power at work, but cannot be certain; much less certain is the power's identity: is it Pan or Hecate, the Korybantes or the Mountain Mother, or Diktynna (all are possible, for Phaedra's strange behaviour seems associated with the wilds); or is it after all a response to some breakdown of family ties; or more mundanely still, just some (ordinary) abnormality inherent in the constitution of women? (Euripides, *Hippolytus* 141–69.) The nurse expresses *her* sense that a divinity is active but suggests that much help from oracles will be needed to identify the god involved (*Hippolytus* 236–8).

Thus among Greeks, as among the Dinka, waywardness in human behaviour is traced to divinity; it is a sign. There are others. Plague and epidemic we have already met: in Athens in 429 and the years that followed; at the beginning of the *Iliad*, and at the beginning of Sophocles' *Oedipus Tyrannus*. And each time the response is the same, to turn to men of god for expert guidance, to *manteis* and to oracles. That is also the characteristic response to other modes of the uncanny: to dreams (repeatedly in Herodotus), to the event that makes no sense, and, equally, to the event that makes too much sense. Thus Herodotus, faced with the capture and execution by Athens of two Spartan heralds on their way with messages for the Persian King, is struck by the uncanny coincidence that these are the grandsons of another pair of Spartan heralds who had been sent to a Persian king (Xerxes), to offer their lives as atonement for the sacrilege involved in killing the Persian heralds who had brought Xerxes' demands for Spartan submission. That offer of atonement had been rejected, and now Herodotus is certain that the anger of Talthybius (patron hero of heralds) has pursued the family into the second generation: it seems to be the guiltlessness of the grandsons which guarantees that this is the action of an ultra-human power. Yet there are puzzles: the Athenians too had put Persian envoys to death; has divine anger pursued them too? And if not, why not? (A characteristically Greek question: the Azande would not have asked it.) Herodotus is uncertain whether the Persian sack of Athens is such a punishment, perhaps because there is not enough of the uncanny about it: there are other, all too human explanations to hand (Herodotus 7.133–7).

Problems of interpretation, where conflict of interest may be reflected in conflict of interpretation, are bound to occur. The horrific self-mutilation and suicide of the Spartan king Cleomenes is uncanny enough to be a sign of divine activity, but in punishment for what? Most Greeks, Herodotus reports, believed that it was for suborning the Pythia at Delphi and persuading her to say that his rival, king Demaratus, was not the son of king Ariston, and thus causing him to be forced into exile; but the Athenians put it about that Cleomenes was punished for devastating land sacred to Demeter and Korē when he attacked Eleusis, and the Argives that it was for sacrilege in enticing the defeated remnants of an Argive army from sanctuary in a sacred grove, massacring them and then burning the grove itself to the ground. Predictably, the Spartans themselves construed his suicide differently and denied any imputation of divine anger: Cleomenes had associated with Scythians and had acquired their disgusting habit of drinking wine neat – hence his insanity. Herodotus feels impelled to adjudicate and gives his opinion as that of 'most Greeks' (in spite of accepting the truth of the Argive story): it was for his villainy against Demaratus that Cleomenes was supernaturally punished.[12] But then Herodotus probably knew Demaratus in his exile in Persia, and treats the information he received from him with great respect: his interpretation of Cleomenes' death also reflects his interests and his commitments.

Incidents might be less grand in scale than shipwreck of the Persian fleet or the grotesque suicide of a Spartan king and still be uncanny. In three generations the descent-group of the Spartan Glaucus, famous for his honesty, was entirely wiped out, so that he had no descendants. It was remembered of him, however, that he had once been tempted into contemplating breaking an oath and not returning a large sum of money entrusted to him years before by a stranger from Miletus. In the event, the story went, he gave it back, but not before he had asked the Delphic oracle whether it was 'better' to break his oath: it was said that the oracle predicted that the 'son of the oath' would destroy his house. And his house was destroyed (Herodotus 6.86). Herodotus tells the story from the other end, but if we reverse his sequence we have a case of the unacceptable (sudden, unaccountable death wiping out a family) being brought within a framework of explanation by interpreting it as a sign of (motivated) divine activity. Such a framework of explanation may work both ways: forwards, creating an expectation of some divinely activated event that will make sense of the senseless and the unacceptable, or backwards (as here, or in the case of the fall of King Croesus of Lydia) in reaching out for a past event, which may be to our sense astonishingly remote, but which will reciprocate meaningfully with what is now seen as senseless, unmotivated, unintelligible.

Indeed the event that is uncanny, the sign of divine activity, may be so in a way that is seemingly trivial but nevertheless not to be understood except within the religious framework of explanation. In the aftermath of the Ionian revolt the younger brother of the tyrant of Salamis in Cyprus, Onesilos, who had led the Cypriot revolt against Persia after ejecting his brother, is killed in battle and his severed head displayed on a stake above the city gate of Amathus, the only town on Cyprus which had refused to join the revolt, and which he had besieged. In time the hollow skull was colonized by a swarm of bees who made their hive in it. The people of Amathus, in face of the uncanniness of these things, consulted an oracle and were told to take down the head, bury it and establish a cult in honour of Onesilos as hero, with an annual sacrifice. Herodotus records that the cult was still maintained in his own day, sixty years or more later (Herodotus 5.114.1).

I have spoken of Greek religion as a system of explanation and response and as constituting a complex statement about what the world of experience is like. In the rest of this essay, I want to consider the sense in which Greek religion is systematic (rather, that is, than a mere agglomeration of unconnected rituals and beliefs), and to explore the nature of the statement that it makes. In order to do this, I will begin with two examples of ritual response: one which seems to suggest that divine powers can be understood in much the same way as we understand other human beings, and responded to accordingly, and another, that of sacrifice, which appears to offer a much more ambiguous image of divinity, and of human relations with the gods. My first example is the language of prayer. There was no 'prayer-book' in classical antiquity and we have no liturgical texts, but Greek literature is full of prayers and from them we can gain a clear idea of the linguistic and conceptual model in terms of which men addressed themselves to divinity. What is perhaps the earliest of such literary prayers can serve as the paradigm case.

In the first book of the *Iliad*, the priest of Apollo, Chryses, turns to his god in order to seek revenge for the public humiliation inflicted on him by Agamemnon before the whole Greek army. This is private speech but it is (seemingly) uttered aloud and it observes the formalities of a public and collective address to divinity:

> 'Hear me,
> lord of the silver bow who set your power above Chryse
> and Killa the sacrosanct, who are lord in strength over Tenedos,
> Smintheus, if ever it pleased your heart that I built your temple,
> if ever it pleased you that I burnt all the rich thigh pieces
> of bulls, of goats, then bring to pass this wish I pray for:
> let your arrows make the Danaans pay for my tears shed.'
>
> (Homer, *Iliad* 1.36–42 trs. Lattimore)

Two assumptions underlie this prayer, and the language of Greek prayer at large: one is that a divinity must be addressed with precision and courtesy, by formal titles and by rehearsal of his powers and attributes (otherwise he may not hear the prayer); the second is that he who utters the prayer must establish and point to ties, bonds of obligation that exist (or will exist) between god and worshipper. Behind the second lies a more fundamental assumption still, one that is central to ancient Greek culture: the assumption of reciprocity, the assumption that lies behind the Greek use of the word *charis*, which is both the doing of good by one person to another but also the (necessary) repayment of that good, the obligation that exists until it is repaid and the feelings of gratitude that should accompany the obligation. The assumption is that any action will be met by a matching and balancing reaction (good for good, evil for evil), and therefore the implication that divinity will respond in kind and reciprocate human action, for good or ill, is one that locates the divine powers squarely within the conceptual framework by means of which ancient Greeks understood the ordering of their world: the divine powers are not anomalous. It also carries the further implication that relations between divinity and worshipper can be construed in the same terms that make sense of relations between men, and that the expectations that men have of one another can be carried over into their expectations of divinity. These are important ground-rules for religious behaviour. Moreover, there is in the language of prayer the further implication (not insignificant, as we shall see later by a comparison with other assumptions) that it is possible for man to converse with divinity in the ordinary language of his interchanges with men: divinity understands Greek, even if it is another question whether he speaks it.

The assumption of reciprocity is one that pervades much of Herodotus' thinking about divinity and the thinking of the characters who appear in his *Histories*. For Croesus, the Lydian king who loses his kingdom to Persia after a defeat caused, as he believes, by his being misled and tricked by an oracle of Apollo, the question whether Apollo does not after all acknowledge the principle of *charis* is one so urgent (in view of the lack of fit between Croesus' enormous benefactions to the god and Apollo's seeming betrayal of him) that the concession of being allowed to ask it is the first he seeks from his new master, the Persian king, Cyrus (Herodotus 1.89–91). So too with the Egyptian pharaoh Mycerinus, son of Cheops, who reacts angrily to the divine pronouncement of Leto's oracle at Buto that in return, as he construes it, for the piety and justice for which he was famed, he was to die young, having already lost his only daughter (Herodotus 2.133).

But if the language of prayer seems transparent, unambiguous in its implication of relations between men and gods that are in all ways similar to relations between men, other rituals are more opaque, even contradictory, in their implied statements about the nature of the relationship. The central ritual of Greek religion, from the pouring of libations onwards, is the offering to the god, and its most characteristic form animal sacrifice. The different forms of animal sacrifice are complex, with significant variations dependent on the god or gods who are to receive the sacrifice. But we can safely take as the starting-point for our questions a composite account of sacrifice to the Olympian deities drawing on our numerous sources.[13]

The animal victim, which will be a domesticated animal, goat, sheep or ox, is festively prepared for the ritual slaughter; if the occasion is grand enough, its horns may be gilded and the whole animal will be groomed for the ritual. It must seem to go willingly and joyfully to its death (the motif is carried over into the stories of human self-sacrifice that Euripides dramatized in plays such as *Iphigeneia at Aulis*). The place of slaughter is ritually marked out as sacred by the carrying round in procession of the sacred basket and by the sprinkling of water over the participants and the victim; the basket contains barley grain (the *oulochytai*), which is thrown at the victim by all the participants, and the sacrificial knife is kept out of sight beneath the grain. The sprinkling of the water and the casting of the grain is the 'beginning' (the term *katarchesthai* is technical) of the ritual, and these are followed by a further step in this 'beginning', by the priest cutting a few hairs from the animal's forehead. Its head is then pulled back and raised towards the sky and its throat cut. Up to this point the participants have maintained a ritual silence (cf. Adrastus' self-slaughter in Herodotus 1.45.3); now at the moment of slaughter the women present must scream the *ololygē*. What follows is not less strange. The animal is skinned and butchered; the entrails (heart, lungs, liver and kidneys – the *splanchna*) are removed, skewered and roasted separately, while of the remainder the tail, gall-bladder and above all the thigh-bones are wrapped in fat and burnt on the altar of the god, and the lean meat roasted and distributed among the participants so that the sacrifice ends in feasting. Before the roast meat is eaten, the *splanchna* are passed round and all taste: in metaphor the *splanchna* are the source and seat of feeling, of love, hatred, anger, anxiety.

All this is *thusia*, the slaughter of a victim, but more properly and specifically the burning of an offering to the god. But considered precisely as offering to a god, what is the meaning of this sequence of actions? Is it a shared meal, a 'communion' between men and gods? Or are men giving food to the gods? Or is it in fact misleading to see it as an offering at all? Should it be seen rather as a process whereby human food and its preparation, cooking, the raw food changed, is consecrated and made acceptable to the gods, and ends in a common meal renewing the community of men? Or is the central act not that of giving or sharing, cooking or eating, but simply that of slaughter? Is the real significance of the ritual that of sacralizing the taking of animal life, of breaking a taboo and by ritual action making harmless the bloody and in itself uncanny business of deliberately killing a living creature: characteristically, moreover, one that is domesticated and taken into the fellowship of human beings, a working companion or a source of food and livelihood while living? (Hunting *wild* animals and killing them is a wholly different operation: it is not *thusia*.)

It is not obvious that any one of these interpretations is right, and we have warrant for thinking that ancient Greeks themselves were conscious of the puzzling and ambiguous nature of the ritual. Poseidon is absent from Olympus at the beginning of the *Odyssey* (and hence Athena's opportunity to protest at Odysseus' inability to return home) because he has gone to join the Ethiopians, 'to receive a hecatomb of bulls and rams. There he sat at the feast and took his pleasure' (Homer, *Odyssey* 1.22–6). And an ancient commentator on a line of the *Iliad* says explicitly: 'they thought of themselves as, as it were, eating jointly with the gods' (Scholiast on *Iliad* 3.310). But not always so: Aristophanes can make comic resource out of the notion that by the smoke of sacrifice on earth men keep the gods in the sky fed. In *Birds* when the revolt of the birds has meant seizing control of the sky and severing communication between men and gods, a delegation of starving gods (led by the glutton Heracles) comes to negotiate a peace. Moreover the distribution as between men and gods of the carcase of the slaughtered animal presents obvious embarrassments, which already (indeed explicitly) underlie the myth of Prometheus in Hesiod's *Theogony* and *Works and Days*, to which I shall return. And Walter Burkert, following the lead of the Swiss folklorist Karl Meuli, has pointed out how much of sacrificial ritual makes sense only by assuming a deep-seated sense of anxiety over the taking of animal life. Hence what Meuli called the 'comedy of innocence', the array of pretence (the self-sacrificing victim, the hidden knife) and the group-involvement of the whole community in the act, in the throwing of barley-grains and the innocuous but symbolic and magical violation of the animal's integrity by cutting off the few hairs. Does this mean that Burkert and Meuli are right in seeing sacrifice as no more than ritualized slaughter?[14] Perhaps at this point we should suspend judgement on the issue, noting for the moment only that non-rationality, paradox and seeming self-contradiction are recurrent features of absolutely central elements in religious ritual and myth in other religious traditions: we may think of such examples as Catholic-Christian 'transsubstantiation' (bread and wine as the body and blood of Christ) in the Mass and the concept of 'virgin birth' in Christian myth.[15]

The problems of interpreting what sacrificial ritual 'says' about relations between man and divinity have been acknowledged ever since Hesiod. If we turn to those religious occasions which we traditionally call 'festivals' (occasions such as the Panathenaia or the Dionysia), which are in effect ritual sequences of greater complexity still, the problem of interpretation (on the face of it more difficult) is often made to seem less pressing because of the assumption that their component parts are (merely) the result of historical accumulation and juxtaposition, perhaps even fortuitous: the supposition that they just 'growed'. Yet that assumption too is no more than an assumption, and perhaps we can take an Athenian festival as an example and see if another approach makes better sense.

The three days of ritual comprising the festival called Anthesteria took place in February each year, in honour of the god Dionysus. The three days, which ran like the Jewish Sabbath from sundown to sundown, were called 'Opening the storage jars (*pithoi*)', 'Jugs' and 'Cooking pots'. The rituals of the first two days centred on the opening and first consumption of the new wine from the previous year's harvest. Their climax was the ritualized drinking of the day called 'Jugs'. The day took its name from a peculiar feature of the ritual: each participant did not merely drink from his own drinking-cup, as at any other drinking party, but his wine was mixed with water also in a personal jug which he took with him to the festival, and, when it was over, dedicated to the god: there was no common mixing bowl. Moreover it was of the essence of the ritual that all participants began to drink simultaneously, when a trumpet sounded, and that they drank in silence: there was a myth to explain why this was so and why each man had his own jug. Once, when the Athenians were celebrating the Anthesteria, Orestes came to Athens still polluted by killing his mother; the Athenian king, rather than break the rules of hospitality by sending him away or risk contamination by incorporating him in the ritual of the community, devised the *cordon sanitaire* of separate vessels and silence.

This is one part of the darker side of the day called 'Jugs'. For the rest, to all appearances, it was a day of festivity, of often riotous drinking. Aristophanes imagines the climax of *Acharnians* as happening on this day, when the hero Dikaiopolis reels back drunk and triumphant as winner of the contest to be the first to empty his wine jug (*Acharnians* 1198ff.). The following day, 'Cooking pots', by contrast, was a day of dark, ominous rituals: the doorposts of all houses were smeared with pitch and men chewed buckthorn, a powerful laxative. These were apotropaic rituals, designed to keep evil at bay and to expel it. Evil, seemingly, was abroad this day and when it ended there were ritual words to say, words whose precise form, even in antiquity, was a matter of uncertainty, but of which the likeliest meaning is an injunction to alien Powers to leave the community: 'Outside ... it is no longer Anthesteria.'

Once more paradox and contradiction. The contradictions between joyful celebration and awe in the face of the threat of evil are palpable, as is the special status of this festival. Its central rituals were carried out in the precinct of Dionysus 'in the Marshes'; all other sanctuaries were closed for this one day of 'Jugs', and conversely the sanctuary in the Marshes was open only on this one day in the year. No 'normal' sacrifices took place, no marriages. All this is readily explained (if explanation it is) on the hypothesis of random accumulation, but Burkert, once more, has pointed out how pervasive the contradictions are of the festival as a whole, and has suggested that they are not to be separated from the ambiguities of the central act of the festival, the opening and drinking of the new wine. The drinking of wine as possession by an alien power; wine as blood; the treading of the grape as wanton destruction and brutality: all these metaphorical and symbolic associations are mirrored in recurring motifs of death and violence in the myths that relate the story of the gift of wine to men by the god Dionysus and in the stories of the dismemberment of the god himself and his rebirth. And if Burkert is right, they are mirrored too in the ritual ambiguities of the Anthesteria, in the precautions taken to ensure that all men jointly and simultaneously drink first of the new wine, and in the taboos and apotropaic rituals that surround this central act.

Again, if Burkert is right (and I think he is), then our attention is instructively drawn to other motifs in the overall pattern of Greek ritual, motifs which seem to imply an ambiguous, even contradictory attitude to the experience of divinity. It is an attitude which seems to suggest that divinity may be a source of disorder rather than order and the rituals are ones which enact the inversion of social normality, the suspension of order, the reversal of roles, rather than their reinforcement. Implicit in Burkert's interpretation of the Anthesteria is the notion that it is the contradictions, tensions and ambiguities of experience itself that may be symbolically enacted in the response of ritual. And such inversions, suspensions and reversals certainly abound. In the ritual of supplication, for example, the force of the ritual acts lies in the self-abasement, the enacted inferiority of the suppliant and that in turn is charged with symbolic meaning precisely because it is a total reversal of normal face-to-face dealings between unrelated individuals. [16] In such behaviour, and in similar ritual motifs, such as the simultaneous putting-out and simultaneous re-lighting of all the hearth-fires of a community, in transvestism as a recurrent element of ritual, in the imposition of total sexual abstinence (as at the festivals called Skira and Arrephoria) or, conversely, in the requirement of sexual promiscuity (as at the Adonia), what is given symbolic expression is the notion that contact and communication with divinity may be contact with the alien and subversive and may involve, not the maintenance, but the subversion of social normality.

Here we have behaviour in communication with a god, or behaviour which invokes the power of a god, which is the reverse of the normal, and with it we seem to have moved to the opposite pole of the interpretation of experience from that which we saw implicit in the language of prayer. There, communication with divinity seemed to be rooted in the notion that divine action could be expected to take forms precisely analogous with those seen as normal among men, and that the appropriate language in which to appeal to a divine power was that in which human beings communicated with one another: so might a human inferior address his superior. But that, as I suggested earlier, is only half the story. We have to take into account also the language of communication between divinity and man. And there we are once more struck at once by paradox. Divinity, it seems, communicates readily with humanity, through dreams and omens, through the utterances of oracles, through the chance speech of men, through the flight of birds. There is no awesome silence on the part of the divine powers, no refusal to speak: even the future is implicitly mapped in the language of divine communication. And yet the messages of divinity are imagined as being systematically ambiguous, inscrutable, opaque: they require the interpretative resources of those specially endowed to understand and transmit them, and more significantly they are systematically misunderstood by those to whom they are addressed.[17] Everywhere they fail to enlighten and clarify the path of men: their truth is revealed, always too late, in the moment of death or of catastrophic discovery. Divinity, it seems, speaks to man but in a language that he cannot understand, a language where words are no more than ambiguous signs and do not mean what they seem to say, and where, characteristically, they are *replaced* by signs: in Heraclitus' words, 'the god whose is the oracle at Delphi neither speaks nor hides: he indicates' (i.e. 'he uses signs': *sēmainei*).[18] He does, and does not, communicate with man.

The notion of ambiguity in divine communication, of a divine language of signs rather than words, seems deeply rooted in the Greek imagination, so that when, in Herodotus, for example, men aspire to the status of divinity and claim the power to predict the future, it is in such a language that they speak. The Scythians predict to Darius the failure of his expedition against them: they send him a present of a bird, a mouse, a frog and five arrows. Darius reads the message (wrongly) as implying surrender: mice live on the ground (and thus stand for earth), frogs live in water (and thus stand for water); birds (which 'are much like horses'!) and the arrows (which represent Scythian power) are surrendered to him. Only Gobryas, his associate from the time of the revolt against the usurping Magus, perhaps reads the signs rightly: 'Unless you Persians turn into birds and fly up in the air, or into mice and burrow under the ground, or into frogs and jump into the lakes, you will never get home again but will stay here in this country and be shot down by Scythian arrows' (Herodotus 4.131–2). And once read the message can be falsified and rendered harmless, if only by withdrawal – unlike the messages of divinity. The prophecies of the divine powers often make use of what the Greeks called an *adynaton*, an impossibility ('When a mule sits on the throne of Media, then, tender-footed Lydian, run . . .'), but in divine language the seeming *adynaton* may be fulfilled and an apparent 'never' may mean 'one day'. When the Pelasgians intend a promise which will never actually be fulfilled, they agree to surrender Lemnos to Athens 'when a ship sails from your land to ours in a single day when the North wind is blowing'. But Miltiades long afterwards reads the message differently and sails from Athenian territory in the Gallipoli peninsula to Lemnos – he makes good his interpretation by force (Herodotus 6.139–40). It is perhaps significant that human attempts to speak the language of divinity can be so easily read and their messages falsified.

To summarize, then. In Greek ritual and in its implicit assumptions about the nature of divinity and of communication between man and god, we encounter contradiction and ambiguity. Construed as a statement about the nature of divinity it seems to say that god both is and is not like man, and that relations between man and god both are and are not like those between men; construed as a statement about experience it seems to say that experience both is and is not humanly intelligible. What man sees in the mirror of his ritual is sometimes himself, sometimes something bafflingly, frighteningly alien. I want now to turn to myth and to suggest that this apparent sense of Greek ritual is borne out and reinforced by what we find in myth.

The first, striking impression of the world of Greek myth is of proliferation, plurality, multiplicity. In myth, as in ritual, it is of the essence that response to experience is embodied in multiplicity: there are many gods, many rituals, many myths, bewilderingly various in their many versions, and it is perhaps not coincidence that it should have been a Belfast-born English poet who was also a Greek scholar who wrote: 'World is crazier and more of it than we think │ Incorrigibly plural. I . . . feel the drunkenness of things being various.'[19] And yet the plurality of many gods and many myths is not disorder or chaos, for all that they are, in Macneice's words, 'soundlessly collateral and incompatible'. In the first instance (first in time as well as in logic) the many gods of Greek myth are not merely 'many'; they form a socialized company already in the imagination of Homer, and it is as a company that they make their most striking impression on us. They are imagined as comprising an extended family of anthropomorphic beings, with Zeus 'the father of gods and men' as head and master of the company. Conceived as a metaphor of human experience this is a brilliant stroke; the model of the family provides a framework within which we can intuitively understand both unity and conflict as the working out of a complex web of loyalties, interests and obligations – conflict (inevitably) of ties, passions and personalities both within and outside the group, but also an ultimate unity, contained within the solidarity of the group and guaranteed in the person of Zeus the Father whose authority embodies the demand for an underlying unity, not chaos, in experience. The Homeric image of divinity is an image of marvellous and compelling adequacy; it underwrites and explains the human sense of contradiction and conflict in experience, and yet contains contradiction within a more fundamental order. It enables divinity to be understood as the source of disorder in the world, and, in the extreme case, mirrored in the myth of war between gods and giants, as the ultimate defence of order against brute chaos, as well as being the unconquerable barrier to human excess and the potentially destructive violence of human self-assertion. We would be quite wrong, I suggest, to set aside the model of divinity that we find in the Homeric poems and imagine it as a purely literary fiction and no part of the 'sense' of Greek religion.[20]

In a famous passage, Herodotus associates Hesiod with Homer as the source of much of what is specific in the ancient Greek conception of divinity (Herodotus 2.53.2). What Hesiod in particular contributes is a sense of depth and perspective to the Homeric model, the awareness (reflected in ritual as well as in myth) of a dark hinterland to the Olympian scene. The Hesiodic succession myth from Ouranos to Kronos, and from Kronos to Zeus, whatever it owes to Near Eastern precedent, confirms our sense that there is more to experience than the Homeric model, in its simplest form, can account for. It asserts that the world has not always been under the control of the Olympians, and that even now, since divinity is indestructible, older and more primitive powers are in and of the world. It speaks of progress (progress whereby dark, anonymous, largely female collectivities – the Moirai, Furies, Gorgons, Graiai, Phorkydes – have given way to the bright splendour of the Olympian gods), but also of the irrepressibility of these more primitive powers: the mindless violence of volcanic eruption is still a fact of human experience; the Fates and Furies have not left us; on the edge of things there are darker powers yet than the company of Zeus.

Moreover even within the Homeric–Hesiodic model of Olympian divinity, there is more room than we perhaps at first allow for a sense of the uncanny and the alien. Homer deeply influenced the whole history of Greek religious imagery, in literature and in art. His gods behave for the most part as men, with the civility and also with the crude brashness, the compulsive self-assertion, of human social existence. It is natural to imagine them (and generations of Greek artists have fixed the iconography of divinity for us) as men who are more than men, physically more perfect, more handsome, taller, enduring timelessly in youth or in maturity: the bronze god from Artemisium in the National Museum at Athens (Zeus or Poseidon), the Apollo of the Olympia pediment, the seated, fraternally conversing divinities of the Parthenon frieze. And it is natural to imagine the gods of the great scenes of Homeric poetry in such guise: Athena speaking with assured civility to Achilles or amused as a connoisseur at the deviousness of Odysseus, Aphrodite sharply reducing Helen to compliance. But there *are* Homeric scenes of a different order. For one, the Apollo who comes 'like the night' to avenge Chryses the priest in the first book of the *Iliad*, 'carrying across his shoulders the bow and the hooded │ quiver; and the shafts clashed on the shoulders of the god walking │ angrily'. He fires his arrows unseen, kneeling 'apart and opposite the ships', and 'the corpse fires burned everywhere and did not stop burning'.

Even further from the image of socialized humanity is the unseen Apollo who 'begins' (the sacrificial image is almost inevitable) the slaughter of Patroclus in *Iliad* 16, a Patroclus who, moments earlier, had swept the Trojans before him 'with the force of the running war-god', 'like something greater │ than human'.

The comparisons, by which a man is made to seem the analogue of a god, are ironic preparation for what comes now:

> . . . there Patroklos, the end of your life was shown forth,
> since Phoibos came against you there in the strong encounter
> dangerously, nor did Patroklos see him as he moved through
> the battle, and shrouded in a deep mist came in against him
> and stood behind him, and struck his back and his broad shoulders
> with a flat stroke of the hand so that his eyes spun. Phoibos
> Apollo now struck away from his head the helmet
> four-horned and hollow-eyed, and under the feet of the horses
> it rolled clattering, and the plumes above it were defiled
> by blood and dust.
>
> (Homer, *Iliad* 16.787–96 trs. Lattimore)

Patroclus has been touched by divinity and his helmet is off; it was Achilles' helmet, and now that Patroclus' wearing of it has doomed him to death, like an animal ritually adorned, the gods transfer ownership of it to Hector, doomed next to die. Patroclus is unwounded but he has begun to die; nothing can save him, as nothing can save the sacrificial victim once the hairs are cut.

Here are hints of a darker, altogether more uncanny aspect of divinity than that seen in the divine assemblies of Olympus. In the Homeric poems they remain hints, but in the world of fifth-century tragedy they are developed into a complex image of dark and light, of human and alien, of the 'self' and the 'other' in the notion of divine power.

In the *Oresteia* of Aeschylus a major theme is the extent to which the past controls and determines present and future. In *Agamemnon*, as the action advances so our sense of the well-springs of the action moves remorselessly backwards into the past: a year, ten years, a generation, perhaps even to the founding of the house. *Agamemnon* is haunted by the presence of the past. But by the end of the trilogy it is not the human past but creatures from the remotest antiquity of the world itself that have come to haunt the play. We have only a momentary and confused sense of the Furies at the end of *Choephoroi*, but in the opening scenes of *Eumenides* we are presented with a compelling image of inhuman powers that defy description: not women but Gorgons, and yet not Gorgons but rather wingless Harpies, unlike anything Apollo's *prophētis* has ever seen. And yet these creatures, who track Orestes like bloodhounds, enticed, almost seduced by the smell of human blood, who whine and howl like animals, are divinities immemorially old; they are of the dark, the children of Night, and to them the Olympian gods are young upstarts who fail to recognize them and will try to strip them of prerogatives which have been theirs since the birth of things, guaranteed by Fate. And in the end their duty of instilling terror into the community of men is acknowledged and underwritten by Athena herself. The Furies are not to be displaced by Olympian persuasive reasoning; they are the fearful face of divinity.

Aeschylus' theatrical image remains astonishingly bold; it testifies to the need to make a space within the world of myth for divinity as terror, as alien, untamed by assimilation to humanity. The same need is apparent, however differently handled, in the work of Sophocles and Euripides. In Euripides' *Hippolytus* the divinities who enclose the play, Aphrodite and Artemis, are terrifying precisely in that their power, their superhuman power, is at the service of a mentality which is in all things human. Their vengefulness, their determination to defend their honour (*timē*) and the respect (*sebas*) that is the prerogative of their power, cannot be rejected as inhuman (we shall see them displayed in their turn by each of the human characters of the play); it is the immediacy, the effortlessness of revenge, not its motivation, which alone sets them apart from men. These divinities speak to us with the clear, ordered articulateness that is the hallmark of Euripidean humanity. For divinity as alien, as 'other', we have to look elsewhere in the play.

Aphrodite's revenge works through human motivations (her own, Phaedra's and Theseus'); it is activated by Theseus' prayer to

Poseidon, a prayer which in this case does not have to establish a divine obligation since its fulfilment is already promised. The fulfilment is conveyed to us in the messenger-speech that follows immediately upon the scene between father and son. Hippolytus leaves Trozen in a chariot drawn by the horses he has lovingly tamed and made his own. On the deserted shore beyond the city a monstrous tidal wave blocks out all sight of familiar points of reference and hurls a bull from the sea up onto the shore in front of the chariot. The terrified horses bolt, the chariot is smashed and Hippolytus is dragged entangled in the reins and battered, almost to outright death, on the rocks. The language and the imagery of this passage powerfully create an awareness that what is happening here is the wreck and destruction of human skills, of a lifetime of effort spent in trying to create a common world of man and animal; it is the untaming of the wild, the utter and instantaneous annihilation of human technology, of culture itself. Seamanship, metallurgy, horse-breaking, wagon-building are all associated in our perception of what is here swept away. At the end Hippolytus is 'outraged', barely recognizable; horses and bull have vanished (*Hippolytus* 1173–242). Euripides' image 'says' that to come face to face with a god is not just to confront a being who thinks and feels like a man but has the power of divinity; it may also be to confront the utterly, destructively alien; impossible, uncanny, sickening, yet undeniably 'there' and beyond us to will away. It is the same with Dionysus' revenge in *Bacchae*, the same with Medea's daemonic revenge in *Medea*.

In these plays we see dramatists expanding the range and reach of Homeric myth to include still more of the darkness of divinity. The imagery of animal forms, in particular, is pervasive and lies always just behind the visible foreground of Olympian humanity. In the *Oresteia*, and in *Hippolytus*, the theatrical realization of myth brings divine powers before us on the stage. I want to end this part of my essay by looking at a play in which divinity is hidden, figured in the language and thematic structure of the play, but unseen even in report.

In Sophocles' *Oedipus Tyrannus* our awareness of divinity, which is essential to our sympathetic response to the events of the play, is created by a complex interweaving of metaphor and dramatic motif, through which we perceive the existence of another world than the world of the stage action; the terrifying interaction of these two worlds destroys Oedipus as a human being, in the ordinary, comfortable sense, and is given added expression in the uncanny role of coincidence and chance in the play. Or rather of coincidence and not of chance. Things fall into place with a fearful impression of inevitability, never foreseen but always felt (it is *as if* Jocasta's prayer to Apollo were at once answered in the arrival of the messenger from Corinth),[21] and the persons of the play fall together with eerie economy (the sole surviving witness of Laius' death turns out to coincide with the slave who was charged with Oedipus' exposure in infancy). These structural ironies in Sophocles' play have often enough been treated, after Aristotle, as 'improbabilities' and dramatic flaws, but that is to miss their essential point, which is to create that sense of a half-seen divine dimension to experience which we have met already in Herodotus.

The two worlds, divine and human, of Sophocles' *Oedipus* are imaged in a series of oppositions that run through the play, oppositions of place and of awareness. Let me take the second of these oppositions first. The image of sightedness and blindness is clearly fundamental: the blind seer Teiresias and the sighted Oedipus blind to the realities of the world about him constitute an opposition absolutely central to Sophocles' meaning.[22] There is another, between Creon and Teiresias, which extends the range of the image. Creon is *par excellence* the political man: his first thought on bringing news of the oracle from Delphi is one of political security, of protecting Oedipus' power by secret, rather than public, discussion of the news he brings. Accused of treason he addresses the chorus as 'citizens' (513) and puts first of what he has to lose his standing 'in the city' (521); he defends himself by subtle and persuasive political reasoning, by analysis of the motivation of power; he counters Oedipus' appeal to the *polis* by asserting his own membership of it (630); and throughout the play he displays a politician's circumspection in anything that affects the *polis*: he will not venture an opinion (569) or a decision (1438f.) without adequate knowledge. Power and a sense of responsibility to the community are things he understands. By total contrast, Teiresias inhabits another world of consciousness; it is above all his complete unawareness of what the city demands of him, his inability to respond to Oedipus' repeated and emphatic use of the word 'city' (five times in forty lines) in appealing to him, that both understandably triggers Oedipus' accusations and seems to place him outside the human community of Thebes. He is Apollo's slave and denies himself status within the *polis* (411). Moreover in opposition to Creon's transparently political language, Teiresias speaks in riddles and thus shares the language of the Sphinx and of Apollo himself.[23] It is as if he does not belong among men.

The issue of belonging as it applies to the communities of men and to the space through which Oedipus moves in his recollected experience is another central part of Sophocles' meaning, and gradually the sense of place in the play is used to reinforce our awareness of the existence of another world than the world we see. Above all it is Oedipus' belonging which comes into question. At the outset of the play, though from elsewhere, he is firmly of Thebes; he belongs there; he is its rescuer from the inhuman Sphinx and now the holder of its power. Beyond Thebes, place seems at first unimportant. The question where Laius was killed is answered only by 'not in Thebes'; beyond that the question seems unimportant. But as the play proceeds its 'geography' grows slowly more complex and more disturbing; is Oedipus rather of Corinth, whose king's son he takes himself to be? Or, as Teiresias asserts, is he a man lost, one who does not know where he is or with whom he lives? By degrees the image of other places, of the cross-roads ('the three ways') and of the mountain (Cithaeron), take on ever greater definition and come to haunt Oedipus' mind and memory as constituting and standing for that other world to which he must return, to which he is in some sense owed and which should have been his tomb. At the end of the play, when he goes for the last time within the palace, he re-enters the house because he belongs nowhere else, nowhere under the sun, and he re-enters the family as one whose story has made nonsense of the language of human community and its relationships (his children's brother, his wife's son) and of its values (his father's killer).

Sophocles' play is one in which no god is seen to be active and no motivation given for Oedipus' destruction. Nonetheless we are given a sense, powerful and terrifying as perhaps nowhere else in Greek literature, of divinity as 'other' in counterpoint with the world of men, reducing the categories of that world to meaninglessness wherever it touches them.

I have been arguing in this essay for a view of Greek religion which tries to take in the whole range of the evidence, liturgical and literary, and to make sense of it as a whole whose parts are meaningfully related to each other. The resulting statement about the nature of divinity, and about man's relation to the divine, is best summed up in a famous remark attributed by Herodotus to the Athenian Solon. Solon replies to Croesus' assumption of lasting human prosperity by observing that 'divinity is envious and disorderly' (Herodotus 1.32.1). Envy (*phthonos*) is an eminently human feeling and a god who displays it is reassuringly intelligible in human terms; but disorder (*tarachē*), as men perceive themselves, is not, and the uniqueness of the divine is the combination of these contradictory aspects, predictable and unpredictable, human and non-human; the essence of divinity lies in the paradoxical coexistence of incompatible truths about human experience. In this there is much that is universal in the creation of religious imagery, and much that is illuminatingly Greek. For if god, as I take it, is made in the image of man (inevitably, as Xenophanes saw), equally inevitably divinity must surpass man in some sense or another, and must reveal the possibility of 'otherness', since the world of man's experience is not one which he could, or would, have made. A god wholly within the compass of man's image of himself explains nothing, offers no reassurance against the fear of chaos, and any religion must extend the range of the explicability of things beyond what men can derive from projection of their own self-awareness on to the external world. Greek religion, if we see it as a whole (and, I believe, only if we see it as a whole) certainly extends the explicability of things, and in ways that are at the same time revealing of fundamental Greek assumptions about the world. The myth of Prometheus, for example, in explaining how the world is what it is, offers a model of two divinities engaged in mutual trickery over the division of rights, the outcome depending on the superiority and intricacy of Zeus's mind; set beside the Hesiodic succession-myth in which, twice over, son ousts father in a combination of guile and force, and beside the model of a conflict of pure force in which the Olympians displace the Titans in a war in Heaven, it tells us much about the experience of tensions within the human family and community as they pass through time: conflict between generations, as sons struggle with an ageing father for control of the patrimony; conflict between siblings for a preferential share of the patrimony for their own dependent families; and conflict between clans for control of territory. Thus these stories not only illuminate 'things as they are' for ancient Greeks, but in drawing on experience to do so, illuminate for us the underlying structural tensions of ancient Greek society.[24] And, if we are prepared to think about our own assumptions, they may perhaps tell us as much about our world and our society.

2

Greek poetry and Greek religion

P. E. EASTERLING

Greek poetry is unquestionably our most extensive, varied and explicit body of evidence for Greek religion in the classical period. It is notoriously difficult to evaluate, but we have a strong incentive to try to make something of it, since the alternatives are so inadequate: there is hardly anything by way of detailed first-hand reporting outside the literary sources, and although inscriptions – records of dedications, priests or festivals – can tell us a good deal about religious life they by no means answer all the questions we need to ask. But although there is good reason to look for ways of approaching Greek poetry as a source for Greek religion we at once find ourselves facing serious problems of interpretation, all the more serious, often enough, for being unacknowledged. There are two main areas of difficulty: first, differing notions of the division between sacred and secular, and second, the tendency on our part, as twentieth-century readers, to monotheistic or rationalistic prejudice, which may lead us to distort the Greek material and even to wonder how seriously the Greeks themselves took their religion.

For us, whether or not we are actually believers, there is a fairly clear-cut distinction between sacred and secular. Religion in the Judaeo-Christian (and particularly the Protestant) tradition means sabbath observance, a sacred book, a fixed liturgy, a church or synagogue or chapel as the principal setting for worship. And in the realm of literature a category of religious poetry can be fairly neatly demarcated (Herbert's *The Temple*, Donne's *Holy Sonnets*, Thompson's *The Hound of Heaven*), just as sacred music is easily identified (plainsong, church cantatas, revivalist hymns . . .). Of course the distinctions are not hard and fast: some of T. S. Eliot's poetry is difficult to classify, and so is Christian rock music, but at least a rough dividing line can be drawn with some confidence.

The Greek situation was radically different. There was no universal sacred book telling religious stories in an 'orthodox' version, no standard liturgy such as we find in the Book of Common Prayer or the Missal, no concept of the sabbath, though of course there were plenty of festival holy days, ritual forms of words for different cults, and sacred texts associated with particular groups such as the Orphics. There were also a great many types of specifically religious song addressed to gods – hymns, paeans, processionals and so on, intended for particular deities and occasions. But the festivals for which they were designed were not held 'in church' – the temples were essentially places where the cult statues lived[1] – and associated with the festivals was a great range of literature and music which might be similar in form but was not obviously religious in content. Indeed it was often performed as part of a competition: tragic and comic plays and dithyrambic song and dance at festivals in honour of Dionysus, and recitations of epic poetry by rhapsodes, as at Delos or the Panathenaia at Athens.

All this makes the 'sacred'/'secular' distinction very difficult to apply. How, for instance, should an Aristophanic comedy be defined? On the 'sacred' side one could mention the fact that the comedies were performed at important festivals in honour of Dionysus, in the holy space of the god's theatre. His statue was brought to the theatre for the performances, which were presumably intended to please him, as entertainments that he would enjoy watching, and at the same time to conduce to his greater glory, since his worshippers were devoting a great deal of time, money and competitive energy to these productions. Besides, there is plenty of evidence to suggest that the specifically cultic aspects of the Dionysiac festivals – the sacrifices and procession – were taken very seriously.[2] Of course these were also occasions of great popular celebration and civic pageantry, but there is no reason for thinking that they were events from which all religious significance had disappeared, like our Easter Monday carnivals or Christmas pantomimes. As K. J. Dover has remarked, 'to the ordinary Greek, festive and ceremonial occasions were the primary constituent of religion; theology came a very bad second'.[3] On the other hand, the plays are not about subjects that one could easily call religious: they are not miracle- or mystery-plays, and when gods are presented as comic characters – Hermes in *Peace*, Poseidon in *Birds* – there is no edifying spiritual message to be deduced from the things they say and do. And although Old Comedy may well have originated in ritual performances it had long since developed into a sophisticated art-form which bore very few traces of its ritual origins; the formal variations between the different plays of Aristophanes strongly suggest that there was no set pattern imposed by religious tradition.[4]

Perhaps, then, the best answer to the question of definition is that it should not be posed in the terms 'sacred *or* secular?' at all. Every play, whether comedy or tragedy, seems in fact to have been both at once, its subject matter free from the constraints of a particular liturgy, ritual or doctrine, but its role in the festival still that of pleasing and honouring the god. Paradoxically even the presiding deity Dionysus could be made fun of in a play, as he is in *Frogs*, where he is an outrageously stupid and cowardly buffoon, but this fact can easily be misinterpreted if it is considered in isolation. Dionysus *is* after all the 'hero', and it is he who wields the ultimate power in the play, he who chooses to bring Aeschylus, not Euripides, back to the world of men. Another point to note is the pervasiveness in Greek drama of religious activity: men are all the time represented as appealing to the gods, praising them, trying to avert their wrath, swearing by them, sacrificing to them, taking part in their festivals. The society mirrored by comedy and tragedy – with whatever satirical or idealizing distortions – is a society full of religious life, a further reason for not separating sacred and secular on the model of our own Western world.

A passage from *Frogs* will illustrate these points, but any other play of Aristophanes would serve the purpose equally well. Dionysus and his slave Xanthias are on a journey to the Under-world to bring back Euripides. They have been warned by Heracles that after crossing a great lake and passing places of torment they will reach the happy region belonging to people who in their life on earth had been initiated into the Mysteries: here amid plan-tations of myrtle they will find bands of men and women singing and dancing to the music of the *aulos*[5] (154–7). This is the first intimation of an important phase in the stage action, the entry of the Chorus in its role as Initiates. The scene opens at 312 with the sound of *aulos* music, then the Chorus are heard summoning Iacchus, and the whole sequence that follows depends on an elaborate development of the idea of worship at the Mysteries. It was an apt dramatic device to choose, since the essence of mystic initiation was ritual preparation for a blessed hereafter – so who better than a Chorus of Initiates to welcome Dionysus to the Underworld? The Athenians were familiar with two main mystery cults, that of Demeter and her daughter Persephone 'the Maiden' (*Korē*) at Eleusis, and that of Orpheus, which had very close con-nections with the worship of Dionysus. Although the mystery cults were not public, and some parts of their ritual were kept strictly secret, they were familiar phenomena, especially the great procession from Athens to Eleusis often mentioned in our literary sources. The god Iacchus who is hymned by the Chorus here was an important figure in the procession to Eleusis and was some-times thought of as a son of Demeter or Persephone, sometimes as Dionysus himself under another name.[6] At all events he had intimate links with Dionysiac worship, so that there is special piquancy in presenting the god in the play as listening to a hymn addressed to Iacchus (325–36; 340–52).

The language the Chorus use in this hymn is wholly appro-priate to the context of ecstatic worship: we can find parallels for the choice of imagery, and the cry 'Iacchus O Iacchus' and the address 'Iacchus of high renown' sound like genuine ritual for-mulas. The metre, based on the ionic (∪ ∪ – –), is one particularly associated with Dionysiac cult songs.[7] Although the whole tone is exuberant and playful, and the two stanzas of the song are separated by a bathetic joke – Xanthias' eager response to a 'whiff of roast pork' from the Initiates' feast – there is nothing to suggest that parody of this affectionate kind deflates or debunks the Mysteries; it is rather a case of the festive and excited atmosphere of the religious event being appropriated as an enhancement of the play:

Chorus	Here in thy home we await thy tread,
	O come Iacchus of high renown.
	Dance o'er this meadow, shake on thy head
	The berries that cluster, thy myrtle crown.
	And lead with the beat of thy tireless feet
	The holy bands in the mystic rite,
	The dance of wantonness and delight,
	Where the Graces find their chiefest pleasure,
	Thy hallowed worshippers' sacred measure.
Xanthias	O queen of high renown, daughter of Demeter, what a lovely whiff of roast pork.
Dionysus	Keep quiet, will you. You may get a bit of sausage if you do.
Chorus	Wake. For the blazing torch he wields,
	Daystar of our nightlong festival.
	He comes, Iacchus, ablaze are the fields;
	See how the old man hears his call,
	And all the tears and the long long years,
	As he moves his limbs, fall away and are gone.
	Blest god, with thy fiery lamp, lead on
	To the flowery marshy floor advancing,
	Lead on the youths in the sacred dancing.

(trs. D. W. Lucas & F. J. A. Cruso)

The Chorus go on to parody the ritual appeal, regular at the beginning of a religious festival, for purity and silence, but this quickly turns into light-hearted social comment: the people who are to abstain from *these* mysteries are to be people who have no taste for comic poetry, who promote civil discord, take bribes, or betray their city. This is followed by the 'festival' proper, with songs to 'Her who saves' (*Sōteira* – presumably Persephone), to Demeter, and finally to Iacchus again. The song to Demeter is interesting: it combines straightforward hymnic language with a direct appeal for victory in the dramatic competition:

> Queen Demeter, stand before us,
> Smile upon your favourite Chorus!
> Grant that when we dance and play
> As befits your holy day,
> Part in earnest, part in jest,
> We may shine above the rest,
> And our play in all men's eyes
> Favour find, and win the prize.
>
> (trs. D. Barrett)

The element of 'play' already much emphasized in the Initiates' songs comes out most strikingly in the Iacchus hymn, which ends in a frolicsome way with jokes about the Chorus' costumes and a reference to a 'pretty little girl' whose breast is seen peeping from her torn tunic. The scene reaches its climax with Dionysus and Xanthias joining in the dance – a thoroughly lively and extremely bawdy comic sequence, but not one that uses religion in order to mock or denigrate it. On the contrary, the religious elements seem to have a very direct function as well as being brilliantly exploited for the comic purposes of the plot. We ought certainly not to overlook the close links between the songs and dances of this scene and the real-life forms of cult activity. For instance, the appeal to Demeter for victory suggests that the hymns might be felt to have effective religious power as well as being part of the light-hearted make-believe of the play.[8]

Clearly there is no hard-and-fast dividing line between sacred and secular in a scene like this one; though perhaps it was bound to be a complex case, since the god Dionysus is a character in the play, and the play was composed for his festival. But even when we consider seemingly more straightforward examples the same problems of interpretation arise. The drinking party seems an unlikely enough context for the expression of religious sentiment, but it was standard Greek practice to begin the proceedings with the pouring of libations to the gods and then to invoke them in a paean,[9] which perhaps suggests that they were thought to be sharing, or at least blessing, the entertainment.[10] Xenophanes gives us a vivid picture of the setting for a *symposion* which shows how misleading it can be to use analogies from our own society:

Now the floor is clean, and so are everybody's hands and the drinking cups. Someone puts plaited garlands on our heads; someone else hands round sweet-scented myrrh in a dish. The mixing bowl stands full of good cheer; and more wine is ready to hand, wine which promises never to fail, sweet wine in the wine jars, smelling of flowers. In the midst incense sends up its holy scent, and there is cold water, sweet and pure. Golden loaves are set out, and there is a magnificent table loaded with cheese and rich honey. The altar in the middle is decorated all round with flowers, and song and festivity fill the house. Men of good cheer must first hymn the god with reverent words and pure speech, pouring libations and praying to be able to do right – for this is more within our reach. It is not bad behaviour for a man to drink as much as he can carry home without the help of an attendant (unless he is very old). We should praise the man who as he drinks reveals noble thoughts, relying on his memory and his striving for virtue. He never recounts the battles of Titans or Giants or Centaurs, the fancies of earlier generations, or violent factions. There is no good in these things; but it is always proper to have respect for the gods. (Xenophanes, fr. 1)

Alongside the food and wine and the atmosphere of revelry there is an equally important place for the incense, the altar, the libations and prayers to the gods. Indeed the specific point of the poem seems to be that there is a right and a wrong kind of poetry to sing at banquets: the right kind is that which shows proper respect for the gods and avoids insulting them by telling stories of their involvement in primitive violence, like Hesiod's tale of the

Battle of Gods and Titans, which Xenophanes evidently found unedifying. The idea of purity which runs through the poem links together what we would think of as sacred and secular elements: the same word *katharos* (pure, clean) is used to describe the floor, the hands of the revellers, the drinking cups, the water which will be mixed with the wine, and the words that are to be used for the celebration of the gods. Ritual purity, aesthetic propriety and moral wholesomeness are all combined in Xenophanes' picture, and we should be wrong to try to separate them out. It would be equally mistaken to think, as some scholars have, that there must be some special explanation for the ideas given emphasis in this poem, and that it was perhaps intended for a gathering of people devoted to the philosophic life, or for some sort of religious fellowship. [11] All the details can be paralleled in 'normal' festive contexts, and we can safely take the poem as evidence for the differences between Greek ways of thought and our own. [12]

Another example from Greek poetry is the genre of *epinikion* or victory ode. The many surviving poems composed (by Pindar and Bacchylides) for victorious athletes show very clearly that the gods and their worship were ever-present in people's minds, even in contexts which we might expect to be far removed from the religious sphere. Success in the Games was an achievement which brought immense prestige to the victor; it was celebrated with grand processions, lavish consumption of food and drink, and if possible a specially composed performance by a choir singing and dancing to the music of the lyre or *aulos*. The poems were expressly designed to honour the individuals who commissioned them, and it was natural that their themes should have a human focus: the victor and the place of his victory, his athletic exploits elsewhere, his family and their sporting record, his city and its distinctions. But at every stage we find the gods and heroes involved: mention of a victory at Olympia brings in Pelops, who was worshipped as a hero in the sacred precinct, and Heracles who founded the games, above all Zeus, to whom they were dedicated, and whose great altar at Olympia was the centre of all the associated cult activities. Similarly the best way to praise the victor's family was to trace it to a divine origin, as in *Olympian* 6 for Hagesias, whose clan, the Iamidai, held the hereditary priesthood of Zeus's altar at Olympia and could claim descent from both Poseidon and Apollo, or in *Olympian* 9 for Epharmostos of Opus, to whom as a member of the local nobility Pindar gives a very grand divine pedigree (rejecting the usual version of a myth in order to do so). Respectful attention is paid, too, to the special divinities of the victor's city: Hera Parthenia at Stymphalos (*Ol.* 6), the Nymphs of the hot springs at Himera in Sicily (*Ol.* 12), the Horae (Seasons) at Corinth (*Ol.* 13). When we look further into the historical evidence we find that the actual occasions marked by performance of the odes were often specifically religious: a procession to one of the altars at Olympia, for example, or back in the victor's home city a procession to the altar of the local hero, and a dedication there of the crown of victory.[13] Finally, whenever Pindar looks for poetic adornment of the facts of the victor's success he turns to myths of heroes, which can never be told without extensive reference to the gods, since the heroes were all closely related to the gods and dependent on them in all their activities.

The effect is both to elevate, to put *this* wrestler or winner of the footrace on a par with the great beings of a glorious past, and at the same time to point the contrast between men and gods, for Pindar all the time reminds his victor and his audience in their moment of celebration that by comparison with the gods men are weak, ephemeral, 'a dream of a shadow'.[14] The point seems to be that in Greek poetry men cannot be defined and discussed without reference to the divine: a great deal of Greek literature from Homer onwards is concerned with the attempt to hold in balance a sense of the distance between men and gods on the one hand and a sense of men's capacity to emulate gods on the other. If men can hope and try within their limits to be godlike it is only because whatever they have is god-given: the valuable achievement of the victor – like that of the poet – is a favour from the gods and must be acknowledged as such.

The comparison between athletic victor and poet reminds us that poets themselves, or their productions, were often in competition for prizes at festivals. In one sense these can be compared with our own festivals of music and the arts: they were certainly cultural events with an intrinsic appeal to their audiences as entertainment, but on the other hand they were always dedicated to a particular deity, and the basic idea seems to have been that since the gods shared the same tastes as mortals they would enjoy the show too, and enjoy it all the more if it was organized as a contest, just as human audiences enjoy the sporting element of any kind of competition. And besides entertainment there was also honour: it was a way of demonstrating one's respect for a divine being to set up an event at his festival in which rival choirs were trying as hard as possible to achieve their best, and the event was not trivialized because the victorious choir won a prize. Once again, the distinction between sacred and secular is hard to draw, and we are better off if we take Greek poetry on its own terms, without trying to replace them with our own.

The other type of prejudice we need to guard against is the notion, which we hardly ever think of questioning, that polytheism must by definition be inferior to monotheism or to some kind of philosophical position such as humanism. We take it for granted that a polytheistic religion, with its manifold divine beings, festivals and rituals and its variant local stories including illogical overlaps and confusions, could not have a serious appeal for sophisticated and thoughtful people: for us, sophistication means theology or systematic philosophical thought. But we should be rash to deny sophistication to a poet like Pindar, an elegant and ambitious writer if ever there was one. He takes a profoundly serious interest in the richness and diversity of Greek cults: he makes no attempt to smooth over local differences or explain them away, but rather dwells on the multiplicity of Greek religious practice as one sign among many of man's intimate involvement with the gods.

This sense of involvement, strongly expressed in all early Greek poetry, has often been overlooked – or distorted into theology – by scholars intent on the search for spirituality, 'inwardness' and doctrine. They have tended to ask the wrong questions, such as 'What did X really believe?', as if the cults – what the worshippers actually did – could only be superficial and superstitious trappings which give no clue to the 'real' emotions underneath.[15] It is here that poetry can be a positive help to us. It may well be highly unreliable as documentary evidence: it may give an idealized and fanciful picture of history, of cult practices and of the supposed relations between men and gods, and it cannot of course tell us what people 'really believed', but it *can* suggest what they thought valuable and important in their religion and what kinds of religious emotion they saw fit to try to express. Some sample passages will perhaps help to illustrate the qualities the Greeks attributed to the gods and the range of what they defined as religious experience (though we should of course allow for the possibility that some of the most intense manifestations were thought too holy to express in literature at all).

Many passages of Greek poetry convey a vivid sense of the divine presence. One of the most memorable is the account (already cited in ch. 1) of Apollo's response when the priest Chryses calls to him for help:

He went in silence along the shore of the loud-resounding sea, and when he was alone he made many prayers to lord Apollo, son of Leto of the lovely hair. 'Hear me, lord of the silver bow, protector of Chryse and Cilla, mighty ruler of Tenedos, O Smintheus! If I ever built a temple that pleased you, if ever I burned in your honour the thigh bones wrapped in fat of bulls and goats, answer my prayer now: let your arrows make the Danaans pay for my tears.' Phoebus Apollo heard his prayer and came down from the peaks of Olympus angered in his heart, with his bow and close-covered quiver on his shoulders. The arrows clattered on his shoulders as he moved in anger; and he came like the night. He took up his position apart from the ships and fired an arrow; there was a dreadful clanging of his silver bow . . .(*Iliad* 1.34–49)

The dire power of Apollo as sender of plague is frighteningly brought out here; but sometimes the epiphany is more benign, as when Poseidon comes down in response to Pelops' prayer for help in Pindar's first *Olympian*:

Going alone in the darkness by the grey-white sea he called aloud on the loud-thundering god of the trident, who appeared to him close at hand. (71–4)

This is all we hear of the moment of meeting between the god and his favourite: it is followed by Pelops' prayer and Poseidon's fulfilment of it, but the sense of closeness to the divine is very powerfully evoked. In the sixth *Olympian* there is a similar scene: the young hero Iamos wades out under the night sky into the river Alpheios and calls on his divine ancestors, his grandfather Poseidon and his father Apollo, for a sign to guide his future. Apollo's voice is heard in response, directing him to the place –the hill of Kronos at Olympia – where he is to have prophetic powers (*Ol.* 6.57–70). The details of setting – the sea-shore, the mid-stream of the river, the night time – emphasize the specialness of these events, just as in *Oedipus at Colonus* the awesome moment when Oedipus is summoned by the gods to a special destiny is heralded by claps of thunder, 'then suddenly a voice called him, making everyone's hair stand on end in fear, for a god called him repeatedly, "Oedipus, Oedipus, why are we delaying?" ' (1623–8). English has no precise way of rendering the intimate and familiar tone of the address to Oedipus: ὦ οὖτος οὖτος Οἰδίπους τί μέλλομεν | χωρεῖν; In all these cases there is a combination of the familiar and the alarmingly different: the god can be approached and may respond effectively, even benignly, to the prayer of a favoured worshipper, but he is also mysterious and terrifying.

All through Greek poetry there is insistent emphasis on the power and easy superiority of the gods: in strength, skill and

beauty they are infinitely greater than human beings, but their activities are conceived in human terms, and the anthropomorphic language that describes them is used comfortably, as if the poets found this an adequate and satisfying way of speaking about the gods. One of the most radiant scenes is in the *Homeric Hymn to Apollo*, when Apollo joins the gods on Olympus and rouses them to song and dance:

The son of glorious Leto goes playing his hollow lyre to rocky Pytho, wearing immortal, fragrant garments, and his lyre makes a lovely sound, played with a golden plectrum. Then he goes from earth to Olympus as swift as thought, to the home of Zeus and the assembly of the other gods. At once the immortals take part in the music, and all the Muses together, singing in response to one another with their fine voices, celebrate the immortal gifts of the gods and the miseries of men – for men live without sense or resource under the sway of the deathless gods and can find no cure for death or defence against old age. And the Graces with their beautiful hair and the cheerful Seasons and Harmonia and Hebe and Zeus's daughter Aphrodite join in the dance, holding each other by the wrists. And among them dances Artemis, shooter of arrows, sister of Apollo, not mean or slight, but tall and splendid to look upon. Ares too and keen-sighted Argeiphontes [Hermes] play among them, and Phoebus Apollo plays the lyre for them, dancing with fine high steps, and a radiance shines about him, as his feet and his fine-spun tunic twinkle. Golden-haired Leto and wise-counselling Zeus take delight in their great hearts as they watch their dear son playing among the immortal gods. (183–206)

We should note in passing that this ideal picture of divine activity mirrors what human poets and musicians and their bands of singers and dancers did in real life, and thereby it makes a great claim for the divine power of human poetry. The *choros* of Muses is the immortal prototype of all human *choroi*, and the subjects of the Muses' songs, just like those of human singers, are 'the immortal gifts of the gods and the miseries of men'. The only difference, as Hesiod makes clear in a passage (*Theogony* 1–103) which in some ways recalls this one, is that for men the enjoyment of poetry is a means of forgetting care, whereas the gods have no cares to forget.

Yet this anthropomorphic vision of the gods never limits them to the merely human, as we see in the stress that is laid here on the 'miseries of men' by contrast with divine happiness. There is always a strong sense of the difference and distance between god and men and an awareness that full epiphany of a god in his or her true form is liable to be more than mortals can bear. Thus the story was told that when Cadmus' daughter Semele asked to see Zeus, her lover, in his true godhead she was consumed in the lightning fire. Behind the radiant iconography lies the idea of a divine power too vast and terrifying for human beings to envisage or describe. Accounts of even the most beneficent epiphanies, like the one in the *Homeric Hymn to Demeter*, when the goddess appears to Metaneira with instructions for the establishment of her cult at Eleusis and we are told of her great stature and beauty, the lovely fragrance of her dress and the radiance about her that fills the house like lightning (275–80), still bring out the fear, shock and speechlessness of the human beings to whom these visions are vouchsafed and the ease with which the divine anger can be aroused.[16] In the *Homeric Hymn to Aphrodite* Anchises has been given the supreme favour of Aphrodite and allowed to share her bed; when she abandons her disguise and wakes him from sleep to tell him who she is his response is one of terror: he turns away his face and begs her to have mercy on him (181–90).

The poets convey a similar sense of mystery in their reflections on the gods' purposes: images suggesting the brilliance of everything divine, like the dazzling light of Olympus or the radiance cast by a god's presence, are counterbalanced by dark language evoking the impenetrability of the mind of Zeus and the terror of his punishment. 'Tangled and dark stretch the paths of his mind, not to be perceived by the sight' sing the Chorus in Aeschylus' *Supplices* (93–5), and more than one poet uses the imagery of the sudden storm to suggest the unexpected and violent nature of his visitations.[17] (Since Zeus was god of the thunder and lightning the storm could be seen both as a literal manifestation of his wrath and as an image evoking something beyond straight description.)

All that the poets say about the gods is echoed in their descriptions of holy places, a very important recurrent subject which surely offers some kind of clue to the quality of Greek religious experience. The reverence felt for sanctuaries – Apollo's at Delos and Delphi, Zeus's at Olympia and Dodona, Athena's on the Acropolis at Athens – or for mountain-tops like Oeta, sacred to Zeus, the site of Heracles' assumption into heaven, is expressed with striking intensity and matched by a powerful sense of the need for purity on the part of the worshipper who approaches these holy but dangerous places. Their holiness evidently depended partly on sacred associations – stories of divine manifestations in certain spots – and partly on the numinous atmosphere of the places themselves. (At Delphi it is easy for even the modern visitor to understand the Greeks' idea that this was the centre of the world.) The opening scene of *Oedipus at Colonus* is concerned with the sanctity of the grove of the Eumenides, a theme which turns out to be highly significant, since much of the play's action is focused on the crossing of boundaries, whether they separate sacred and unhallowed ground, the city and foreign land, or life and death:

This place is holy, burgeoning with bay, olive and vine. And within the grove the close-feathered nightingales sing their lovely song. (16–18)

Oedipus, who at last successfully crosses all the boundaries, is of course a great tragic figure, and there is the utmost interest in the play in his moral condition, but this is always closely associated with his ritual state in relation to the holy places and their divinities. If we try to interpret the play without taking account of its religious dimension we are liable to make a very limited reading of it.

The matter of the worshipper's ritual condition – pure or polluted, clean or unclean – is one of great importance in the texts we have been briefly considering.[18] It contrasts sharply with our modern emphasis on inward spiritual experience, but it should not therefore be too easily dismissed as 'primitive'. It may be true that the Greeks made comparatively modest claims on their gods, hoping at most for favour and support, and not – unless they were devotees of a special orgiastic cult or initiates in the Mysteries –for transfiguring inner experience, but we should not therefore be tempted to assume that their religion was quite inadequate for thinking people. Certainly the evidence of their very articulate and sophisticated literature points to different conclusions. It is hard to read Homer, Pindar, Aeschylus or Sophocles without gaining the impression that Greek religion made a profoundly serious imaginative appeal, at least to the poets who were its guardians. And, since the poets were usually composing for performance at popular festivals, it is natural to think that they were expressing feelings that other worshippers might recognize and share. Our task is to try, however imperfectly, to read their signals.

3

Early Greek views about life after death

N. J. RICHARDSON

The particulars of future beings must needs be dark unto ancient Theories, which Christian Philosophy yet determines but in a cloud of opinions.

Sir Thomas Browne, *Hydriotaphia* ch. iv

There is surely no society in which people's views about death and the after-life are entirely coherent and consistent, and the Greeks were no exception. Rituals of burial and mourning did not really change fundamentally throughout antiquity, but beliefs about what happened to a person at the point of death and afterwards were never fixed and always remained a subject for debate. The Greeks were faced here with the same problem which has confronted men at all times, and although some of the answers which they offered were different from those of other societies, it is not so difficult to understand the processes of thinking which led them to put forward the solutions which they gave.

The Greeks practised both inhumation and cremation of their dead, and the dominant method of burial varied from place to place and from one period to another. At almost all periods, however, in antiquity both methods could be found in use side by side, as is the case today. It is not easy to determine whether, or to what extent, variation of this practice reflects differences of belief. In the Homeric poems the prevailing view appears to be that when the body has been burnt the soul (*psychē*) is free to enter Hades, the realm of the dead (*Il.* 23.71–6; *Od.* 11.51–4, 216–22), and it is possible that cremation was thought to release the soul

50

from this world more rapidly and effectively than inhumation. But already in Homer the soul regularly leaves the body at the point of death and begins its journey towards Hades, and later it is clear that what really mattered was that the body should receive proper burial rites, whether these involved cremation or inhumation. It was a most solemn duty for the family or companions of the dead man to ensure that this was done. The *Iliad* ends with Priam's perilous journey to recover the body of his son Hector from Achilles, and the ensuing funeral, and Sophocles' *Ajax* and *Antigone* show how a dead person's relatives will risk or suffer death, rather than leave the body unburied. To fail in this duty was at all times regarded as one of the worst offences one could commit. It aroused the anger of the dead man, and brought down upon one divine punishment administered by the Erinyes, who were regarded as spirits of just vengeance activated by the dead man's curses. To refuse burial even to an enemy of one's state was an abnormal act. It is clear that in Sophocles' *Antigone* Creon has gone too far in decreeing that Polyneices' body should be left unburied where it fell. His corpse pollutes the land and prevents religious ceremonies from continuing in a way acceptable to the gods (*Ant.* 1016–22). Athenian law forbade the burial within Attica of traitors and those who had stolen sacred property, but even here burial could presumably be conducted outside the boundaries of the state.

After the death of a relative or friend certain natural human desires manifest themselves. First of all there is the need to show one's grief in a significant manner at the loss, which normally requires a period of mourning. Then it is felt to be necessary to ensure that the burial is conducted in a decent and honourable manner, and that suitable tributes are paid to the dead person's good qualities. Finally there is the more enduring desire to commemorate the dead in future, by both visible and non-material forms of monument. In ancient Greece, as elsewhere, these needs found satisfaction in a series of elaborate funeral rituals, and in the creation of memorials which sometimes reached a very high peak indeed of artistic and literary achievement. There was a constant tendency towards extravagance in these ceremonies and acts of commemoration, both because grief naturally seeks vehement expression, and also because such displays have always been thought to be a way of demonstrating the importance of the dead person. Greek political reformers frequently attempted to limit the expenditure and other excesses connected with funerals. At Athens, for example, there were at least three attempts to do so, one in the sixth century B.C. by Solon, another some time later, and a third by Demetrius of Phalerum at the end of the fourth century B.C. (Cicero, *De legibus* 2.26.64–6).

Nevertheless, mourning and funeral customs continued to arouse criticism from some members of society. There is an amusing satire on the subject by the second-century A.D. writer Lucian (*On Mourning*), which incidentally gives us a graphic picture of what usually took place on such occasions. Lucian says that when someone dies the family puts an *obol* in his mouth to pay Charon the ferryman for taking him across the Styx, without stopping to consider what coinage is current in the underworld. Then they bathe the body,

as though the lake below were not big enough for people there to bathe in, and after anointing with the finest perfume that corpse which is already hastening towards corruption, and crowning it with lovely flowers, they lay it in state dressed in fine clothes, apparently so that the dead person should not be cold on his journey or be seen naked by Cerberus.

There follow elaborate displays of grief, which even include tearing of clothes, rolling in the dust and beating one's head on the ground,

while the dead man, all decent, handsome and elaborately crowned with wreaths, lies in lofty and exalted state as though dressed up for a procession.

Some people even hire professional mourners to lead their laments, and after the funeral they hold contests and deliver orations at the tomb. As for the procession to the grave (*ekphora*), this is often an opportunity for an elaborate display of wealth on the part of the family, and at the funeral itself they make all kinds of offerings of food and wine, household goods and other possessions, burning or burying them with the body, as if these are of any use to the dead man. For that matter, what is the good (says Lucian) of all the elaborate forms of grave-mounds, tombstones, epitaphs and so on? Finally after the funeral the mourners hold a feast (*perideipnon*) after three days of fasting, as the lying-in-state (*prothesis*) took place on the day after death, and the burial on the third day. Even here Lucian finds material for satire, mocking the mourners for pretending to be unwilling to break their fast, and for feeling shame at the display of simple human appetites after the death of their dearest. Surely, Lucian says, if the dead man were able to answer the laments of his family he would tell them to stop making such a fuss, since he is in many ways far better off now than when he was alive, and all this rigmarole means nothing to him!

These customs, which the satirist found so absurd, all arise from those natural human needs which we have mentioned, combined with the prevailing popular notions about what happened to someone after he died. For these, as Lucian says, people took their ideas from 'Homer, Hesiod and the other myth-makers, treating their poetry as if it were law'. In the Homeric poems the soul goes down beneath the earth to the realm of Hades and Persephone, a kingdom of bloodless images which resemble their bodily forms but have no strength or real life. It is not entirely clear how far these images are still supposed to possess consciousness or intelligence. When Odysseus summons up the ghosts, it is said that only the prophet Teiresias is in full possession of his intellectual faculties, whereas all the other ghosts are merely fluttering shadows (*Od.* 11.494–5). None of the other ghosts except Elpenor, whose body is still unburied, recognize or speak to

Odysseus before they have drunk blood (139ff.). Later in this episode Odysseus claims to have had a vision of scenes inside the underworld in which various characters pursue activities similar to those on earth (including Minos who is portrayed as a judge for the dead), or suffer punishment for crimes committed in their lifetime (568–635). But the Hellenistic scholars of Alexandria dismissed this passage, probably rightly, as a later addition to the poem. There is no other mention in Homer of punishment after death, apart from one possible allusion in a solemn formula of oath-taking, which seems to say that perjurors can be punished after death (*Il.* 3.278–9). This suggests that, as one might have expected, the belief in punishment in the underworld may have already been a popular one in Homer's time, as it certainly was later, but the poet has chosen not to give it any prominence. The *Iliad* in particular presents a very austere picture of the after-life as a total contrast with life on earth, and neither rewards nor punishments would have suited the poet's bleak conception of death as the common end for all men alike, whether good or bad, humble or great.

Such was not, it seems, the universal belief of those times, as we can see from passing allusions to characters who do escape this common lot. Even in the *Iliad* we hear of Ganymede, who was carried off to heaven (20.232ff.), and of Tithonus as the husband of Dawn (11.1–2). The number of those who escape death is greater in the *Odyssey*. Here Menelaus is told that as the son-in-law of Zeus he is fated to go to the Elysian plain at the ends of the earth, where Rhadamanthys lives (4.561ff.). Ino was once a mortal, but now she lives in the sea and 'has a share of honour from the gods' (5.333–5). Castor and Polydeuces, sons of Zeus, live and die on alternate days (11.302–4), and Kleitos was carried off by Dawn to join the immortals (15.250–1). Calypso even promised Odysseus immortality if he stayed with her, although she complains that the gods have always begrudged such honours to those with whom goddesses fall in love (5.118ff.).

Other early epic poets were more generous in distributing

these privileges to men of the past.[1] Hesiod even tells of whole generations who had a special destiny after death. In his myth of the Ages of Mankind the men of his Golden Age later become immortal guardians of justice on earth (*Works and Days* 121–6), and those of the Silver Age receive honour as 'blessed mortals', although they are below the earth (140–2), whilst some or possibly all of the heroes who fought in the wars at Troy and Thebes are said to live in the Islands of the Blest at the ends of the earth, where Kronos rules over them (161–73).

Here then we already have, in addition to the normal Homeric view, two other possibilities open to specially distinguished mortals. One can either be removed from the world of men to a distant place where one lives a happy life, or one exists beneath the earth, but has a different fate from other men and continues to receive special honours after death. This last possibility looks like the germ of what was to become a very common view later, that if one honoured certain men of the past with worship and offerings they still had power to help or harm those on earth. It seems as if this belief, also, may have been already current at the time of the Homeric poems, but again the poet chose not to emphasize it. For we are told that Erechtheus, the legendary king of Athens, is worshipped there with regular sacrifices (*Il.* 2.546–51), and from time to time in the poems tombs are mentioned which seem to be treated with particular reverence. Archaeological evidence shows that the practice of making offerings at tombs of men of the past was becoming common before the end of the eighth century B.C., especially in connection with Bronze Age tombs.[2] It is not until later that we learn of the regular worship of heroes from literary evidence, but the law-code of Dracon at Athens in the late seventh century B.C. prescribed that the heroes of the land should be honoured 'according to ancestral custom', and this implies earlier worship (Porphyry, *De abstinentia* 4.22).

Such heroes were often honoured as the ancestors or founders of a particular community (whether this was a country or a local community, or a kinship group of some kind), and when new colonies were sent out their leaders were also worshipped as heroes after death. This practice was extended to include other classes of men, such as lawgivers, poets, athletes, and other famous men, throughout the classical period. Often the Delphic oracle was said to be responsible for ordering the institution of such cults, but there were also many legends of miraculous events connected with these figures, either in their lifetime or after death, and these stories were linked to the beginnings of worship of them. The parallels with the cult of saints are striking, particularly if one considers the importance which was attached to the possession of the physical remains of the hero, especially as a protection of one's land against attack. The bones of Orestes, which the Spartans claimed to have discovered in Tegea and brought to Sparta, were thought to have given them success in battle (Hdt. 1.67–8), and in the fifth century B.C. Cimon brought what were believed to be the bones of Theseus from the island of Skyros to Athens. It was also thought that some heroes had special powers of healing, and even their statues were credited with powers of this kind.

On the other hand a significant difference between the cult of heroes and that of saints is that it was relatively rare for anyone to claim possession of only one part of a hero's remains, whereas in the case of saints such relics have been a regular feature of their worship in many countries. Occasionally we do hear (for example) of the head of a hero being buried in one place and the rest of him elsewhere, and there were also special cases such as the ivory shoulder of Pelops, which was supposed to have been preserved at Olympia. But in general it looks as if the fact that the heroes were thought to be firmly anchored in the earth and in some way still attached to their physical remains led people to be very wary of inflicting on their remains the kind of dismemberment suffered by the saints. In their case, as they were believed to be in heaven, the fate of their relics might be presumed to be a matter of relative indifference to them.

Hero-cults form a large and important part of Greek religious practice in the historical period. They could often be used as a way of giving a sense of unity and social identity to any particular group, whether large or small, and heroes and heroines also performed a crucial function as a mediating factor (or 'middle term') between gods and ordinary men, in a similar way to the saints. For the Greeks of the classical period the heroes of the legendary past were very far from being remote or shadowy figures. On the contrary their practical assistance was constantly invoked, especially in times of crisis (such as war or disease) when they were expected to respond in a powerful and effective way. Many of them were essentially local figures, closely tied to their supposed tombs, but some of the major figures (such as Heracles, a borderline case between hero and god) were worshipped all over Greece, and could be immensely popular. ('Dumb is the man who does not encompass Heracles with his voice', says Pindar, *Pyth.* 9.94.)

Heroic honours, however, were not for the generality of mankind. Yet one can hardly believe that the Greeks would have remained content with Homer's gloomy picture of the fate which awaited most men after death; and in fact we soon find evidence to the contrary. One of the early Greek hymns which circulated under the name of Homer tells the story of how Persephone was carried off by the god of the underworld, and how her mother Demeter came in the course of searching for her to Eleusis in Attica, where she ordered the people to build her a temple. Later, after her daughter's recovery she taught the Eleusinians her rites, which are said to be secret, and the poet ends his narrative by proclaiming: 'blessed is he among men on earth who has seen these rites; whereas whoever is uninitiated and has no share in them has no part in the same things when he has died, down in the murky gloom' (*Homeric Hymn to Demeter* 480–2). The hymn also states that whoever does wrong and fails to honour and propitiate Persephone as he ought to do will suffer eternal punishment (367–9).

This hymn attests to the belief that if one performed certain secret rituals in honour of Demeter and Persephone one would thereby be guaranteed exemption from the common fate of men after death, whereas on the contrary those who offended Persephone would suffer punishment in the after-life. Such beliefs were again probably current long before the Homeric poems, but we do not find clear literary evidence of them before this poem, which was probably composed in the seventh century B.C. Later, with the powerful assistance of Athenian propaganda, Eleusis maintained her position as the most important of Demeter's sanctuaries, but there were many other places throughout the Greek world where similar rituals were cele-brated. In the classical period initiation into the Mysteries (as they were called) at Eleusis was open to anyone who could speak Greek, provided that he was not polluted by bloodshed, and par-ticipation was later extended to the Graeco-Roman world in general. Consequently secrecy, although always very solemnly stressed (with the penalty of death if it was broken), was to some extent a nominal matter, and the real point of it seems to have been not so much to limit the range of those who could hope to benefit from initiation, but rather to stress the awe-inspiring character of the deities who were being honoured and of the benefits which they could confer.

There appears to be no very clear indication to begin with that much more was expected of the initiates than that they should undergo the various rituals which took place on these occasions. One might however assume that those who offended the gods in general, for example by perjury, crimes against members of their own families, and offences against strangers (*xenoi*), would also be liable to incur the anger of the deities of the underworld. This is indeed the natural implication of the situation we find in Homer, where (in spite of the previously noted absence of references to punishment *after* death) it is the underworld deities known as the Erinyes, or alternatively Hades and Persephone, who hear and respond to appeals to punish those guilty of precisely these types of crimes. Consequently the allusion in the Homeric hymn to punishment for those who 'commit injustice, and fail to appease

Persephone' (367–9) might be taken as implying that initiation was not altogether divorced from moral considerations, even at this early period.

Later, in any case, it was thought to be paradoxical that the satisfaction of purely ritual requirements should act as a passport to happiness after death. This view stimulated the celebrated pro-test of the Cynic Diogenes, who asked why the thief Pataikion should be better off than Epaminondas in the after-life, merely because he had been initiated. The same objection is made in Plato's *Republic* to the idea which was current at the time, that by performing certain rites of purification in accordance with instructions ascribed to the mythical figures of Orpheus and Musaeus, one could avoid the consequences of one's misdeeds and escape punishment after death (363a–66b). As a reaction to this sort of criticism it was natural that the moral connotations of the Mysteries at Eleusis should come to be emphasized much more. Thus for example in Aristophanes' *Frogs* the chorus of initiates in the underworld sing of how they alone have light and joy, because they have not only been initiated but have also behaved piously towards both citizens and strangers alike (454–9).

This moral emphasis was strengthened at Athens by the claim (which was probably first made in the mid-sixth century B.C.) that the people of Attica had been the first to receive from Demeter not only the Mysteries but also the science of agriculture. She had instructed Triptolemus, one of the rulers of Eleusis, in this art, and he in turn passed on this knowledge to the world in general. It was said that this had led men to live a settled and civilized life, forming societies and learning how to unite for mutual benefit. Demeter herself was worshipped as *Thesmophoros*, which was taken to mean 'Bringer of law', and Triptolemus himself was regarded as one of the earliest law-givers. As a consequence it was not possible to receive the favour of this deity, either in life as the giver of the wealth of the earth, or after death, unless one behaved in a civilized manner towards one's fellow-men as well as the gods.

The picture which Aristophanes paints in *Frogs* of the life of the initiates after death is similar to earlier descriptions of Elysium or the Islands of the Blest. By contrast those who are punished for crimes committed while on earth lie in mud and filth (*Frogs* 145–51). In other accounts they may, like the sinners Tityus, Tantalus and Sisyphus in Homer's Underworld (*Od.* 11.576–600), be condemned to the perpetual performance of useless tasks. In Polygnotus' picture of the underworld at Delphi, for example, a man named Oknos ('Sloth') was shown plaiting a rope, while a donkey stood next to him and ate it as he plaited it, and some women who were depicted carrying water in broken pitchers were identified on the painting as the uninitiated (Pausanias 10.29.1–2; 31.9–11). We already have here something similar to the later Christian ideas of Paradise and Hell in such portrayals of the after-life. Evidently notions of this kind were already widespread by the end of the fifth century B.C. It looks as if there was no very clear attempt in such cases to distinguish between ritual and moral requirements. The initiates were rewarded and the uninitiated suffered punishment after death, but at the same time rewards and penalties were allotted to those who had lived morally good or bad lives on earth. In both cases this implied some form of judgement of souls after death. In the reference to Minos as judge of the dead in the *Odyssey* (11.568–71) it looks as if he is simply settling disputes among them, as he had done on earth. He appears again as a judge, together with Rhadamanthys, Aeacus, Triptolemus and other unnamed heroes, in Plato's *Apology* (41a), but it is only in Plato's *Gorgias* (523e ff.) that the first three of these are named as judges who assess men's lives on earth after they have died. Earlier, however, Aeschylus already mentions this idea of judgement, and ascribes it to the god of the underworld (Aeschylus, *Supplices* 230–1; *Eumenides* 273–5).

In such popular portrayals there is no indication that life on earth is more than a single stage in the soul's existence, which is followed by judgement after death and assignation to an appropriate sphere of further existence, happy or unhappy. But if one were prepared to see earthly life as merely one stage in a longer span of time, it was theoretically possible to suppose that the soul had not only existed before it belonged to an earthly body, but also might go through a series of reincarnations in successive lives. As the Greeks were familiar with myths of bodily transformation (*metempsychōsis*), where for example human beings are turned into animals, or gods take human form for a certain period, it was not extraordinary for them to think of a single person as taking different forms and living out different lives. It is not known for certain how the Greeks first came to believe in the possibility of reincarnation. Herodotus thought that they took the idea over from the Egyptians (2.123), but this is probably wrong. Some modern scholars have thought that they derived it from the Thracians or Scythians, others again that the Greeks invented it for themselves.[3] In any case, it is clear that it began to become popular in Greece in the later part of the sixth century B.C., especially through the influence of Pythagoras of Samos, whose personal belief in *metempsychōsis* is attested by his contemporary Xenophanes (Diels–Kranz 21B7).

It is also in the course of the sixth century B.C. that we begin to find evidence of the composition and circulation of works of poetry attributed to the legendary singer Orpheus and his follower Musaeus, in which various theological doctrines were put forward which are relevant here. Those who adopted such beliefs held that the soul was ultimately divine in origin, and that one should attempt to free it as far as possible from the contamination of the body, by strict rules of diet and conduct such as abstention from eating meat, and by special rituals of purification. By such means they believed it possible for the soul to progress through an ascending series of earthly lives, until finally, after also undergoing various forms of purgatory in the underworld, it was freed from the cycle of rebirth and could return to its original divine state.

To account for this state of affairs the 'followers of Orpheus' put forward a myth, whose originally esoteric character is indicated by the fact that in the classical period we meet with only a few very oblique and uncertain references to it.[4] This related how the rebellious Titans, the generation of gods who were older than Zeus and the other Olympian deities, had torn in pieces the god Dionysus, who in this myth was the son of Zeus and Persephone. Then the Titans ate his limbs, but his heart was rescued by Athena and a new Dionysus was formed from it. The Titans themselves were burnt by the lightning of Zeus, and from the soot men were born. Thus mankind has a share in what Plato calls 'the old Titanic nature' (*Laws* 701c), and pays the penalty for this ancestral crime. But men have also inherited a share in the divine nature of Dionysus. Consequently those who held such beliefs paid particular attention to the worship of Dionysus, calling themselves *Bacchoi* after this god, and believing that the rituals of his cult had special power to free them from fears of what might await them after death.

It is not easy to say how far these ideas of reincarnation and of man's ancestral guilt won acceptance at any time from the Greeks. But they were clearly familiar to both the philosopher Empedocles and the poet Pindar in the early fifth century, and they left a deep mark later on Plato. More important, however, in the long run was the emphasis on the divine character of the soul (*psychē*). The early Greek philosophers before Socrates held a very wide variety of views on the nature of the soul. Some said that it consisted of fire, others of air, others again that it was composed of various kinds of atomic particles which could be dissolved on death, whilst another school argued that it was only a harmony of bodily constituents, and so ceased to exist when the body perished. Uncertainty on this subject is reflected in the literature of this period, where a whole spectrum of different views can be discerned. Thus for example the idea that the soul is composed of air or *aithēr* and returns to it after death is echoed by Euripides (*Supplices* 531–6, 1140; *Helen* 1014–16, etc.), and also in a famous epigram on the Athenians who were killed in 432 B.C. at Potidaea

(*I. G.* 1².945). It seems, however, to have been Socrates himself who was the first to stress the need to 'take care of one's soul' (e.g. Plato, *Apology* 29d ff.), an expression which at an earlier period would have meant simply looking after one's material life and making it as comfortable as possible (*psychē* being sometimes used simply as a synonym for 'life'). For Socrates, however, this implied a concern for one's own intellectual and moral nature, to the exclusion of other objectives in life. This was in accordance with his understanding of the Delphic command to know one's own self. For Socrates, self-knowledge involved understanding the nature and purpose of one's own soul (cf. Plato, *Alcibiades* I, 128b–30e, 124a; *Phaedrus* 229e; Xenophon, *Memorabilia* 3.9.6; 4.2.24; Plutarch, *Moralia* 1118C). How far he himself was prepared to go in defining the soul's nature it is probably impossible to say, as his own views have been absorbed into those of his followers. In Plato's *Apology* he is made to express uncertainty about what happens after death, combined with the belief that, whatever it is, it cannot be bad. It is only in the *Phaedo* that we find a more confident assertion of belief in the soul's immortality, which certainly reflects Plato's own belief, together with philosophical arguments in favour of this view. Here this doctrine is supported by the theory of reincarnation, which is linked to Plato's own theory of Forms – those eternal entities of which things in the world are mere copies, and which the soul's own nature is said to resemble.

For Plato it was the intellectual character of the soul which was most important, and through this it shared in the nature of divinity. Aristotle took over and stressed even further this intellectual aspect. For him the mind (*nous*) was the only immortal part of personality, and this could not be in any way contaminated by the material world. The mind alone survived after death, but Aristotle shows remarkably little interest in this question of survival or of what happens thereafter. Consequently his views on mind and soul, although philosophically important, had little influence on later popular thought, by contrast with the impact of Plato's teaching on the subject.

This very brief sketch of early Greek views about death and life after death will have shown the lack of any universally accepted dogmas on this subject, in contrast to the relative uniformity of actual practice in the matter of funeral and mourning customs which seems to have prevailed throughout antiquity. At the same time it is possible to see how the various views which we have considered can be related to each other. It is not so much a question of independent strands of thought and belief, but rather of a nexus of interrelated ideas. The Greeks themselves did not see a direct conflict between the older 'mythological' views of the early poets and those later ideas which we have considered. Although the Homeric poems present a one-sided picture, one can catch glimpses of other beliefs in them, such as the possibility of punishments or rewards after death. The idea that the heroic dead can continue to have some influence over what goes on in the world of the living is one which the Homeric poems seem to have relegated to the background, but it was clearly not new at that time. The notion of special favours after death for initiates into the mystery cults of Demeter and Persephone is really only a particular version of the general belief that individual deities could reward those whom they loved in various ways, and, as we have seen, the moral aspect of these cults, although more emphasized in the classical period, may have been already to some extent implicit from the beginning.

Belief in reincarnation is a very striking development, and this does look like something quite novel. Yet here again it does not contradict earlier views and can in fact be seen as a development from them. Equally, the strange myth of the dismemberment of Dionysus by the Titans has many elements which recur elsewhere. Opposition to Dionysus is a fundamental feature of the stories about this god (as in Euripides' *Bacchae*, for example, or earlier in the story of his persecution by King Lycurgus of Thrace at *Iliad* 6.130–40), and dismemberment is a fate usually suffered by

Dionysus' opponents (e.g. Pentheus). The Titans are the opponents of the Olympian gods already in Hesiod's *Theogony*. The idea that men suffer as a result of a crime committed by their remote ancestors is an extension of the general Greek belief that guilt can be inherited and continue over a series of generations. Thus although at first sight this story of Dionysus and the Titans seems to stand apart from the normal course of Greek mythology, one can see how a myth of this kind could have been created within this framework.

Finally there is the most significant of all the developments in this field, the belief in the originally divine nature of the soul and its immortality. There is clearly a great difference here between the Homeric idea of the soul as little more than a shadow or image of the body, and Plato's insistence that the soul represents the real and enduring personality. Yet even this might be viewed rather as a shift of emphasis than as a radical contradiction. The Homeric poems allow glimpses of the idea that divine parentage or some other relationship with the gods might enable one to escape death and become immortal. This privilege, severely restricted in Homer, is as we have seen more widespread in other early epic poems. But if all men in general, rather than merely certain heroes, could be seen as having some element of divinity in their origins and hence in their nature, it followed that there must be a part of oneself which shared the divine characteristic of immortality. Clearly this must be the most important part, and consequently it was essential to recognize its existence, to define (if possible) its nature, and to ensure that its interests were made paramount in one's life and not impeded by other aspects of one's personality. From this one arrives quite naturally at Socrates' insistence on the need to care for one's soul, and (by a further stage of analysis) at the Platonic and Aristotelian emphasis on the rational or intellectual element of the personality as the divine part which has been designed to dominate the rest.

Thus one can see how the philosophers, who criticized so severely the ideas of their poetic forerunners, nevertheless tried to assimilate and re-interpret these ideas in the light of their own assumptions. This process can be observed at work in other areas of Greek religion, as for example in the case of beliefs about the nature of the gods themselves. This perhaps explains why in the field of ideas about life after death, as elsewhere, earlier and more primitive notions survived alongside the more advanced and sophisticated views of the philosophers, and continued to exercise a powerful influence over men's minds throughout the whole course of later antiquity.

4

Greek temples: Why and where?

J. N. COLDSTREAM

This chapter is concerned chiefly with the purpose and function of the temple in the ancient Greek world. First we must enquire how, when, and why the Greek temple, as a free-standing architectural form, came into being. Then we must examine several temples and sanctuaries in various parts of the Greek world, considering not merely their architecture, but their surroundings too, and the widely different cults which they served: cults carried out in the midst of a *polis*, in honour of the city's patron deity and protector; cults practised far away from any city, in a wild mountainous setting; cults connected with the great panhellenic sanctuaries, independent of any one *polis*, and somehow transcending the differences and rivalries between cities; secret cults associated with mystery religions, to which none save initiates had access; cults connected with a god of healing and medicine; and finally, oracular cults, including the greatest oracular shrine of all which claimed to be the centre of the earth. In each case we shall see how the character of the architecture was to some extent dictated by the needs of the cult.

In the Minoan and Mycenaean civilizations of the Aegean Bronze Age, the temple as an independent building had been virtually unknown. Indeed, there was then no need for such buildings. Absolute monarchy was the universal rule; the monarch was also high priest, and the 'temples' which served the official cults would be small rooms within his palace, often tucked away in remote corners. In the town beyond the palace walls, his subjects would likewise set aside rooms within their houses for private worship. And far away from the towns, other cults were practised

67

on mountain peaks, or within caves, or in small rural enclosures. Scenes of worship in Minoan art are most often set in the open air, around sacred trees or isolated pillars, or around small portable altars – a kind of worship which may leave no architectural traces at all.

After the collapse of the Mycenaean civilization, and after the destruction of its palaces around 1200 B.C., traces of domestic religion disappear. During the ensuing Dark Age it seems that all worship took place in the open air, usually around a fixed and raised altar for burnt sacrifices. And then, suddenly, in the great dawn after the Dark Age in the eighth century B.C., the free-standing temple emerges as a new architectural form. But this does not mean that religious worship then went indoors. On the contrary, the open-air altar in most places remained the focus of the cult. As a general rule the temple was never a place for con-gregational worship, like a Christian church; it was simply the house of the god, the place where the god's image resided.

Why, then, should it have been during the eighth century that the Greek temple has its origin? Its appearance coincides with many other symptoms of a great awakening after the Dark Age, and it has been reasonably claimed that the building of a free-standing temple was one of the first corporate enterprises of the emergent city-state. Doubtless there are other important signs of the arrival of the true *polis*, not least the construction of massive fortification walls and the provision of a central space for public gatherings. Nevertheless a broad historical point can be made with regard to the first temples, if we bear in mind the political changes between Mycenaean and archaic times – the change from monarchy to aristocracy, and eventually to constitutional govern-ment. The corporate effort which had once gone into the building of palaces and royal tombs for Mycenaean kings was now diverted to the service of the gods, the supreme protectors of the *polis*; and a god's house must at least be worthy of a king. Thus the acropolis of Tiryns, which had once been the seat of a Mycenaean monarch, had by the eighth century been set apart for the worship of the patron deity, Hera; her temple was actually built upon the ruins of the Mycenaean palace, making use of its solid stone foundations. Likewise, on the Athenian acropolis, the temples of Athena are preceded by the scanty ruins of another Mycenaean royal palace.

Some of the best preserved traces of early temples are in Crete, partly because their sites were left undisturbed by later generations, and partly because their walls were constructed entirely in rough stone, rather than in fragile mud-brick. At Dreros in the east of the island, the temple of Apollo Delphinios was built in the late eighth century, and its rubble walls still stand some ten feet high. Crete, during the troubles of the Dark Age, had been less disrupted than any other Aegean land, so that there are reminiscences here of the Bronze Age: reminiscences of a Minoan palace shrine in the offering bench at the back of the temple, and the altar nearby; and reminiscences of the Mycenaean throne room in the central hearth-altar flanked by columns. This hearth had been used for burnt sacrifices, Crete providing the exception to the general rule of open-air ritual. Here, presumably, the priests had roasted the goats whose horns were found in the debris of the altar together with the sacrificial knife. But the most remarkable discovery at Dreros was of the three cult-statues of hammered bronze representing Apollo, Artemis and Leto, by far the earliest cult-images found in any Greek temple. This is indeed the house of the deities who presided over the city.

On the Greek mainland, traces of early temples are much less well preserved because of the local tradition of building the upper walls in mud-brick – and, of course, in major cities like Athens and Corinth the flimsy masonry of the earliest temples had little chance of being well preserved under the deep and massive stone foundations of Classical and later structures. And so, to get an idea of the elevation of early mainland temples, we must fall back on clay models dedicated at the temples which they represent. A model from the sanctuary of Hera at Perachora [1], on the Corinthian Gulf, shows a small building with a round, apsidal end

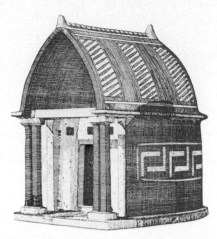

1 Perachora, clay model of a temple, restored.

and a high-pitched roof, probably covered with thatch. It has a
shallow porch, supported by pairs of small posts standing in front
of the side walls. The painted meander dates it to the Geometric
style of the eighth century B.C. Another such model, of rectangular plan, is from the sanctuary of Hera near Argos; it has in
addition an even shallower porch at the back. Such buildings will
have had walls of mud-brick, perhaps reinforced by a timber
frame. The *cella* – or main chamber – would have been very much
at the mercy of the elements without some form of protection.
Thus the porches were functionally necessary to shelter the *cella*'s
front wall; as for the side walls, the projecting eaves could throw
rain-drops off the vulnerable mud-brick. But although these
devices might be sufficient for a small building, for larger temples
something more drastic was needed to protect them from
rain.

   In this respect the first temple of Hera on Samos, built around
800 B.C. [2a], is a landmark in the history of Greek temple
architecture. It is the first *Hekatompedon*, the earliest temple to
establish the canonical length of a hundred feet, a precedent often
followed in archaic times. The width is only twenty-one feet, but

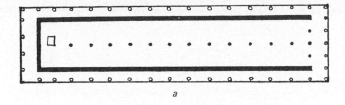

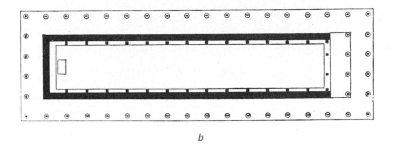

2 Samos, early temples of Hera, plans: (a) first temple, (b) second temple.

still wide enough to need a row of internal wooden posts to support the high-pitched roof. At the back of the *cella*, the stone base
of the cult-statue was placed slightly off centre, so that the internal
supports should not obscure it. The statue itself does not survive;
it was almost certainly of wood, and at this early date perhaps not
representational at all – a local historian mentions a primitive
wooden image of Hera resembling a plank, which was carried
around in processions. When the temple needed repair later in the
eighth century, the *cella* was surrounded by one of the earliest
known peristyles, of wooden columns: in this early context, a
most lavish and spectacular way of protecting the mud-brick walls
against the elements. Indeed, for a Greece just emerging from its
Dark Age, there is something grandiose and adventurous about
the whole building; even in the most sumptuous of Mycenaean
palaces, no single room had ever had a length of more than forty
feet. When this Samian architect designed the first *Hekatompedon*,
what sort of model did he have in mind? Nearest in space and time
(though probably a little later) is a large aristocratic *megaron* house

on the acropolis of Emporio on the neighbouring island of Chios. Like the Samian temple, it is a long hall with an internal row of columns down the middle, approached by a porch with columns across the front; its width is approximately that of the temple, but its length is only sixty feet. So the grandest of house-plans could be elongated in the service of the gods; but even for the gods it was impossible at this early stage to make the building any wider, since the length of timbers for a simple pitched roof limited the width to an absolute maximum of about twenty-five feet.

Here, then, we have one of the very first public buildings in Greece, in the service of the patron deity. Its erection implies careful planning by the sovereign *polis* of Samos, situated one hour's walk away along the island's shore. The temple must have been a great source of pride to the inhabitants; and yet the centre of Hera's cult still remained outside, round the open-air altar built for burnt sacrifices. And this altar is sited above earlier altars which had existed long before there was any thought of building a temple.

In the early seventh century this temple was destroyed by a river flood, and its successor [2b] shows several obvious improvements. The shape is less absurdly narrow, and the architect now felt happy about spanning the width without the clumsy internal supports; instead he used half-columns attached to the side walls. Perhaps these walls were more solid; at all events, they now rested on a fine stone footing of dressed rectangular blocks. The whole appearance is becoming more monumental. And there is also more thought now for the temple's surroundings. The seventh-century sanctuary was approached through a monumental entrance, or *propylon*. Beyond the altar was a large open space where crowds could gather at festivals. This area lay between the temple and a long open colonnade, or *stoa* – one of the earliest examples known. Its form was very simple: a back wall, and a roof resting on two rows of wooden posts. Here, no doubt, were the booths where visitors could obtain suitable offerings to Hera; here, too, they would find shelter from hot sun and rain.

The seventh century saw the rebirth of monumental architecture as a fine art. In temple building the greatest advances were made on the Greek mainland, where we witness the birth of the Doric order. The idea probably originated in Corinth, and the first truly Doric temple of which we know lies in a rather backward area very much under Corinthian influence, at Thermon in Aetolia. There for the first time we find the characteristic adornment of Doric superstructure: the metopes and triglyphs above the architrave, the antefixes and water-spouts for attachment to the cornices, and the clay rooftiles (for these terms see ch. 7, pp. 174f.). But the use of stone is still confined to the foundations; the walls are still of mud-brick, the beams of the superstructure and the peristyle columns would still have been of wood, while the metopes and other revetments are of clay with painted designs. The heavy clay tiles, however, were to have a decisive effect on the future development of temple architecture. When they were substituted for the older method of thatching, the pitch of the roof changed from high to low, giving rise to the familiar shape of the gable or pediment. Furthermore, the tiles increased the weight of the superstructure to the point where there was real danger of overloading the wooden columns and the mud-brick walls; and so the whole masonry was eventually translated into stone in all temples built after the beginning of the sixth century. The temple of Hera at Olympia [3], erected around 600 B.C., was one of the latest to be built in the older manner, with wooden columns, wooden beams, and mud-brick walls. The columns here were gradually replaced in stone at different times – hence the wide variety in the shape of the capitals; in fact, one wooden column was still standing there when Pausanias visited Olympia in the second century A.D.

Only a few years afterwards, the temple of Artemis at Kerkyra (Corfu) [4] was built wholly of stone – columns, superstructure, and all. This temple is also the first to have sculpture filling its pediments: in this case, the formidable Gorgon shown as a nature goddess, flanked by her children Pegasus and Chrysaor, and attended

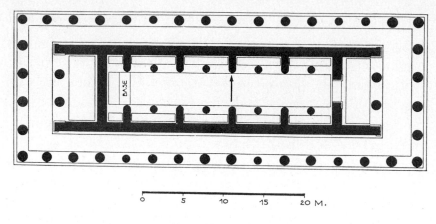

3 Olympia, temple of Hera, plan.

by a pair of vast lion-panthers. In this building all the essential elements of the Doric order are there; the Greek temple has already
reached a monumental maturity at a time when secular architecture was still in its infancy.

So much, then, for the origins. The next three centuries saw no
drastic changes in the ground plan of a Greek temple: a *cella*
approached through a porch (*pronaos*), often with a second porch
at the back (*opisthodomos*), and surrounded by a peristyle of free-
standing columns. There were subtle adjustments in proportions,
and interior arrangements might vary considerably according to
the needs of the local cult; in the Sicilian colonies the basic plan
might be enlarged to a colossal size, while in the eastern Aegean
world the Ionic order was usually preferred to Doric. But in
general there was remarkably little development in temple design,
as can be seen if we compare a late fourth-century plan [5] with
those already considered. Let us turn our attention, then, to the
setting of these temples, and to the different cults which they
served.

The temple just now mentioned is that of Athena Polias at
Priene, the Ionic city in Asia Minor, overlooking the river Maeander.
The Priene we know is a new foundation of *c.* 350 B.C., replacing
an older Priene (as yet undiscovered by archaeologists) which had

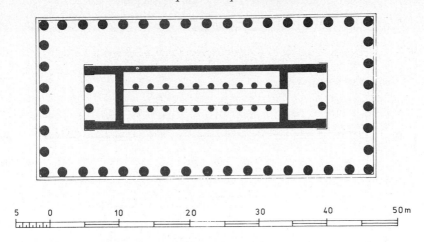

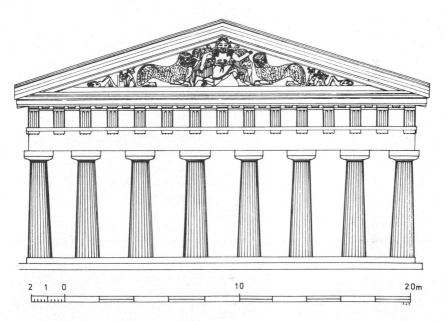

4 Kerkyra (Corfu), temple of Artemis, plan and restored elevation.

been deserted after the silting-up of its harbour by the sluggish
river. The new city was laid out on a regular grid-plan, in accordance with the method of town-planning established by
Hippodamus of Miletus. High up on the slope and not far below
the great rocky acropolis, a prominent platform was set aside for

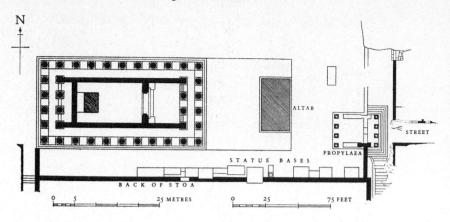

5 Priene, temple of Athena Polias, plan.

the temple and sanctuary of Athena in her attribute of Polias, the protector of the *polis*. Much admired in antiquity, her temple was designed by Pythios who was also the architect of the Mausoleum at Halicarnassus. Indeed Mausolus himself, while he ruled over these parts as satrap, may have had much to do with the foundation of the new Priene; there was plenty of room for a Carian garrison on the acropolis. But during its most flourishing period in the third century Priene was a completely independent *polis* with its own democratic constitution. Almost the whole city has been excavated, and a model reconstruction [6] shows the temple of Athena in its urban context. The grid-plan consisted mainly of private houses in blocks between streets, usually four to a block; two whole blocks have been allotted to the sanctuary. On the terrace immediately below lies the open space of the agora, centre of public life, overlooked by the *bouleutērion* where the elected council met; above, to the right, the full assembly of citizens would have gathered in the remarkably well preserved little theatre. There is room in this town for approximately five thousand citizens, a figure close to that suggested by Plato (*Laws* 737e) for his ideal state. Priene is a remarkably pleasant site to visit, partly because everything is kept within the human scale; no building is oppressively large. The temple, with the other public buildings, takes its place amidst the regular plan of court-yard houses.

6 Priene: model reconstruction of the town, with the temple of Athena Polias.

For a complete contrast to this urban setting let us examine the temple of Zeus at Olympia, built in the 460s B.C. through the initiative of the neighbouring city of Elis. Olympia, one of the great panhellenic sanctuaries of the Greek world, was the scene of the Games held every four years from 776 B.C. almost continuously until late antiquity. Olympia was never a *polis*; but some administrative buildings were made necessary by the sheer scale of the festival, which must have been one of the most powerful unifying forces in an otherwise deeply divided Greek world. The central part of the sanctuary is the Altis, the sacred grove, dominated by the old temple of Hera which we have already mentioned, and the early classical temple of Zeus, one of the largest on the Greek mainland. Its surviving ruins will not bear any reconstruction *in situ*; the original stucco coating of the columns has nearly all worn off, leaving the shelly and crumbly limestone exposed. Even so, the vast Doric capitals lying on the ground, six feet across, are sufficiently impressive. A reconstructed elevation [7] shows the position of the celebrated sculptures: the pediments, the east end portraying the fatal chariot race between Pelops and King Oenomaos over which Zeus himself presides as arbiter; at the west end, the battle between Lapiths and Centaurs in the presence of Apollo; inside, above the entrances to the porches, are the metopes showing the labours of Heracles, six at each end. The plan [8] is completely orthodox, but the chief interest here lies in the arrangements inside the *cella* to receive the cult statue. If we think back to the first primitive *Hekatompedon* of Samos over three centuries earlier, a *cella* one hundred feet long might seem rather prodigal for housing a crude wooden image in the form of a plank. At Olympia the case is very different: a much larger temple is barely able to accommodate a cult-statue which became one of the Seven Wonders of the ancient world. This is the colossal gold and ivory (chryselephantine) statute of the seated Zeus [9], which Pheidias was commissioned to design some thirty years after the temple was built. This colossal figure, over forty feet high, is now known to us only through imitations on coins and other small

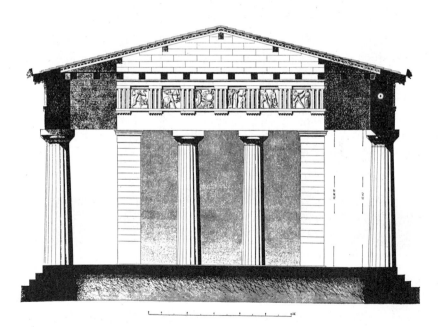

7 Olympia, temple of Zeus, restored elevation with east pediment, and cross-section with view of metopes.

orthodoxy by placing the cult-statue in a small chamber of its own with east–west orientation; the statue is imagined as being set up against the west wall of this rear chamber, so as to catch the first rays of the rising sun streaming through the eastern side door. An objection to this theory is that no trace of a cult-statue, or even of its base, has ever been found; and as we come to know more and more about Arcadian sanctuaries, it emerges that the Arcadians actually preferred the north–south orientation as a matter of course. Quite recently a novel and imaginative explanation has been advanced, demonstrating the prehistoric survivals in Arcadian religion. While most other Greeks had come to portray their deities as anthropomorphic, the Arcadians even in classical times still adhered to Bronze Age beliefs in the sanctity of pillars and trees as divine objects of worship. Hence, in the absence of any trace of a normal cult-image, it follows that the role of the cult-statue was played by a remarkable free-standing column at the end of the *cella*, a tree and pillar combined: in fact, the very earliest of Corinthian columns. An intriguing theory indeed, but we should still have to account for the rear chamber with the side door.

From a backward part of mainland Greece we pass to the hinterland of western Sicily, just beyond the limits of the Greek world. The temple of Segesta [12] is superbly situated in a wide valley and, like the Bassae temple, appears at first sight to stand in splendid isolation. On the nearby hill, however, scant traces of a contemporary settlement have been found, razed by the Saracens during the tenth century A.D. with unusual thoroughness. Segesta had been a town of the indigenous Elymians, who by the fifth century B.C. had become thoroughly hellenized under the influence of the colonial Greek cities of Sicily. They remained, however, consistently hostile to their nearest Greek neighbours, the Dorians of Selinus; and against the Selinuntines on more than one occasion they looked far overseas for support, to Athens. In the narrative of Thucydides (6.8ff.) we read how, by pretending to more wealth than their city possessed, in 416 B.C. they lured a powerful Athenian armament to Sicily to attack the Dorian states,

12 Segesta, the temple.

with consequences which were to prove disastrous for Athens. The fine-looking temple, possibly designed by an Athenian architect not long before these events, gives us a similar impression of the Elymian character; for it was never finished. It is an empty shell. The *peripteron* was erected, but the funds appear to have run out before the *cella* could be constructed. The columns of the *peripteron* had been smoothed, ready for fluting; but no fluting had been achieved. Since Sicily possesses no fine marble, these columns of shelly limestone would eventually have received a coating of white stucco. Furthermore, on the stepped foundations of the stylobate, one can still see the bosses by which the blocks had been lifted into position; on a finished temple these bosses would have been removed and the blocks properly dressed. Although we know nothing of the cult for which the temple was intended, it gives us some impressive evidence of the spread of Hellenism through religious architecture; it also reveals one way of building a Greek temple – though not necessarily the only way: that is, from the outside inwards.

Among the ruins of neighbouring Selinus, the remains of eight

Doric temples attest the astonishing prosperity of the city in archaic and classical times. One of them, Temple G, is one of the largest known anywhere in the Greek world, 361 feet long, 164 feet wide, and with columns eleven feet in diameter. This grand-iose building, however, was still incomplete when the city was captured and destroyed by the Carthaginians in 409 B.C. Here we shall single out for attention the archaic Temple F for its unique plan [13]. Instead of forming the usual open colonnade, the external columns are joined to one another by stone barriers, leaving narrow doors for admission only on the short eastern side. This unusual enclosing of the *peripteron* implies some kind of mystery religion, to which not everyone had access. And yet there was

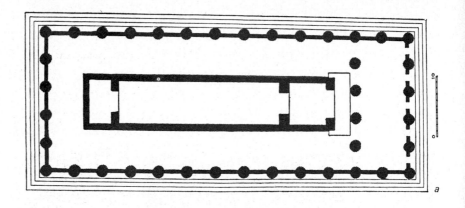

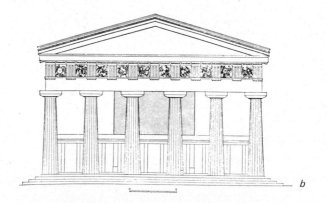

13 Selinus, Temple F, plan and restored elevation.

room for a large gathering in the unusually wide spaces between the peripteral columns and the *cella* walls. The ritual associated with the temple must have taken place within this enclosure, in the absence of the normal open-air altar.

The greatest of all mystery cults was celebrated in the sanctuary of Demeter and Persephone at Eleusis. Today many visitors to Greece are discouraged from going to the site by its unpleasant industrial surroundings. Nevertheless, for those who have passed within the outer walls of the sanctuary, it is not difficult to forget the nearby factories and recapture something of the ancient atmosphere. There one can see evidence for at least eighteen centuries of continuous worship, from Mycenaean times until the suppression of pagan cults in A.D. 395. The sanctuary [14] rises up a series of terraces on the flank of a small hill; on the broadest of these was the *Telestērion*, the Hall of the Mysteries held in honour of Demeter and Persephone. Little of this building survives except for the ground plan, but roughly in its centre is a deep hole, where excavators have discovered a series of earlier temples going well back into the Mycenaean period. Each was larger than its pre-

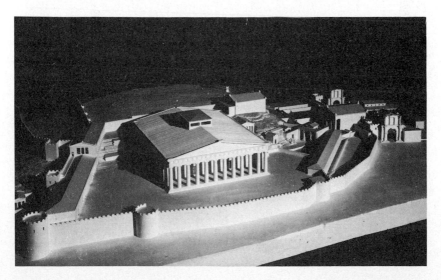

14 Eleusis: model reconstruction of the sanctuary of Demeter and Persephone. In the centre, the final *Telestērion*, with a skylight above the *Anaktoron*.

decessor, until by the Periclean age this Hall of the Mysteries occupied the whole terrace, including some steps cut into the rock at the back. This vast temple, another building designed by Iktinos, was supported on a forest of columns, of which the bases can still be seen. In this form, with minor alterations in Roman times, the *Telestērion* stood for eight hundred more years, the place where the secret mystery-rites were celebrated every year.

For the myth which explains the cult, our fullest source is the *Homeric Hymn to Demeter*. The poet tells us how, after the loss of her daughter Persephone to Hades, Demeter came to Eleusis as a *mater dolorosa*, disguised as an old woman from Crete. On a stone near the entrance to her later sanctuary, she sat down and wept; that stone became known as the *Agelastos Petra*, the 'mirthless rock'. Then the king and queen of Eleusis took pity on her, and engaged her as a nurse for their young son, the prince Demophon. While nursing the child Demeter planned one night to make him immortal by baptizing him with fire; but the queen caught her in the act and was deeply distressed. Thereupon the goddess revealed herself in her full beauty, and with terrible anger denounced the king and queen for rejecting the gift of eternal life for their son, and commanded them to atone by building her a fair temple and altar. This was done; but Demeter still remained in mourning, and caused a dreadful famine all over the earth for a whole year. At last Zeus intervened, and ordered his brother Hades to release Persephone from the underworld. Demeter now became reconciled to the Eleusinians, and taught them – and them only – the secret mystery-rites of her cult. So there grew up at Eleusis the cult which answers one of the fundamental needs of humankind: the need for food, and hence the need for the rebirth of the corn crops each year. The corn, like Persephone, must stay below ground all through the winter months; but when it grows up in spring, it becomes an earnest of immortal life for mankind, provided that they observe the secret Mysteries. 'Happy is he among men on earth who has seen these Mysteries', says the poet of the *Hymn*; 'but he who is uninitiate and has no part in them never experiences such good things when he is dead, down in darkness and gloom' (480–2).

As we have seen, the sanctuary had an extraordinarily long life. On the *Telestērion* site nine successive temples were erected [15]. The original Mycenaean building went through two architectural stages, and is thought to have survived all through the Dark Age in a third and fourth stage with the addition of a curved terrace wall,

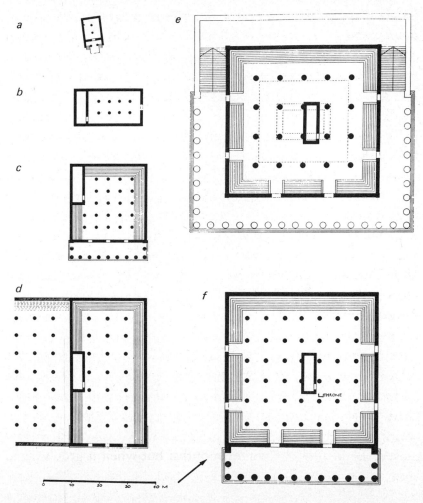

15 Eleusis, *Telestērion*, successive temples: (a) Mycenaean, (b) time of Solon, (c) time of Pisistratus, (d) time of Cimon, (e) plan of Iktinos, (f) fifth-fourth century B.C., repaired in second century A.D.

and then with a new enclosure. Then, in the time of Solon, a new temple was built, with a 'holy-of-holies' at the back known as the *Anaktoron* or 'Palace', sited approximately over the spot where the very first Mycenaean shrine had been. This *Anaktoron* was to remain sacrosanct for the next thousand years, as the very centre of the mystery-rites. Meanwhile the temple, the *Telestērion*, was rebuilt on a larger scale by the tyrant Pisistratus (who added the rock-cut steps), then by Cimon; then came Iktinos' large square building in the time of Pericles, which was remodelled in Roman times; but every successive *Telestērion* incorporated the Solonian *Anaktoron*, itself a temple within a temple; today it leaves its trace as a narrow rectangle within one avenue of internal columns.

This little chapel is thought to have housed the original primitive wooden image of Demeter; it was also the scene of the climax in the mystery-rites, which occupied nine days in September. The first four were devoted to various preparations in and around Athens: the initiates would bathe in the sea, purifying themselves and also the pigs which they would sacrifice to Demeter. On the fifth day they marched in procession to Eleusis, carrying with them the sacred wooden image of Iacchus, and pausing at the bridge of the river Kephisos to warn off evil spirits. On arrival at Eleusis they rested all through the sixth day, but during the night the Great Mysteries took place, culminating in the initiation ceremony. Of these rites we can know nothing for certain, because officially everything which took place inside the sanctuary on this occasion was a close secret, guarded on pain of death, and never revealed. On the seventh day the initiates rested once again; the eighth was devoted to libations and rites for the dead; on the ninth the procession returned to Athens.

Our only clue to the nature of the mystery-rites is that they took place in three stages: first there were the *drōmena*, things done; then the *legomena*, things said; and finally the *deiknumena*, things displayed. The *drōmena* might have been a sort of nocturnal pageant, re-enacting the sufferings of Demeter on the spots associated with the mythical story. Of the *legomena* we know nothing, except that they were in Greek, and were meant to be intelligible to the initiates; hence the exclusion from initiation of barbarians who could not understand Greek. Equally obscure are the *deiknumena*, but it has been conjectured that they might have been some sacred relics preserved from Mycenaean times. After these rites came the *epopteia*, the revelation for those who had been initiated the previous year. An imaginative attempt to reconstruct this climax of the Mysteries [16] is staged around the *Anaktoron*, under the forest of columns within the *Telestērion*; in an otherwise dark hall lit only by torches, the moment of vision or revelation is achieved by the sudden admission of early-morning daylight through a lantern or skylight immediately above the *Anaktoron*.

Quite another kind of sanctuary is to be seen on the island of Kos: a sanctuary of healing, with Asclepius the son of Apollo as its presiding deity. Sanctuaries of this nature are always situated in well-watered countryside; this one lies on a hill slope, about forty minutes' walk from the ancient town of Kos. Constructed mainly

16 Eleusis, *Anaktoron*, imaginative reconstruction of Mysteries.

in Hellenistic times, it is carefully planned on three broad terraces [17]. On the lowest level are three stoas which enclose sulphurous springs, waters which invalid visitors would drink as a cure; later a Roman bath was added. The festivals of Asclepius were held on the middle terrace, round the altar and the two small temples; there, too, were the priests' quarters. The uppermost terrace was occupied by the large Doric temple of Asclepius and its surrounding stoas. At other healing sanctuaries, such as Epidaurus, the treatment of invalids was largely auto-suggestive; they offered their votives and their prayers, and then expected to see healing visions in their dreams while they slept on the stone benches of the sanctuary. Kos, however, is the home of Hippocrates (*c.* 450–370 B.C.), father of scientific medicine; as one might expect, visitors here received real medical treatment, though probably in the school of medicine established in the town by Hippocrates himself rather than in the sanctuary. The siting of the temple [18] is truly superb; from it one looks far out to sea, to the coast of Asia Minor beyond; just by the conical hill in the far distance the site of Halicarnassus is clearly visible. Even today, a visit to the Asklepieion of Kos is indeed a healing experience.

Finally we come to the oracular shrines of Apollo, and let us

17 Kos, sanctuary of Asclepius, restoration.

18 Kos, sanctuary of Asclepius.

first consider the sanctuary of Didyma in western Asia Minor, in the territory of Miletus. The temple which we see today was begun around 300 B.C.; like some other buildings planned on this grandiose scale, it was never finished. The slender Ionic columns, sixty-four feet high [19a], were never crowned with a pediment. To give some idea of the scale: a man of average height is as tall as the column bases and the cushions immediately above. The plan [19b] is a vast enlargement of the usual design, encircled by a double *peripteron*, and with three rows of columns in the porch. There are also a number of unusual features, especially designed for the working of the oracle. Beyond the porch lies an extra ante-chamber, with two interior columns; but access to it from the porch was impossible, since its floor lies five feet higher up. Beyond, a monumental flight of steps sweeps about sixteen feet down into the *cella*, which was left open to the sky. Within this open court lay a small temple [20] (foreground), which housed the cult-image of Apollo. Visitors who came to consult the oracle reached the court not through the antechamber, but by the two passages on either side. These sloped down under barrel vaults, in

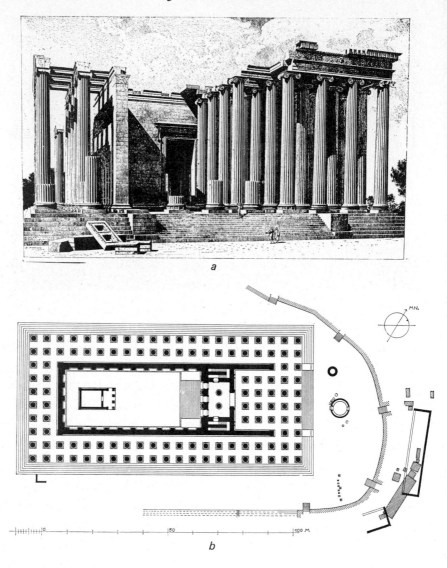

a

b

19 Didyma, temple of Apollo: (a) restored elevation, (b) plan.

almost complete darkness, into two small rectangular rooms on either side of the great stairway. Thence visitors would pass through doors into the blazing light of the court which served as the *adyton* of Apollo; there a sacred grove surrounded the small Ionic temple with the cult-statues, within which the prophetess

20 Didyma, temple of Apollo: interior court, or *adyton*.

took her seat by the oracular spring. Only the priesthood had access to the monumental steps leading up to the antechamber, which may have served as the *chrēsmographeion* where the oracular response was interpreted. Thereupon the priests, standing upon the platform which barred direct access from outside, would deliver the oracles to anxious visitors waiting among the porch columns – a fine example of Hellenistic stage-management.

Delphi, the 'navel of the earth', is the seat of Apollo's most pan-hellenic oracular shrine. Its early history has yet to be clarified, but already in Mycenaean times there may well have been a cult of a female deity on the lower part of the site, later occupied by the Marmaria sanctuary of Athena; over two hundred female figurines of the twelfth century B.C. were found on this terrace, and the goddess to whom they were offered would have been remembered in later times as Gē, the earth-goddess who was Apollo's predecessor in local myth. By the eighth century, however, Apollo had already become the presiding deity. One of his special functions was as *Archēgetēs*, the guide of colonists seeking new homes overseas; from the Delphic oracle it was his custom to give his counsel and blessing to leaders of colonial expeditions – and here lies one of the main reasons why Delphi rose to pan-hellenic fame.

Apollo's own sanctuary (*Hieron*) is overlooked by the awe-inspiring Phaidriades, the two Shining Rocks, situated in the foothills of Mount Parnassus. Between the two lies the Castalian spring, whose function was originally limited to cleansing and purifying (it was not until Roman times that it was associated in any way with poetic inspiration). Within the *Hieron* [27, ch. 6] the Sacred Way winds up the successive terraces, past the treasuries set up each by a different city to house the most impressive of its dedications, jostling one another in competition for Apollo's favour. Prominent among them is the late archaic Treasury of the Athenians, notable for its metopal sculptures depicting the labours of Theseus and Heracles, and also for the long Hellenistic in-scription which includes the musical notation for a *Hymn to Apollo*. The corniche of the Sacred Way eventually reaches the broad terrace of Apollo's temple, and farther up the hill are the theatre, and the stadium for the four-yearly Pythian Games.

Unlike the Mysteries of Eleusis, there was nothing secret about the procedure for consulting the oracle. This topic is treated more fully in chapter 6; here we are primarily concerned with the temple itself, within which the oracle was housed. The building whose scanty remains we see today was erected during the fourth century B.C.; it was a most conservative temple for its time, keeping exactly the same elongated proportions as its archaic predecessor which had perished in a fire or earthquake. One has the impression that a special effort was being made to preserve or restore the interior arrangements of the older temple. Of these arrangements there is nothing left *in situ*; the modern visitor, faced with the bare foun-dations of the temple, must therefore make an effort of the imagination, armed with many clues from literary sources.

For ancient visitors to Delphi, entry to the temple was restricted to nine days in the year, and permitted only to those wishing to consult the oracle after they had paid for a preliminary sacrifice.

Once inside the porch, the visitor would be reminded of the Delphic precepts ('know thyself', 'nothing too much', etc.) inscribed on marble herms, or busts. The *cella*, supported on two rows of internal columns like most classical interiors, would have had an oppressively subfusc atmosphere; for somewhere in its central part was the eternal oracular hearth, the *Pythomantis Hestia*, which could never be extinguished. To consult the oracle he would descend into Apollo's *adyton*, which cannot have been a separate room since no internal walls have been found inside the *cella*. Instead, at its far end, there is a rectangular area where no foundations were discovered, and it has been suggested that none were ever laid. Here, then, is the most likely place for the sunken *adyton*, where we must visualize the gold image of Apollo, the stone *omphalos* representing the navel of the earth, the sacred laurel tree, and the Pythian priestess seated upon her tripod and mouthing the oracular responses in an ecstatic trance [28, 30, 31, ch. 6].

From this brief survey it will have become apparent that the theme of the Greek temple permits many variations, especially in the management of interior space. Many temples were specially sited, and specially designed, to meet the needs of a particular kind of cult. The buildings can be appreciated simply as consummate masterpieces of ancient Greek architecture. But our appreciation and enjoyment will be considerably enhanced if we enquire into the various forms of worship which they served.

5

The Greek religious festivals

PAUL CARTLEDGE

In the new *Legacy of Greece* recently edited by Sir Moses Finley there is no chapter on religion. The reason is straightforward. The ancient world's religious legacy to mediaeval Europe and the modern world was Christianity, not some version of the classical Greeks' polytheistic paganism. But this creates a major difficulty for anyone wishing to understand the society of classical Greece. For few aspects of antiquity are harder to comprehend than the mental universe of paganism, a universe inhabited by and full of a multiplicity of gods rather than governed by one omnipotent deity. One thing, though, is pretty clear. Classical Greek religion was at bottom a question of doing not of believing, of behaviour rather than faith. Or, as Finley puts it in his introduction to *The Legacy of Greece*, 'Greek piety, Greek religion, . . . appear to be a matter of rituals, festivals, processions, games, oracles, sacrifices – actions, in sum – and of stories, myths, about concrete instances in the working of the deities, not of abstract dogmas.'[1]

It would scarcely be an exaggeration to say that within this practical, social frame of reference festivals were the single most important feature of classical Greek religion in its public aspect. That religion, it could be argued, was above all the totality of public festivals celebrated by each of the hundreds of political communities; and the total was extraordinarily high, both absolutely and as a proportion of the days in the year given over to festivals by the cities. Our evidence is unfortunately very incomplete and uneven. But altogether in excess of 300 public, state-run religious festivals are known to have been celebrated at over 250 places in honour of more than 400 deities (counting Athena Polias, for example, as separate from Athena Parthenos, Athena Nikē, and so on). The festivals of Athens are far better documented than those of any other state: here in the fifth and fourth centuries B.C. not less than 120 days of the calendar (thirty-three per cent) were devoted to festivals, and the number may have been as great as 144. Athens, as we shall see, was somewhat exceptional in this regard, but among the countries of the Mediterranean today it is perhaps only in Italy that the percentage of festival days is anything like so large.[2]

Festivals are representative expressions of classical Greek religion in another sense too. They exemplify that unity in diversity which is the hallmark of ancient Greek civilization as a whole. The following story from Herodotus illustrates this cardinal point. When it looked as if the Athenians might turn traitor during the Persian Wars of 480–479, the Spartans hastily sent a delegation to try to persuade them to stay loyal to the Greek cause. They need not have bothered, as the Athenians were quick to tell them. For there were many reasons, they said, why they could not possibly go over to the Persian side. 'The first and chief of these is the burning and destruction of our temples and the images of our gods . . . Again, there is our common brotherhood with the Greeks: our common language, the altars and the sacrifices of which we all partake, the common character which we bear.'[3] The two Greek words translated here as 'our common brotherhood with the Greeks' mean literally 'the Greek thing' (*to Hellēnikon*); another paraphrase might be 'the fact of being Greek'. Notice that, after language, religion is the next most important ingredient of Greekness and that a shared religion served to mark off the Greeks in their own eyes from the rest of the human race.

So far as festivals specifically are concerned, a Western Greek from Massilia (modern Marseilles) would therefore feel instantly at home in Trapezous (Trebizond, Trabzon) as he watched the familiar basic rituals of the procession, sacrifice and feasting being enacted. Yet this fundamental homogeneity of festival structure coexisted with a remarkable heterogeneity of local festival content. A quick dip into the standard reference works turns up an astonishingly wide range of activities all taking place within the general framework of religious festivals: girls on swings; cult images being washed in the sea; sword-dancing; criminals being flogged with green branches and ritually expelled from the community; even exchanges of obscenities between groups of men and women. A longer perusal, though, reveals the more important fact that the greater number of state religious festivals had their roots in the soil. They were, that is to say, originally agricultural rites celebrated by peasants in their villages and fields in order to secure continuity of existence, a perpetual increase of men, animals and crops. And their rhythm was originally that of the seasons, following the cycle of the agricultural year. As Aristotle wrote, 'the traditional sacrifices and festivals are, as we can see, held after the gathering in of the harvest, as a sort of harvest-home, because it was at this time that the people had most leisure'.[4]

'Festivals' here translates Aristotle's *synodoi*, a word which literally means 'goings-together' and so could be used for any form of meeting or association, sacred or secular, peaceful or hostile. (Thanks to its later ecclesiastical usage, it gives us our 'synods'.) This was just one among several expressions in current use for festivals, a further indication if one is needed of the importance of festivals in Greek social life. Thus another term, meaning literally a gathering or assembly, is *panēgyris*, though strictly this applied only to festivals like the Olympic Games which attracted participants (*theōroi*) from more than one community. But the commonest and most general expression of all was *heortē*. Like our 'holiday', which is derived from holy day, *heortē* could mean simply amusement or entertainment as well as religious festival, and, in the sentence just before the one quoted above, Aristotle says that through holding festivals men 'pay due honour to the gods and at the same time provide pleasant relaxations for themselves'. Plato, less down-to-earth than his pupil, preferred a more spiritual interpretation:

The gods . . . took pity on the human race, born to suffer as it was, and gave it relief in the form of religious festivals to serve as periods of rest from its labours. They gave us the Muses, with Apollo their leader, and Dionysus; by having these gods to share their holidays, men were to be made whole again, and thanks to them, we find refreshment in the celebration of these festivals. (Plato, *Laws* 2.653D trs. T. J. Saunders)

Apart from these three general words, there are three which refer more particularly to special features of festivals. First, and possibly linked etymologically to *heortē*, is *eranos*. This originally signified a collective feast, but since feasting was as indispensable a part of festivals as the animal sacrifice that preceded it, *eranos* came to be used for the festival as a whole too. Secondly, a festival accompanied by rites of initiation, most famously the mystery cult of Demeter and Persephone at Eleusis, might be called *teletē*. Thirdly, and finally, a *panēgyris* like the Olympic Games which involved competitions might also be described as an *agōn*, the Greek for 'contest'; competitive excellence was thought to be a peculiarly appropriate way of showing due respect for the gods, as we shall see.

Most *heortai*, then, stemmed ultimately from rural, agricultural celebrations. Not surprisingly, therefore, the festival most widely attested throughout the Greek world is the Thesmophoria, which was held in honour of Demeter, the earth-mother goddess of agricultural increase. But between the time of Homer, our earliest literary source, and the classical fifth and fourth centuries B.C. the tie between festivals and the agricultural year visibly weakened. Hardly any harvest festivals properly so called are attested, and at Athens in the fifth century what were technically agricultural festivals were being celebrated up to three months out of season, with the consequence that the ritual ploughing at the Skira festival, for instance, had 'no correlation with the actual ploughing of the peasants'.[5] This was because the Athenian state calendar, which tried to reconcile the lunar year of 354 days with the solar one of 365¼, had not been kept properly adjusted, despite this humorous protest by the Chorus of Aristophanes' *Clouds*: 'The moon says she treats you well, while you fail to keep your calendar straight, but jumble it up, with the result that the gods get cross with her whenever they are cheated of their dinner and have to return home without enjoying the feast appointed for the day.'[6]

In other words, a process of secularization, or more precisely politicization, can be detected as the Greek world became organized into city-states (*poleis*) and these states gradually developed urban centres increasingly divorced from their rural hinterland. Indeed, the very act of fixing a day of the month for a festival represented a move away from the natural, peasant basis of its original celebration. This process of secularization was not hindered by the fact that in classical Greece 'the sacred and the secular were intermingled in a manner which is sometimes astonishing to us'.[7] On the other hand, secularization should not be over-emphasized. For the peaceful coexistence of the mundane and the celestial, the sacred with the profane, also meant that even the most secularized of festivals never lost touch entirely with its religious roots. Sacred things could not be treated as profane, and festivals took place in a precinct dedicated to some god and were accompanied by sacrifices.

All this makes it virtually impossible to convey in words the atmosphere of an *heortē*. But anyone who has imbibed the mixed carnival and devotional atmosphere of a village *festa* in southern Italy or Sicily, or a village *paneyiri* in Greece will have gained some, though of course an inexact, notion of what it may have felt like to participate in an ancient Greek religious festival.

So much by way of general introduction. The rest of this chapter will be given over to a more detailed account of just two festivals, the Olympia (or Olympic Games, as we know them) and the Great or City Dionysia at Athens. These two have been specially selected for several reasons. Each is the ultimate source of an idea that is still potent in our contemporary world – respectively, competitive athletic sports, and the theatre – and yet the contexts in which those ideas were originally generated are fundamentally different from those of the modern, revived Olympics or a current theatrical production. The understanding of such basic cultural differences is just as important a reason for studying ancient Greece as the flattering recognition of cultural similarities. Next, both the Olympia and the Dionysia festivals admirably illustrate most of the general features of festivals sketched above: the unity in diversity that was classical Greek religion; the origin of festivals in peasants' agricultural celebrations; the common structural elements of the procession, the sacrifice and the feast; the holidaymaking interruption of the routine daily grind; the religious conception of competitive excellence; and the process of secularization. Finally, each of these religious festivals is relatively well documented by literary texts, by the epigraphical evidence of inscriptions and by archaeology.

The Olympic Games

The Olympia, held every four years in honour of Zeus Olympios (from Mt Olympus in Thessaly, the highest peak in Greece), became the largest *panēgyris* of the Greeks. This was only fitting for the worship of the senior deity of the Olympian pantheon, the father of the gods. It was, besides, the panhellenic festival *par excellence*, both because all and only Greeks were eligible to participate in the Games, and because at its zenith it attracted participants from all corners of the Greek world [21]. But although Greece was a religious unity from early times, the institutions which were the organs of that unity developed relatively late. The four major panhellenic athletics festivals, for example – the Olympic, Pythian, Isthmian and Nemean Games – were not organized into an interlocking *periodos* or circuit until the sixth century B.C.

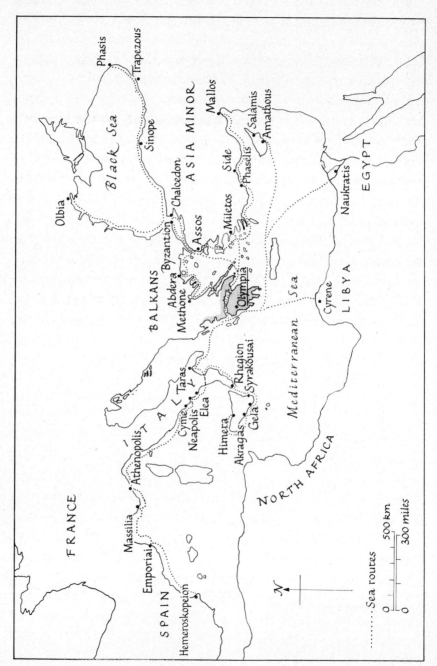

21 The world of the competitors at Olympia.

Of these four, the Olympics were traditionally and rightly regarded as the senior festival. The conventional foundation date of 776 B.C. was perhaps first computed by the local polymath and sophist, Hippias of Elis. Whether this date is precisely accurate or not, it is certain that the Games were an appreciably later addition to the cult of Zeus in the Altis or sacred grove at Olympia whose beginnings can be traced back archaeologically to the eleventh century B.C. (but no earlier). Why this particular cult of Zeus Olympios, which seems to have taken over an earlier oracle of Gē (Earth), grew to be the most important in the Greek world is unclear. But this development was undoubtedly assisted by geography and politics. The site of Olympia on the banks of the River Alpheios in the north-west Peloponnese was remote from the main centres of habitation in early Greece [22], and at first the cult was not tied to any one state. Indeed, long after the Games were inaugurated the right to organize them was disputed by neighbouring states. In these circumstances it was impossible for

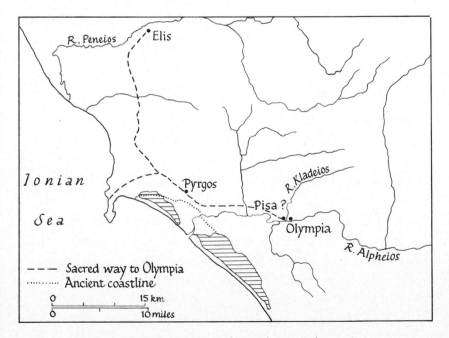

22 The site of Olympia in the north-west Peloponnese.

the festival to be exploited as a source of political power. Then, too, like Delphi the site still breathes an air of numinous calm, and again like Apollo's at Delphi the oracle of Zeus may well have spread its fame before ever anyone thought to hold games at the sanctuary.

It is also unclear why the Games were in fact added to the cult of Olympian Zeus. Pelops, who is closely associated with their origins in myth, was worshipped through them as a hero-god rather than as a founder; and in any case the old theory which explained all athletic games as originating in burial rites for heroes, such as the funeral games held by Achilles for Patroclus in the *Iliad*, is now discredited. All we can confidently assert is that the material preconditions for the holding of games at Olympia on a regular and more than narrowly local basis were satisfied by the early eighth century B.C., and not much, if at all, before. By then there was available a sufficiently large, homogeneous, stable and wealthy population; communications between the relevant communities, mostly at first in the Peloponnese, were sufficiently peaceful and close; and the lush pastureland of the Alpheios valley supported sufficient cattle for ritual slaughter and consumption as sacrificial victims.[8]

In 776 B.C., too, to broaden the perspective, the Greek world was poised on the threshold of momentous change. The creation of the *polis* and the idea of citizenship; the dispatch of the first overseas colonies; the invention of a fully phonetic alphabetic script – these are just some of the early manifestations of this 'age of experiment'.[9] Spearheading these revolutionary changes were the various local aristocracies, who combined a monopoly of political power with a controlling share of the ideas serving to reinforce their rule, including control of the religious apparatus of their incipient city-states. Central to aristocratic ideology from as early as we have evidence for it was the ideal of competitiveness: 'ever to be first and to surpass the rest', as one Homeric hero says to another – this was the leitmotiv of the noblemen's existence. It was from the ranks of such *kaloikagathoi*, true gentlemen, that the first competitors at the Olympic Games were drawn.

'Games', though, is a rather grand title for what was until 724 B.C. a single running race, the stade (*stadion* – roughly 200 metres). But the isolation of this event for the first half-century of the Games' history reminds us that this was primarily a religious occasion. The suggestion that running races and competitive games in general were conceived originally as contributing to maintain the energies of nature, following a regular cycle, is attractive. The competitive element, which was present in practically all public ceremonies in ancient Greece, may have carried with it the general implication of efficaciousness inherent in all fertility rites. Certainly, the Greeks found it natural to pursue human excellence in religious occasions such as this and to reward it according to its degree in tangible, material ways.

By the mid-seventh century B.C. it is appropriate to speak of an Olympic Games, which then comprised the nine events that remained part of the programme until the Games were closed down, as being pagan, by a Christian Roman Emperor in A.D. 393 [23]. These were the *stadion, diaulos* (roughly 400 metres), *dolichos* (roughly 5,000 metres), *pentathlon* (discus; standing jump; javelin; *stadion*; wrestling), wrestling, boxing, chariot-race, horse-race, and *pankration* (a brutal, even lethal combination of boxing, wrestling and judo).[10] Events for boys (aged twelve to eighteen), the race in heavy armour, and one or two other events were added subsequently so that by 472 B.C. when the Games were reorganized after the Persian Wars under the management of Elis they had swollen into a five-day festival. The construction of a proper stadium in the sixth century marked the growing autonomy of track and field events from the more narrowly religious manifestations.

On the other hand, the athletics never broke entirely free from their cultic moorings. To approach the ancient Olympics in a spirit appropriate to their modern imitation is to let oneself in for

Olympiad	Year BC	Event
1	776	Stade-race (short foot-race)
14	724	*Diaulos* (double-length foot-race)
15	720	*Dolichos* (long-distance foot-race)
18	708	*Pentathlon* and wrestling
23	688	Boxing
25	680	*Tethrippon* (four-horse chariot-race)
33	648	*Pankration* (type of all-in wrestling) and horse-race
37	632	Foot-race and wrestling for boys
38	628	*Pentathlon* for boys (immediately discontinued)
41	616	Boxing for boys
65	520	Race-in-armour
70	500	*Apēnē* (mule-cart race)
71	496	*Calpē* or *anabatēs* (race for mares)
84	444	*Apēnē* and *calpē* discontinued
93	408	*Synoris* (two-horse chariot-race)
96	396	Competitions for heralds and trumpeters
99	384	Chariot-racing for teams of four colts
128	268	Chariot-racing for teams of two colts
131	256	Races for colts
145	200	*Pankration* for boys

23 The development of the Olympic programme.

a grave shock. It would be 'as if a sports correspondent, setting out to cover the Montreal Olympics, should find that he had been sent, instead, to cover the Holy Week ceremonies at Seville'.[11] Scholars cannot agree on the order of the athletics programme, but there is unanimity that the festival began, ended and was punctuated with individual and collective religious worship and that it was timed to coincide with a full moon, probably the second after the summer solstice.

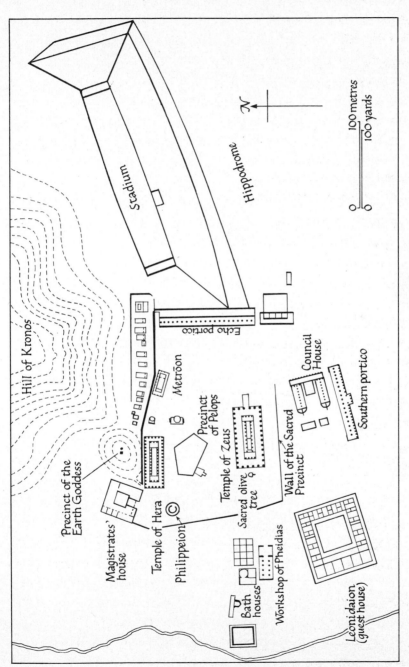

24 The sanctuary at Zeus at Olympia.

The first day was reserved for ceremonial within the Altis. Sacrifices, dedications and prayers were offered up to Zeus by officials and competitors, and the solemnly binding oath was sworn by all participants before the altar and statue of Zeus Horkios (Guardian of Oaths). Breach of this oath could lead to disqualification and a heavy fine. During the Games there were two more public sacrifices; the one held on the day of the full moon following the procession to the great ash altar of Zeus was the festival's central event. The final day was concluded with a general feast after the crowning of the victors.

But if it would be wrong to ignore the fundamental religious components of the ancient Olympics, it would be hardly less erroneous to ignore the more purely secular elements too. Of these, three may be picked out for special mention: the economics of the festival and its accompaniments; the character of the athletic competition; and the relationship between politics and sport.

Far, far more people came to watch the athletics than the comparative handful of leisured and affluent gentlemen who could afford the time and expense of the intensive training necessary to compete in them. This vast throng (perhaps as many as 40,000 could have crowded into the fourth-century stadium, the one visible at Olympia today) had to find food and shelter, and probably the great majority of them expected also to be entertained when there were no athletic or religious activities going on. Hence the Olympics, like the Ascension Day festivities of Renaissance Venice and many another such occasion, attracted a multifarious fringe of lodging-house keepers, stall-holders, peddlers, cooks, jugglers, musicians, prostitutes – in short, all the fun of the fair. So important economically might these festival fairs be that a Greek geographer writing around the turn of our era could refer to the main festival of Delos as 'a sort of commercial affair'.[12] At a rather higher level, the craftsmen who made objects suitable for dedication to Zeus or some other god or hero in the Altis profited greatly; and the considerable building and repair activity in the many shrines brought work to skilled artists of international repute like Pheidias (who made the gold and ivory statue of Zeus, adjudged one of the Seven Wonders of antiquity) and, more important economically, to local unskilled manual labourers. At the most elevated level of all in cultic terms, sacrificed animals provided hides for privileged officials and other VIPs, and a rare meat meal for the humbler celebrants.

Turning from economics to the character of the athletic competition, it is essential to rid our minds of the notion of amateurism so dear to Pierre, Baron de Coubertin, the inspiration behind the revival of the Olympics in 1896.[13] Competitors in the ancient Olympics may often have been self-styled gentlemen, but they were not amateurs either in the sense that they disdained material rewards or in the sense that they were dilettantes who merely played at athletics.[14] Aristocrats of all ages, whose claim to superiority rests ultimately on an accident of birth, are of course apt to overstress innate talent at the expense of training. But an aristocrat like Theagenes of Thasos, who is alleged to have won around 1,300 victories in boxing and the *pankration* in just twenty-two years of the early fifth century, was hardly a dilettante; and he of course won most of his victories in competitions where the prize was not just a token olive-crown as at Olympia. In other words, Theagenes was a professional, that is full-time, athlete, who must have devoted his youth and early manhood almost exclusively to the single-minded (or mindless, according to some ancient as well as modern critics) pursuit of athletic success.

From the Greek word *agōn* our 'agony' is derived. However, it is not only the strain and toughness of Greek competitiveness that strike us so forcefully today but also its all-pervasiveness. As we shall see, it was no less in evidence in the Theatre of Dionysus at Athens than in the stadium at Olympia. Still, there are probably no nicer illustrations of the peculiar quality of Greek competitiveness than Pindar's epinician odes, written to celebrate victors at the four major panhellenic games. From many possible examples space permits just two selections, one from the eighth Olympian

Ode, the other from the eighth Pythian. Both were commissioned for victors in the boys' wrestling who were scions of the island aristocracy of Aegina not far from Athens:

> On the limbs of four boys he put away from him
> The hateful return, the dishonouring tongue,
> The secret by-path,
> And into his father's father he breathed
> Strength to resist old age.
> A man forgets death when all goes well.
>
> (*Olympian* 8.67–73)

And now four times you came down with bodies beneath you,
(You meant them harm),
To whom the Pythian feast has given
No glad home-coming like yours.
They, when they meet their mothers,
Have no sweet laughter around them moving delight.
In back streets out of their enemies' way
They cower; disaster has bitten them.

(*Pythian* 8.81–7 trs. C. M. Bowra)

Competition at Olympia, then, was a paramilitary exercise. It will come as no surprise to learn that *agōn* in one of its senses can mean 'war', and war in the ancient Greeks' view was a male preserve. Not only were women not allowed to compete in person in the Olympics (though they might enter their chariots), they were actually debarred from watching the Games, where their men channelled their competitive aggression into action that only just stayed this side of outright martial violence. What George Orwell wrote of modern sport is even more true of the ancient Olympics: 'Serious sport has nothing to do with fair play. It is bound up with hatred, jealousy, boastfulness, disregard of all rules, and sadistic pleasure in witnessing violence: in other words, it is war minus the shooting.'[15] In ancient Greece they sometimes had the shooting too, in the sense that deaths, above all in the boxing and *pankration*, were by no means unknown; indeed, death in Olympic competition was revealingly placed in the Greek scale of values on a par with the highest glory of all, death in battle on behalf of one's city.

This provides a convenient link to my final topic, the relation between politics and sport. The ancient Greeks would have shared the modern criticism of Nazi Germany in 1936 and Soviet Russia in 1980, that the host nation ought not to make political capital out of hosting the Games. This was an eventuality they sidestepped by keeping the Games in one venue and under the management of a state that was not of the first political importance. On the other hand, the ancient Greeks would not have understood the official attempts made today to distinguish in principle between international politics and international sport, and to keep the former out of the latter. The Olympic sacred truce, for example, was not designed to promote panhellenic amity, as de Coubertin fondly imagined. It was an armistice (*ekecheiria*), a supremely realistic measure aimed at protecting pilgrims and participants in the festival from hostile military activity by states through whose territory they might have to pass or in which the Games were held. The truce never stopped wars between Greek states; it merely prevented wars from stopping the Games. Even so, in 420 B.C. the Games were threatened by an invasion, as we shall see, and in 364 B.C. they were actually interrupted as fighting spilled over into the Altis.[16]

If General von Clausewitz was right to hold that war is the continuation of politics by or with other means, then the ancient Olympics were the continuation of war with or by other, political means. It is true that competitors entered individually, but the state took the liveliest possible interest in an Olympic victory gained by one of its citizens, while conversely citizens sought to turn their victories to political account. The following examples will demonstrate that politics and sport were inseparably intertwined in ancient Greece, as they are today, though in very different ways.

In the recent past, nation states have boycotted the Olympics in order to make various political points. No ancient Greek state would have deprived itself of the chance to bask in the reflected glory of an Olympic victory by one of its native sons. If the citizens of a particular state were barred from competing in antiquity, this was because Elis decreed it so, as she did, for instance, to the Spartans in 420. Nevertheless, a prominent and very wealthy Spartan entered his four-horse chariot under an assumed name, won, and then made bold to throw off the disguise and claim his prize as a Spartan. Whereupon the Eleian judges not merely disqualified him but even had him whipped – a singular exception to the rule that corporal punishment in antiquity was reserved for slaves.[17]

The Spartans were banned in 420 B.C. for political, not religious, reasons, and political tensions were running so high that the participants feared Sparta might actually invade Olympia to get the ban lifted. But that a ban of this kind was highly unusual is shown by the fact that in 480 B.C. the tyrant of Greek Rhegion in South Italy was not debarred from competing (and winning) even though earlier that same summer he had collaborated with the Carthaginians in their invasion of Greek Sicily.[18] The panhellenism of the Olympic Games, in other words, served not only to emphasize what the Greeks had in common culturally, but also to point up their irreconcilable political differences. Otherwise it would be hard to explain how the Greeks of Taras, for example, could unashamedly dedicate at the panhellenic shrine of Olympia a tithe of booty taken from their South Italian neighbours, the Greeks of Thourioi.[19]

There are several specific instances of states taking an interest in citizens of theirs who competed or, best of all, won at Olympia. Perhaps the most spectacular of these concerns the citizen of Akragas (modern Agrigento in Sicily) who in 412 B.C. won the prestigious stade race. He was escorted back within the walls of his city by no less than 300 chariots, each drawn by a pair of white horses.[20] From about 600 B.C., too, Greek states had built public *gymnasia*, exercise-grounds. This was mainly of course to encourage their warriors to keep strong and fit, but gymnastic exercises had an obvious practical application at Olympia as well. By the later fifth century some states were offering good trainers material inducements, and by the end of the fourth they were also subsidizing promising athletes whose ancestral wealth was not equal to the huge demands in time and financial outlay made by Olympic competition. One final example of state encouragement of Olympic success: at Sparta, the most powerful military state in Greece from the seventh to the fourth century, Olympic victors had the enormous privilege of being stationed in front of their king in battle.[21]

As for individuals who used an Olympic victory as a form of political credit, the classic example is surely that of Alcibiades. Athens in his day was a radical democracy, whose expressed ideology was egalitarian. Yet even so Alcibiades could justifiably hope to gain political advantage from a victory in the most aristocratic of Olympic events, the four-horse chariot-race. In the year in question, probably 416 B.C., he entered no less than seven chariots and took second and fourth places as well as the crown itself.[22] It would be hard to think of a modern parallel for a politician trading on his athletic success in order to secure the adoption by a democratic assembly of a controversial foreign policy involving war in a distant land. That is perhaps as good an illustration as any of just how alien to our way of thinking was the mixture of the religious and the secular, of sport and politics, represented by the ancient Olympic festival.

The Great or City Dionysia at Athens

It is impossible to establish in full detail the *Fasti* or festival calendar of any Greek state, as can be done for, say, Republican Rome.[23] But the calendar of democratic Athens in the fifth and fourth centuries B.C. allows by far the most complete reconstruction of any of the hundreds of calendars then in use in the Greek world.[24] According to an anonymous pamphleteer of the later fifth century, the Athenians celebrated more festivals than any other Greek city, allegedly twice as many.[25] Certainly they were very numerous, the reasons being that the state of Athens had been created from an earlier unification of a large number of local communities and that there was felt a need to integrate as many traditional religious forces as possible for the benefit of the new collectivity.

Two texts will bring out just how important festivals were to the social life of democratic Athens. In 431 B.C. the Peloponnesian War broke out as a result of irreconcilable tensions between the two Greek 'super powers', Athens and Sparta. In the winter of 431–430 B.C. following the first season's campaigning the Athenians honoured their leading statesman Pericles by choosing him to deliver the funeral oration over the Athenian dead. His actual words are not known, but the great historian of the Peloponnesian War, Thucydides, has given us an immortal version of his speech, which preserves at least the general sense of what Pericles actually said in the Kerameikos cemetery. The speech was a hymn of praise to the Athenians' democratic way of life, which Pericles claimed to be a model for other Greeks to follow. Essential to that way of life, he said, were festivals. 'When our work is over, we are in a position to enjoy all kinds of recreation for our spirits. There are various kinds of contests (*agōnes*) and sacrifices (*thusiai*) regularly throughout the year.'[26]

Twenty-seven years later Athens had lost the disastrous Peloponnesian War and been compelled by the Spartans to abolish its democratic constitution. A vicious oligarchic junta, later known as the Thirty Tyrants, exercised a bloody sway for some months until they provoked a determined democratic resistance led from outside Athens by a small and heroic band of exiles. These exiles succeeded in re-entering Athens under arms, a battle was fought in the staunchly democratic port of Piraeus, and the forces of the Thirty were defeated. This defeat was the undoing of their regime. Not long after, Athens became a democracy once more and remained so until 322 B.C. when the Macedonians again put democracy down, this time for good. Following the battle of the Piraeus in 403 B.C. the herald of those initiated into the Eleusinian Mysteries addressed a ringing plea for national reconciliation to those who had fought for the Thirty. A version of his speech was given by Xenophon in his *History of Greece*:

Fellow-citizens, why are you driving us out of the city? Why do you want to kill us? We have never done you any harm. We have shared with you in the most holy religious services, in sacrifices and in splendid festivals (*heortai*); we have joined in dances with you . . . In the name of the gods of our fathers and mothers, of the bonds of kinship and marriage and friendship, which are shared by so many of us on both sides, I beg you to feel some shame in front of gods and men and to give up this sin against your fatherland. (Xenophon, *Hellenica* 2.4.20–1)[27]

Festivals, then, were important in democratic Athens. But so were they in any Greek city, whatever its political constitution, and even a citizen of a non-democratic state could agree with Pericles that they provided spiritual recreation, and with the Eleusinian herald that they reinforced communal solidarity. What gave them their special flavour in Athens in the fifth and fourth centuries therefore was precisely the fact that Athens was a democracy, the world's first and the most long-lived, radical and successful in classical Greece. This is how the so-called 'Old Oligarch' explained, in his biased way, the function of festivals in democratic Athens:

However, for the staging of dramatic and choral festivals, the superintending of the *gymnasia* and the games and the provision of triremes, they realize that it is the rich who pay, and the common people for whom such things are arranged and who serve in the triremes. At all events, they think it right to receive pay for singing, running and dancing, and for sailing in the fleet so that they may have money and the rich may become poor. In the courts too, they are as much interested in their own advantage as they are in justice. ('Old Oligarch' 1.13 trs. J. M. Moore)[28]

What he is saying, in other words, is that the Athenian democracy was run by and for the majority of poor citizens, the *dēmos*, who used their control of the constitution to soak the rich minority of citizens, men like our anonymous pamphleteer who would prefer to live under some form of oligarchy, the rule of the rich few (*oligoi*). Needless to say, a democrat would hardly have seen things this way and would stress the honour and prestige that the wealthy derived individually from their financial contributions and the power and glory that accrued to the state of Athens collectively thanks to its control of the sea and its magnificent cultural productions. As good a way as any of evaluating these competing claims is to examine the Great or City Dionysia, a festival second in importance only to the Panathenaia devoted to Athens' patron goddess, Athena Polias.[29]

Today it is the tragedies and comedies produced at the festival that immediately spring to mind in connection with the Dionysia; and the following account will give most space to their staging and reception. But for the Athenians these were but one, and not necessarily the most important, element. To put the plays into proper historical perspective, it is necessary to examine as a whole the occasion of which they formed an integral part; the way in which that occasion was organized; and what the occasion and its organization tell us about democratic Athenian society.

The Great Dionysia festival was also known as the City Dionysia to distinguish it from the various rural Dionysia celebrated in the demes or parishes of Attica, the city-state territory of Athens. Dionysus, a latecomer to the Olympian pantheon, is of uncertain geographical origin, but he functioned as a god of fertility in general and wine in particular. No less unclear is the reason why the ecstatic dancing and revelry (*kōmos*) associated with his cult should have given rise to drama, especially as the rites

were traditionally performed by women and yet all the acting personnel of tragedy, satyr-drama and comedy were men. Comedy,
as its etymology indicates, is directly descended from the singing
that accompanied the *kōmos*, though that still leaves the genesis of
its dramatic form to be explained. As for tragedy, it is only a
hypothesis that it had its origins in mystic initiation into the rites of
Dionysus, that all tragedy was originally about Dionysus, and that
the satyr-play attached to the tragedies is a vestige of these
initiatory origins.

Whatever the merits of that hypothesis, it is clear that, just as
the Games were added to the cult of Zeus Olympios at Olympia,
so the plays were grafted on to an original cult of Dionysus
Eleuthereus (from Eleutherai, a village on Attica's northern bor-
der); this consisted in the bringing of his statue from outside
Athens to his sanctuary at the foot of the Acropolis, the solemn
sacrifice, and the ensuing revel. The date by which the drama had
taken recognizable shape is tied to the careers of the benevolent
dictator Pisistratus and the actor-playwright Thespis. Towards the
end of his reign Pisistratus, for political rather than religious or
cultural reasons, 'gave tragedy an official blessing by bringing
rural mumming to the city'.[30] The *floruit* of Thespis was given in
antiquity as 534, six years before Pisistratus' death. The democracy, therefore, which was not instituted until 508–507 B.C., did
not inaugurate the enlarged Dionysia but took it over and in the
process transformed its political significance.

The Greek Dionysia occurred in Elaphēbolion, the ninth
month of the Athenian year, which was named after Artemis
Elaphēbolos ('Deerhunter'). As with other Athenian months, the
festival that had at first been the most important and after which
the month was named had ceased to be so by the time of the
democracy. A couple of days before the festival proper began two
preliminary ceremonies were conducted. The old wooden statue
of Dionysus was removed from its precinct and placed tem-
porarily in a temple outside the city-walls on the road to
Eleutherai. This was so that every year the festival's original

transfer from Eleutherai to Athens might be symbolically re-enacted, at least in part. Secondly, on Elaphēbolion 8 the *Proagōn* or 'ceremony preceding the contest' was held. From 444 B.C. this took place in a building constructed at the instigation of Pericles and called the Odeion or Singing-Hall. Here the competing playwrights, accompanied by their actors, announced what plays were to be performed. At the *Proagōn* of 406 B.C., for example, just after the death of Euripides had been announced, Sophocles appeared in mourning, and introduced his actors and chorus without the customary garlands on their heads; the audience, we are told, dissolved into tears.

The festival proper began on Elaphēbolion 10 with a great pro-cession (*pompē*); this was distinct from the procession that brought back the statue. Participants in the grand opening procession included not only Athenian citizens, but resident aliens and, in the fifth century, Athenian colonists who had been settled elsewhere in the Aegean area for economic and strategic reasons. All were dressed in gorgeous robes; many carried a model of an erect phallus, the Dionysiac fertility symbol; others drove along the cows and bulls that were to be sacrificed in the Theatre of Dionysus as the culmination of the procession, no less than 240 of them in 333 B.C. In the evening there was a great communal beef supper, a rare treat, washed down with litres of diluted wine; then followed a gigantic revel. Since this was the holiest day of the fes-tival, there is not surprisingly no record of a political Assembly being held on this day. So out of the ordinary was it, in fact, that even prisoners were released from custody on bail.

The next day, the first of the three tragedians whose work had been selected had his three tragedies and a satyr-play performed. But before the plays could commence there were more ceremonies, some religious, most wholly secular. The saying of prayers and the pouring of libations are to be expected. But in the fifth century, before defeat in the Peloponnesian War put paid to their vaulting ambitions, the Athenians also used this occasion as a grand demonstration of their imperial might. They had the year's tribute from their subject-allies, some of whom will have been in the audience, paraded by some 400 hired bearers who each carried a sack containing one talent's worth of silver.[31] This parade, which served as a kind of collective receipt, formed a natural complement to the Parthenon and other splendid buildings on the Acropolis above the Theatre which had been financed from the imperial tribute. Then there was another, smaller parade, this time in full armour by newly-adult orphans whose fathers had been killed in war and who had therefore been raised at state expense. This was a neat way of celebrating both military patriotism and a kind of welfare-state democratic paternalism. Finally, this was the moment for the conduct of some civic business: the renewal of a treaty, perhaps, or the proclamation of honours for individual citizens. Only when these preliminaries were out of the way could the first play start.

There were four days of plays, three for tragedies and their accompanying satyr-plays, the fourth for the five comedies chosen. On the day after the comedies an Assembly was held to scrutinize, in quintessentially democratic fashion, the conduct of the festival by the relevant state officials. It was now that complaints could be made, and court cases might arise from allegations of misconduct. A brief description of what was involved in the staging of the plays and the spirit in which they were presented and received will readily show why litigation, oddly to our way of thinking, might result from participation in a religious ritual.

The plays were put on in the open air during the hours of daylight. *Theatron* was originally the collective noun for a group of spectators (*theatai*) and so became attached to the place where the *theatai* spectated. At Athens this meant the south-east slope of the Acropolis, a doubly appropriate site. Not only was the Acropolis the focus of Athenian religious and civic activity, but it was also geographically suitable. The abrupt rock of the hill provided shelter from the north winds apt to blow in early spring when the Dionysia normally fell; while the hill's moderate south-east slope could be specially prepared to accommodate superimposed rows of seating [25] – beaten earth and wooden benches down to the later fourth century, when the stone seating visible today was constructed. It is estimated that the theatre could hold up to 17,000 spectators, who looked down on the drama and beyond to the plain that stretched to Mt Hymettus and the sea. 'The whole setting was drawn into the dramatic scene rather than shut out or obliterated.'[32] Nothing could be further from our theatre-buildings with their enclosed space and artificial, man-made atmosphere.

The drama took place in a prepared area at the foot of the hill. To repeat, the origins of drama are obscure, but it somehow crystallized out of ritual miming, singing and dancing that told and retold traditional myths about the Athenians' gods and heroic ancestors. Thus the essential and irreducible component of the theatre was the *orchēstra*, a circular dancing-floor of beaten earth perhaps modelled on a threshing-floor. Here the Chorus of masked

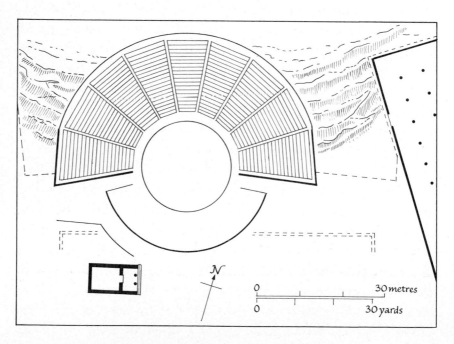

25 The Theatre of Dionysus in the fifth century B.C.

men chanted and danced to the accompaniment of an oboe-like instrument (*aulos*). The actors, also masked men, occupied a separately defined space behind the *orchēstra*, a raised wooden stage to which they gained access from the *skēnē*. The latter, which means literally a tent or booth (like those erected at Olympia), was a rectangular building of light wooden construction that served both as the main prop and as the actors' dressing- and mask-changing room. There had been, to begin with, just one actor in tragedy, the playwright himself, who enacted the drama in dialogue with the Chorus. Aeschylus added a second, Sophocles a third, and three remained the fixed number of speaking actors in tragedy, though some plays of Aristophanes demanded a minimum of five.

The play's the thing. *Drama* in Greek means 'something done', a reminder that the plays were seen and heard rather than read. In fact, the playwright (*poiētēs* or 'maker') was not said to 'write' his plays but to 'produce' or 'teach' them. For though most Athenian citizens were sufficiently literate to enable the democracy to function, they lived in a fundamentally oral culture in which information in the broadest sense was normally communicated by word of mouth and in face-to-face contact. They were thereby far more habituated than we are to the spoken word as a medium of communication – a pre-condition for the successful operation of the Dionysia in their extended form, since play-going in democratic Athens provided a rich and highly concentrated bill of fare.

Individual Greek plays were by our standards short, one-acters; Aeschylus' *Agamemnon* is unusually long with 1,673 lines. But then no tragedian (unlike the comic playwright) composed a single, self-sufficient play. Instead, he wrote three tragedies, sometimes as a connected trilogy, and a kind of burlesque masque in which the Chorus impersonated animals rather than humans. These together made up a day's bill and, like the five comedies, provided something like six solid hours of performance. Besides, the language of tragedy was artificially elevated to match the unrelieved moral earnestness of the drama. The mere fact of the presentation of nine such plays each year before an audience well in excess of 10,000 in the open air seems an extraordinary feat to most of us, who find it easier to comprehend the light relief afforded by the satyr-plays and comedies. And this is not to mention the quality of the surviving plays, several of which have established themselves as classics of the theatre. Which reminds us that it was the Greeks or rather the Athenians who in the fifth century B.C. created the idea of a theatre.[33] But they did so in a religious context.

However, since there was no division between church and state, there being no church, the running of the Dionysia was subsumed under the normal administration of the Athenian democratic state. The civic official in overall charge of the festival was the eponymous chief Archon, who was appointed annually (after 487 B.C. by the democratic procedure of the lot) and was accountable to the Athenian people as a whole, again in accordance with a basic democratic principle. Management of the Great Dionysia was only one of his responsibilities, and he was not chosen for his special dramatic sensitivity.

Nevertheless, he it was who selected the three tragedians and the five writers of comedies from those interested in 'applying for a Chorus'. We do not know the criteria on which he made his selection, though he perhaps asked the prospective playwrights to recite passages to him. However the selection was made, we can only applaud those Archons who decided for Aeschylus, Sophocles, Euripides and Aristophanes, and feel sorry for the one who preferred the unknown Gnesippos to Sophocles. The Archon's next task was to appoint *chorēgoi*, Chorus-masters or impresarios, one for each of the lucky playwrights. Here the drama and the political economy of democratic Athens met each other head on. For to act as *chorēgos* was to perform a *leitourgia*, a legally enforceable, necessary public service; and the requirement to carry out a liturgy was a form of indirect tax levied only on the richest Athenian citizens and resident aliens. On the liberality or meanness of the

chorēgos the success of a playwright depended to a considerable
degree. For he found, paid and kitted out the Chorus and, when
required, provided for a retinue of mute characters or even
occasionally a second Chorus. He also paid the *aulos*-player and,
from the late fifth century, a professional Chorus-trainer.
Perhaps, too, he covered the cost of any special effects. When the
performances were over, he was expected to provide a banquet
for all concerned.

All this was unavoidably expensive, and it could be hugely so.
There happens to survive part of a law-court speech written for a
man being prosecuted on the potentially capital charge of em-
bezzlement in about 400 B.C.[34] The defendant begins with a
monumental catalogue of all the liturgies he has performed,
including that of acting as *chorēgos* for tragedy at the Great
Dionysia which, he claims, cost him no less than half a talent. But
this was an extraordinary amount, well above the required
minimum, and the defendant indirectly explains why he paid out
so much. For he overspent in order to benefit the city and to build
up a large store of credit with the Athenian people against precisely such an eventuality as the prosecution he was then facing.
The trial was being held before a jury of 501 ordinary Athenian
citizens in the politically charged atmosphere described earlier in
this chapter. It is an easy inference that our *chorēgos*, an enormously
wealthy man, was anxious to allay any suspicion that his wealth
had made him sympathetic to oligarchic counter-revolution. This
is why he stresses his exceptional public-spiritedness and does not
dwell on the prestige and influence wealth commanded even in
this ostensibly egalitarian society.

After the playwrights and the *chorēgoi* it remained for the
Archon to select the actors. Or rather, it seems, he chose the leading
actor for each poet, and then those actors selected their supporting
actors for themselves. The general term for actor was *hypokritēs*, so
called because he answered the Chorus. But the titles used to distinguish between the actors are sociologically far more revealing.
They make explicit that element which largely shaped the

6
Delphi and divination

SIMON PRICE

Delphi is a place which most tourists in Greece visit [26].[1] The oracle of Apollo has an obvious fascination for us, but understanding the place is difficult. The diligent visitor might turn for guidance to one of the standard histories of Greece, but unfortunately they only mention Delphi from time to time in the course of their narratives and do not pause to consider, as I want to do, Delphi as an institution.[2] Many visitors will therefore consult a guide-book. One of the best of these, the *Blue Guide*, starts with the statutory

26 Delphi: from the left can be seen the Treasury of the Athenians, the Sacred Way up to the Temple of Apollo, the theatre and the stadium (the large new building is the museum). In the distance is Itéa.

purple passage about the picturesqueness of Delphi (an attitude to landscape which goes back to the nineteenth century): the towering rocks and the mountains, while 'the View down the sacred plain to Itéa, with its myriad olive-trees, is not the least of the delights which make Delphi the goal of countless excursions every day of the year'. More helpfully, the guide-book has a synopsis of the history of Delphi and also an account of the operation of the oracle. The priestess of the oracle, the Pythia, purified herself and:

munching a laurel leaf, took her seat upon the tripod, which was placed over the chasm in the Adyton. Intoxicated by the exhalations from the chasm, she uttered incoherent sounds, which were interpreted in hexa-meter verse by a poet in waiting. The interpretation, which was always obscure and frequently equivocal, was handed over to the enquirer, who not seldom returned more mystified than he had come.[3]

This view of the roles of the Pythia and of the attendant 'prophets' is very widespread, but it succeeds in making Delphi completely baffling. How can one understand the gibberings of an intoxicated priestess? Why on earth should people consult Delphi if they generally went away more mystified than they had come?

Before considering how to improve on this view of the oracle, it might be useful to pause and recall some of the uncontroversial facts about Delphi. They form the framework within which all the various interpretations of Delphi operate. The archaeological excavations of the site have shown that the sanctuary [27] is first attested at the end of the ninth century B.C. It can only have been of local significance at this time; Greek communities in the ninth century were still small and isolated. In the eighth century Delphi grew in importance as the Greek world began to expand and com-munities looked outwards, both towards other Greek com-munities and towards their 'barbarian' neighbours. There were other oracles, such as the one at Dodona in north-west Greece, but Delphi became the most important oracle in mainland Greece. It was consulted by numerous Greek communities and at

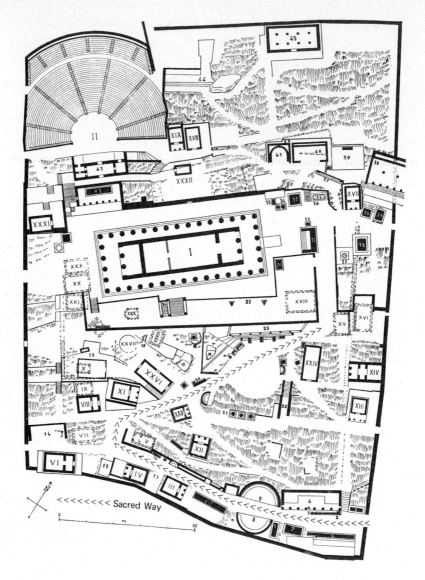

27 The Sanctuary of Apollo bounded by a wall: I Temple of Apollo; II theatre; III–
XXXI Treasuries; 1–59 dedications of statues and other offerings by various
Greek peoples. The gymnasia and stadium lie off this plan.

the end of the eighth century the sanctuary was defined by a boun-
dary wall. The temple was sufficiently notable to be mentioned in
Homer (*Iliad* 9.404–5; *Odyssey* 8.79–82), but in the seventh century the houses in the sanctuary were removed and an elaborate

new temple was built on the site of the present temple. By the sixth century the sanctuary had become one of the unquestioned centres of the Greek world. Like Olympia, Delphi held games, in honour of Apollo, which from the early sixth century were open to all Greeks; for these games there were a gymnasium, stadium and theatre, which in due course were rebuilt in stone. The sanctuary became more splendid as cities from all over the Greek world made dedications there. By the end of the fifth century there were twenty-seven special buildings – 'treasuries' – put up by different cities to house dedications. The oracle itself was consulted by Greeks from South Italy, North Africa, mainland Greece, as well as by Croesus, king of Lydia, in what is now western Turkey.

A pre-condition for the international position of Delphi was that the sanctuary, like Olympia, was in principle independent of the political struggles of the Greek cities. Though people lived at Delphi, they could not depend for their livelihood on agricultural territory like any normal Greek city. Nor did the local inhabitants control the administration of the sanctuary (such as the upkeep of the temple) like any normal city sanctuary. They simply provided the personnel for the oracle (the priests, the Pythia etc.). From the beginning of the sixth century an association of Greeks from central Greece and the north-east Peloponnese (the ancient Amphictyonic League) organized the sanctuary itself.

This outline of the position of Delphi in the Greek world does not, however, help us much to understand why Delphi was so important. Why was it that the sane, rational Greeks went to hear the rantings of an old woman up in the hills of central Greece? I want to start my answer to this question by pointing to the dangers of making the Greeks too like ourselves. I shall then examine the procedure of the oracle and the problems of understanding which it poses. What was the mental state of the Pythia? Was she helped by munching laurel leaves or sniffing vapours? Was the gibberish she uttered reduced to order by the 'prophets', who thus manipulated the oracle? Having done that we can move on to look at the position of Delphi in Greek society. Why was so much importance attached to the oracle? What function did it serve? Finally I want to ask how much doubt and scepticism there was about the validity of the oracle and whether this explains changes in the role of Delphi. The period on which I shall focus runs roughly from the seventh century down to the Persian Wars in the early fifth century B.C., when the role of Delphi is well attested in the work of Herodotus, from whom I shall draw my evidence whenever possible.[4] Herodotus, however, has little to say about the procedures of consultation and here we are largely dependent on later testimony, especially Plutarch's two very important treatises on Delphi. Plutarch wrote them in the late first century A.D., five hundred years after Herodotus, but Plutarch was actually a priest at Delphi and thus knew well the procedure of his own day.[5]

We find Delphi difficult to understand because we do not have anything in our own culture which fully corresponds to it. Our political leaders do not attempt to discover the will of the gods before going to war. In Western Europe the only widespread form of divination is the astrological predictions in the newspapers, despised and read by millions. But these predictions are very general and tend not to give advice on specific problems. We expect people to make their own rational judgements about their problems. No educated modern person could take seriously the wild utterances of the Pythia, especially if they purported to foretell the future.

Some scholars have felt that, for the Greeks to be comprehensible, they have to be just like us, but that the picture of Delphi presented by the *Blue Guide* does not make sense. One scholar has suggested that the utterances of the Pythia herself were less important than quite another form of oracle practised at the site, the so-called lottery oracle. Under this procedure the enquirer would ask a direct question ('Should we build a temple to Demeter?'), and would receive in reply either a black or a white bean drawn out of a jar by the Pythia, whose colour indicated the answer yes or no. Rationalizing scholars, understanding well the principle of tossing a coin, certainly find this easier to understand than the utterances of the Pythia, but the lottery-oracle is rarely attested, in contrast to the numerous references to oracles given orally by the Pythia herself. Other scholars have attempted to solve the problem by rejecting as frauds all oracles which go beyond simple yes/no answers to the question and which give positive guidance or instruction. In its most extreme version this argument dismisses all oracles, including those in Herodotus, which were allegedly delivered before the mid-fifth century B.C.[6] No doubt some oracles were composed after the event which they purported to predict,[7] but to write off all the oracles found in Herodotus is again to evade the problem. There is no doubt that those oracles, and many others like them, were accepted as authentic utterances of the Pythia in the fifth century. They therefore demand explanation.

How can we avoid the danger of applying the standards of our culture to Delphi? One of the best ways is to get some understanding of other modern cultures quite different from our own. For our present purposes the best single book is one written by the British anthropologist Evans-Pritchard about the oracles of the Azande of the Southern Sudan.[8] He lived for some time with the Azande, investigating in person how their system of oracles worked. The most important of these oracles was the 'poison oracle'. When a man had an important decision to make or wanted to discover the truth about a current situation, he would consult this oracle. Special poison was carefully administered to a fowl and the problem was put to the oracle. For example, in a case of suspected adultery, the poison oracle was asked to kill the fowl if the suspect was guilty and to spare it if the person was innocent. A second test was then carried out on another bird to confirm the first test.

The Zande oracles played an important role in decision-making. Because Evans-Pritchard actually participated in the oracular sessions, he was able to show that it was quite wrong to project our scepticism on to the Azande. As he says:

No important venture is undertaken without authorisation of the poison oracle. In important collective undertakings, in all crises of life, in all serious legal disputes, in all matters seriously affecting individual welfare, in short, on all occasions regarded by Azande as dangerous or socially important, the activity is preceded by consultation of the poison oracle.[9]

To compare this oracular system to Delphi is difficult. Ideally one should not compare the two systems torn from their full contexts, but Evans-Pritchard's description of the poison oracle does bring alive for us the possible significance of an oracular system. Was Delphi like this?

Consultations of the oracle were organized probably once a month, but extra consultations were possible at other times. There were elaborate preliminary procedures; these were controlled by the priests (who are to be distinguished both from the 'prophets' who wrote down the words of the Pythia for the enquirer, and also from other cult officials). Someone might come as a delegate from Sparta or Athens to consult the oracle about some pressing affair of state (should the Spartans fight the Athenians?) or he might come on some personal matter (should he go and serve as a mercenary in Persia?). Those who came to consult the oracle were always men rather than women, who lacked an official voice in decision-making. The oracle was always busy, but if the person belonged to a privileged city he could jump the queue. He then had to pay a consultation fee and make a preliminary sacrifice of a goat to ascertain whether Apollo was happy for the consultation to take place. As Plutarch says:

When the priests and the cult officials say that they are sacrificing the victim, sprinkling holy water over it and observing its movements and its trembling, of what else do they take this to be the sign except that the god is ready to give an oracle? (*Moralia* 437A)

If the animal's shaking gave sufficient indication of Apollo's favour, it was sacrificed on the great altar outside the temple.

Then the enquirer, after paying further taxes, entered the temple where he made a final sacrifice. After these elaborate pre-liminaries the consultation could begin.

Within the temple the enquirer approached the sacred area (the *adyton*) where the oracle would be given [28]. Unfortunately the results of the excavations of this area have been inconclusive and some of what I shall say about it is rather hypothetical. It is clear, however, that the *adyton* was complicated, not to say cluttered. Against the rear wall, protected by a stone canopy, was the *omphalos* or 'navel', which was supposed to mark the centre of the world. Two statues of Apollo, one of wood, the other of gold, stood in the temple; at least one of them was probably in the *adyton*. But Apollo was not the only god honoured there. The tomb of Dionysus was sited in the *adyton*. It may seem odd to find another god in Apollo's temple, but Dionysus was an important deity at Delphi. Plutarch says that Delphi belonged to him no less than to Apollo and there was a major festival of Dionysus on the hills above Delphi every other year, though he was not involved in the giving of oracles (*Moralia* 388E).

When the enquirer reached the far end of the temple, he prob-ably went with the 'prophets' and cult officials into a special room

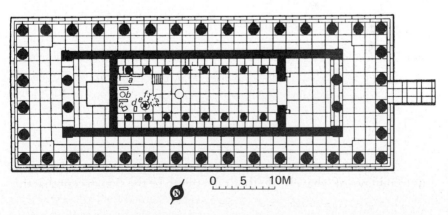

28 The Temple of Apollo: (a) room for enquirers; (b) *omphalos* with stone canopy; (c) gold statue of Apollo; (d) tomb of Dionysus; (e) oracular 'chasm' under the tripod; (f) sacred laurel.

which prevented them from seeing the *adyton* itself where the Pythia herself sat on Apollo's tripod. Beside her, probably, grew a laurel tree sacred to Apollo (there may have been windows in the roof to give it light). The actual enquiry (e.g. Does Apollo approve of the truce between Sparta and Argos?) was put to the Pythia either orally or written on a tablet. Then she prophesied.

What were her utterances like and how can we explain them? It is clear from the ancient accounts that she did not have a normal conversation with the enquirer, but it is clear also that the picture of her ranting and raving is an exaggeration, created largely by pagan and Christian writers hostile to Delphi. Plutarch gives an

29 Dionysus, carrying a thyrsus, greets Apollo with his laurel branch, perhaps on the return of Apollo from his regular winter stay with the Hyperboreans. A woman prepares a seat for the traveller. To the right, a maenad, and two satyrs with Apollonian lyre and flute. In front, the *omphalos*. To the left, a satyr and a maenad with Dionysiac tympanon, and the tripod. (Athenian vase, about 425 B.C.)

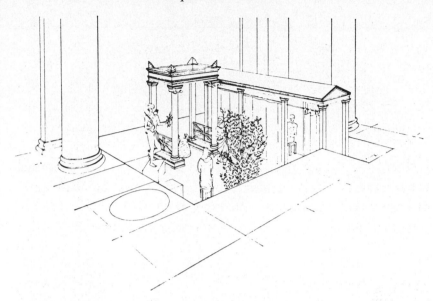

30 The *adyton* (hypothetical reconstruction).

interesting account of one recent consultation which had gone ahead despite the fact that the preliminary sacrifice had scarcely worked:

[The Pythia] went down into the *adyton* unwillingly, they say, and half-heartedly; and at her first response it was at once clear from the harshness of her voice that she was not responding properly and was like a labouring ship, as if she was filled with a mighty and baleful spirit. Finally she became hysterical and with a frightful shriek rushed towards the exit and threw herself down, with the result that not only the members of the deputation, but also the 'prophet' Nicander and the cult officials that were present fled. (*Moralia* 438B)

From this disaster (the Pythia died a few days later) we get a picture not only of the enquirers and the officials listening to the Pythia (from inside the room), but also of their expectations of her response. Her voice was supposed to change, but not in this bizarre and extreme manner.

Many explanations have been offered of how the Pythia prophesied. One scholar has suggested that the Pythia 'would show her-

31 Themis, a mythical forerunner of the Pythia, seated on a tripod and holding a spray of laurel, prophesies to Aegeus, king of Athens. Aegeus, who was enquiring about his lack of children, later fathered Theseus. (Athenian vase, about 440 B.C.)

self inspired, enthusiastic; her emotion would affect her utterance, just as an actress in the role of Medea or Clytemnestra or Lady Macbeth does not speak in her normal voice, but suits her utterance to the role she plays'.[10] This is hardly a helpful suggestion. Apart from the singular inappropriateness of the comparison with the three female 'monsters', the Pythia was not an actress. She *was* the Pythia. She lived in the sanctuary in permanent chastity and served Apollo for life.[11]

Did the chewing of laurel help? One German professor solemnly ate a pile of leaves and pronounced that he did not feel at all ecstatic.[12] Prophets and poets of the classical period did indeed consume laurel leaves to induce inspiration, but the practice is alleged at Delphi only by two late critics of the oracle. They were attempting to bring the oracle into disrepute; their sceptical point of view has certainly prevailed in modern times. But even if the Pythia did chew laurel, the experiment carried out by the German professor shows that the eating of laurel is in itself insufficient to bring on an attack of prophecy. It was far more important that the Pythia was expected to be possessed by Apollo and to be his mouthpiece.

We come now to the prophetic vapours which allegedly emerged from the ground. These play a great part not only in the modern imagination but also in some ancient accounts of Delphi. There is firstly the myth told by an historian of the first century B.C. about the origins of the oracle. Some goats grazing on the mountain-side one day discovered a hole in the ground. Whenever one of them leaned into it, the animal started to leap and shriek in a bizarre fashion. The goatherd came to see what was happening and the same thing happened to him, except that he actually started to prophesy the future. The news of this spread and others came to the spot.

In time, as many people leaped down the hole because of their state of possession and all disappeared, the locals, to eliminate the danger, appointed one woman as prophetess for all, through whom the giving of oracles was to take place. They built her an apparatus on which she could be safe during her trances and the giving of oracles to those who wanted them. The apparatus had three feet and was therefore called a tripod; presumably all the bronze tripods which are constructed to this day are made in imitation of this apparatus. About the manner in which the oracle was discovered and the reasons which led to the creation of the tripod I think I have said enough. (Diodorus Siculus 16.26)

The story clearly presupposes that something coming out of the ground inspired the prophecy, but it does not discuss the nature of the emanation.

Plutarch, however, who was a philosopher and not a historian, does devote considerable attention to the vapour, which he argued varied in strength:

As for the proof on which I depend, I have as witnesses many strangers and all the attendants of the shrine. It is a fact that the room in which they seat those who would consult the oracle is filled, not frequently or regularly, but as it happens from time to time, with a delightful fragrance coming on a current of air from the *adyton* as from a spring; the fragrance is like the aroma which the most exquisite and costly perfumes give off; it is probable that this phenomenon occurs because of heat or some other influence of this sort. (*Moralia* 437 C)

Plutarch uses the variability of the vapour as his explanation of why the oracle was not as active in his day as in the past. Many have been tempted to take Plutarch's account at face value and they have sought for traces of this heavenly aroma. Unfortunately modern geological examination of the area has shown conclusively that there can never have been any natural emanations from the rocks under the temple. Even worse, the most recent archaeological theory about the temple itself is that there was no natural chasm in the *adyton* for the Pythia to sit over. The *adyton* was indeed a little lower than the floor level of the main part of the temple, but there can only have been a representation of the mouth of a chasm. In other words, it was a symbol and we should not attempt to convert a symbol of the way that the god inspired the Pythia into a simple physical explanation of the giving of oracles.

If we can be certain that there was no natural emanation from the rock through a chasm, where does that leave Plutarch's account? We need to look in more detail at the work in which this passage occurs. Four quite different explanations are offered by different speakers in the dialogue of the relative inactivity of the oracle in Plutarch's day. One speaker argued that the moral perversion of mankind had led to their abandonment by the gods, another that Greece had simply been depopulated. The third suggested that *daimones* – 'spirits' – were responsible for divination

and that they had departed. The last speaker objects that the
theory of *daimones* fails to account for how the oracle had worked;
he believes that the soul has a natural aptitude for divination,
which could be stimulated by the vapours from the ground. These
four very different arguments illustrate very neatly the range of
educated speculation about the workings of Delphi. The diversity
of opinion shows that in fact no one *knew* the answer.

I have no startling explanation of my own to put in place of
these ancient accounts. Indeed I do not feel that it is a worthwhile
enterprise to seek to discover some deeper explanation at the level
of the mental state of the Pythia. We might think it essential to
locate an explanation at that level, but this is only because we do
not accept the power of Apollo. For most Greeks, however, the
issue was only to account in detail, if one chose, for how the
power of Apollo worked. There were different ancient explanations, but we cannot go behind them to discover 'the real facts'.
These various accounts of the procedure themselves formed the
context in which those involved in the oracle understood it. They
also provide the framework within which we can begin to make
sense of Delphi.

In order to understand Delphi more fully we need to look not
only at the details of the consultation but also, more generally, at
the role of Delphi in Greek society. It is important to see what forces
sustained the general acceptance of the Pythia's powers of prophecy. Many have believed that the standing of Delphi was due to
the 'prophets'; as the importance of Delphi was not due to
geography or the political weight of the Amphictyonic League,
how else could one explain Delphi? These prophets, who actually
composed the oracles, are seen as the conscious supporters of particular cities or political movements. More flatteringly, they are
said to be responsible for making Delphic religious policy support
not the old formal ritual observances of Greek religion, but new
moral values such as purity of the spirit; it was allegedly 'the high-
water mark of religious ethic in pagan antiquity'.[13]

These theories, going back to eighteenth-century attacks on religion, which attempt to attribute the importance of Delphi to the prophets, are highly unsatisfactory. The procedure which they presuppose is that the Pythia uttered gibberish which the prophets, who were, as we saw earlier, in the room with the baffled enquirer, then put into coherent form. This process of redaction allowed them in effect total control over the issuing of oracles. But, as we have already seen, the Pythia did not rant and rave and the enquirer would have been able to hear and understand much of what she said.[14] Thus the role of the prophets was limited to the ordering and writing down (in prose or verse) of the Pythia's responses. This view of the more restricted role of the prophets is supported by the occasional instances of bribery and corruption which are attested at Delphi. It was the Pythia rather than the prophets who was accused of corruptly issuing oracles. For example, when Cleomenes, king of Sparta, wished to have the other Spartan king, Demaratus, deposed on the ground that he was a bastard, he 'managed to induce Kobon . . . who was a very influential person in Delphi, to persuade Perialla the Pythia to give the answer (to the Spartan enquiry) which Cleomenes wanted'. But when this became known, Kobon was exiled, Perialla deprived of her office, and 'most Greeks think that Cleomenes' unpleasant death was due to the fact that he corrupted the Pythia and induced her to say what she did about Demaratus'.[15] Not only were the prophets never accused of corruption, but the ancient critics of Delphi never attacked the oracle on the grounds that it was controlled by scheming prophets. The Pythia was the person held responsible.

The proponents of this view of the prophets might, however, point to what looks like systematic policy as evidence for conscious control. For example, Delphi is associated with one of the two groups of cities who sent out colonies in the eighth and seventh centuries.[16] But this pattern of consultation is not enough to prove conscious control. Indeed such control was precisely one of the rationalizing theories which Evans-Pritchard showed did not work in the case of his Zande oracles (*Witchcraft, Oracles and Magic* 173–4); it is perfectly possible for oracular responses to be remarkably convenient for the oracle and the enquirer without any conscious manipulation by those giving the oracle. The good faith of the oracle was of course generally accepted by the Greeks. Why else should anyone bother to go there?

The theory of Delphic propaganda and manipulation also makes a more general mistake. It assumes that Delphi was something set apart from Greek society which had its own independent motivations. No doubt the interests of the inhabitants of Delphi lay in the success of the oracle; as Apollo told the first priests of the oracle, they would gain their livelihood from the visitors to the oracle (*Homeric Hymn to Apollo* 531–7). But none of the officials of the oracle had any specialized theological training and we should not picture the oracle as a positive source of progressive theological or political doctrines which showed the way to the other Greeks. Delphi was indeed regarded as a source of authority, but it was there to be consulted, not to lead. In other words it was a focus to which people were attracted and onto which they sometimes projected views of their own. Therefore, we need to start our investigation of the role of Delphi in Greek society not with Delphi itself but with the needs of Greek society.

The basic purpose of the Delphic oracle is explicitly stated in the *Homeric Hymn to Apollo*, which gives an account of Apollo's foundation of the oracle. Apollo explains that he wished to build an oracular temple for people from all over Greece 'to whom I could give unfailing advice (*nēmertea boulēn*) through the prophetic responses in the rich temple' (247–53). When his plan came to fruition he told his first officials that they would 'know the plans of the immortals, by whose will you will always be honoured for all days' (480–5). Delphi was to give advice to the Greeks, advice which would be unfailing because of the oracle's access to the plans of the immortal gods.

The Greeks, like the Azande, sought advice from their oracle on a wide range of problems. For information about particular enquiries our sources are naturally biased in favour of the major enquiries by cities, but it is clear that private individuals also travelled to Delphi to seek advice from the god before undertaking a particularly important venture. For convenience, the enquiries may be divided into three overlapping categories, the personal, the religious and the political.

Plutarch gives a list of the questions put to the oracle which illustrates the range of personal problems. People ask 'if they shall be victorious, if they shall marry, if it is to their advantage to sail, to farm, to go abroad' (*Moralia* 386C; cf. 407D, 408C). Of course not everyone who was considering marriage or farming or travel went to Delphi; most such decisions would not have been difficult to take, but Delphi was always there in case of need. Thus when Miltiades of Athens was asked by a Thracian tribe, the Dolonkoi (who were acting on the advice of Delphi), to be in charge of their affairs, 'he immediately went to Delphi to ask the oracle if he should do what the Dolonkoi asked of him' (6.34–6). How else could he be sure that such a momentous step was the right one for him?

Many of the questions put to Delphi arose out of specifically religious problems. For example, in the fourth century the Athenians were uncertain what action to take over the sacred land of the Eleusinian goddesses which had been impiously put to cultivation. Should they expel the farmers, or charge them rent for the profit of the goddesses? They asked Delphi to decide. Ritual purification, especially of murderers, such as Orestes, was also a speciality of Apollo. This did not necessarily take place at Delphi, but Apollo gave advice, directly or indirectly. At Athens there was a board of three civic officials, known as *Pythochrēstoi*, who were responsible for expounding the ancestral lore if, for example, a servant had been killed by burglars. They were selected by Delphi, but they did not refer to the oracle themselves on individual cases. Direct consultation of Delphi did, however, take place. After the battle of Thermopylae, the Spartans received an oracle from Delphi telling them to seek reparation from Xerxes

32 Crisis and Purification. Orestes flees for protection from the Furies to the *omphalos*. In fear the Pythia runs out of the *adyton*, dropping the key to the temple. But Artemis and Apollo ward off the flying Fury. Notice also the laurel tree, and the dedications of helmets and chariot wheels which hang in the temple. (South Italian vase, about 370 B.C.)

for the killing of their king Leonidas and to accept whatever he offered (8.114).

In addition to these religious problems, cities often appealed to Delphi if they faced some more general political problem. For example, the city of Cyrene in North Africa fell into misfortune because of strife in its royal family: 'they sent people to Delphi to ask how they should order their affairs so as to achieve the best form of government' (4.161). There might also be difficulties with one's neighbours. In response to Aeginetan attacks on Attica, the Athenians were about to take counter-measures when they received 'an oracle from Delphi that they should hold back for thirty years and then in the thirty-first year after the Aeginetans had started the trouble, they should consecrate a piece of ground to Aeacus (an Aeginetan hero) and declare war against the

Aeginetans' (5.89). 'Natural' disasters, such as plague or drought, were also problems which often faced Greek cities. The island of Thera once suffered from a seven-year drought which caused all the trees on the island bar one to wither up. The Therans therefore consulted the oracle and were told to found a colony in North Africa, which they had in fact been told to do before (4.151).[17] Indeed it was standard practice if someone thought of founding a colony to seek Delphic advice. It was thought peculiar and foolish that Dorieus, when debarred from succeeding to the Spartan throne, took a body of men to found a colony 'without previously consulting the Delphic oracle on a suitable site or observing any of the customary practices' (5.42). His settlement failed.

A wide range of personal, religious and political problems was thus put to Delphi, but the question for us still remains, Why? Why did the intelligent, rational Greeks not think about these problems for themselves and reach their own decisions? Oracular decision-making is surely unnecessary and stupid. It might help us to break this prejudice of ours if we turn again to the Zande poison oracle. Evans-Pritchard, who lived with the Azande, writes: 'I always kept a supply of poison for the use of my household and neighbours and we regulated our affairs in accordance with the oracle's decisions. I may remark that I found this as satisfactory a way of running my house and my affairs as any other I know of' (*Witchcraft, Oracles and Magic* 126). We too might have found that the Greek system actually worked for us. It will certainly help us to appreciate the need for it if we realize that the problems put to it were of singular difficulty. Those involved had formulated the problem and thought about it so far as they could, but how could the Athenians decide what to do about the sacred land? If they took the wrong decision, the goddesses would be angry. How could Miltiades be sure that he should emigrate, or the Therans know what action to take over a drought? The imponderables were too great.

The actions of the Athenians faced with the threat of Persian invasion in 481 B.C. will illustrate these points (7.140–4). The

Athenians, being prepared to listen to the oracle's advice, had sent
envoys to Delphi, who heard with great dismay a terrifying
prophecy warning them to flee from the Persians to the world's
end. The envoys were about to abandon themselves to despair
when a distinguished Delphian advised them to seek another oracle.
As suppliants, therefore, the envoys begged Apollo for a more
favourable prophecy:

Thereupon the Pythia uttered her second prophecy, which ran as
follows:
    Not wholly can Pallas win the heart of Olympian Zeus,
    Though she prays him with many words and all her subtlety;
    Yet will I speak to you this other word, as firm as adamant:
    Though all else shall be taken within the bounds of Cecrops
    And the valley of the holy mountain of Cithaeron,
    Yet Zeus the all-seeing grants to Athena's prayer
    That the wooden wall only shall not fall, but help you and
        your children.
    But await not the host of horses and foot coming from Asia,
    Nor be still, but turn your back and withdraw from the foe.
    Truly a day will come when you will meet him face to face.
    Divine Salamis, you will bring death to women's sons
    When the corn is scattered, or the harvest gathered in. (7.141)

   The envoys were heartened by this second oracle and returned
with it to Athens. They then reported the oracle to the assembly
where a debate took place. There two incompatible interpretations were offered of the oracle. Some of the older men took the
oracle to mean that the Acropolis would be saved by a 'wooden
wall', as in the old days, but others argued that the 'wooden wall'
referred to ships which would save Athens. The difficulty with
this interpretation was the last two lines, which the professional
(but unofficial) oracle-interpreters understood to mean an Athenian
defeat at Salamis. In their opinion the Athenians should abandon
Attica altogether. Themistocles, however, suggested that because
the oracle called Salamis 'divine' the defeat would not be Athenian
but Persian; therefore the Athenians should make preparations to

fight the invaders at sea. The Athenians were convinced by his interpretation and 'decided after the debate on the oracle to take the god's advice and to meet the invader at sea with all the force they possessed, and with any other Greeks who were willing to join them'.

This incident shows very clearly the roles of human intelligence and the divine will in the context of oracles.[18] The Athenians had identified a problem which they were uncertain how to handle. The first oracle was too black, but rather than disregard it, the envoys repeated their question to the oracle. This was not because they were relying on the 'chance' procedures of a lottery-oracle to provide a preferable answer, but because they hoped to persuade the gods as suppliants to give them a more kindly prophecy. As the second oracle makes clear, they had tried to sway the will of Zeus. This reference to the will of Zeus reminds us that the oracles of Apollo were based, as the *Homeric Hymn to Apollo* said, on knowledge of the will of the immortal gods. The application of human intelligence was continued in the debate in the Athenian assembly as to the meaning of the oracle.[19] It was crucially important to establish what the advice of the oracle actually was. Careful and logical arguments were deployed. Though the proponents of the wooden walls on the Acropolis maintained their interpretation (and met their deaths for it at the hands of the Persians: 8.51–5), Themistocles' argument won the day because it succeeded in accounting for the whole text of the oracle.

The problem of communication between gods and humans meant that attention to the interpretation of the oracle was vital. The meaning of an oracle was not necessarily obvious. The Athenians in this case clearly reached the correct interpretation; they did win the battle of Salamis. This is not to say that all oracles were bafflingly obscure or ambiguous, but that it was the responsibility of the recipient to ensure that he had interpreted correctly. Failure to do so could lead to disaster. Thus the Spartans once made an attack on Tegea in neighbouring Arcadia relying on an oracle which turned out to be ambiguous:

> Arcadia? Great is the thing you ask me. I will not grant it.
> In Arcadia are many men, acorn-eaters,
> And they will keep you out. Yet, as I am not grudging,
> I will give you Tegea to dance in with stamping feet
> And her fair plain to measure out with the line.

The Spartans lost the battle against the Tegeans, and the chains which they had expected to fix on the Tegeans were put on their own men (1.66). Notoriously, Croesus, king of Lydia, also failed to perceive the true meaning of two oracles. He was told that his line would last until a mule sat on the Median throne and that if he attacked Persia he would destroy a mighty empire. He did not realize that Cyrus, king of Persia, whose parents were of different races, was a metaphorical mule and that the mighty empire he would destroy was his own (1.53–6 and 91).

Though access to divine guidance normally followed the paths which I have outlined, there were no barriers preventing different types of questions, or different types of divine guidance. From time to time people placed before Delphi more general questions which did not relate to specific decisions. Croesus' question about the length of his line was of this sort. So too the Siphnians asked at the height of their prosperity whether it would last for long (3.57–8). We might be tempted to put enquiries of this sort into an entirely different 'prophetic' category in which Apollo does not give advice but simply predicts the future. But the distinction does not hold. Advice was given on the basis of knowledge of the future; the Athenian enquiry about the Persian invasion not only sought advice but also begged that the will of the gods be changed. Conversely both Croesus and the Siphnians no doubt intended to take decisions on the basis of Apollo's response to their general questions.

Apollo was also able to offer advice on matters where he had

not been consulted. The most famous case of this is the oracle concerning Battus of Thera and the foundation of Cyrene (which preceded the Theran enquiry which we have already noted).
Herodotus reports two accounts, one Theran and the other Cyrenean
(4.150–6). According to the Therans, the king of Thera was consulting the oracle about other matters but got the reply that he
should found a city in Libya. He felt he was too old and asked
whether Apollo could tell one of the younger men present, for
example Battus, to go. The Cyrenean story lays much more
emphasis on Battus. He was a stammerer and went to Delphi
about his voice, but received an oracle addressing him as Battus
and telling him to found a colony in Libya. Herodotus believes
that he was known by another name at this time and that the oracle
addressed him as Battus in a bilingual pun; Battus in Greek meant
'stammerer', but in Libyan 'king'. The different accounts are not
reconcilable, but the significant point is that in both stories the
oracle took the initiative. This leading role of Delphi is
emphasized in a document from Cyrene itself, purporting to give
the oath of the founders of the colony, which begins: 'since Apollo
spontaneously told Battus and the Therans to colonize Cyrene
. . .'[20] It was a mark of peculiar favour for Apollo to vouchsafe
advice spontaneously.

We have seen how the Greeks received advice from Apollo,
either in response to questions or occasionally spontaneously, on a
range of difficult and important problems, and we have also
examined the need for the application of human intelligence to
the oracles. This leads us to consider now some possible consequences of this active attitude to oracles. What happened if the
oracle went against the intentions of the enquirer? What sort of
doubts were there about the validity of oracles? Did scepticism
grow in the course of the fifth century?

Oracles sometimes gave advice that was unwelcome, such as
the oracle recommending the Athenians to flee from the Persian
invasion, but people acted in trepidation against oracular advice

(7.149 – Argos). It was naturally better to find some way of evading the oracle. For example, the Athenians were strongly advised by an oracle to wait for thirty years before attacking Aegina; to attack immediately would be extremely hazardous, though they would in the end win (5.89). But the Athenians wanted to attack immediately, and so they consecrated the sanctuary to Aeacus straight away, no doubt hoping to modify the bleakness of the Delphic warning. Unfortunately we do not know how this plan would have come out as their preparations for war were interrupted by other events. A similar problem of unwelcome advice faced Cleisthenes of Sicyon who, as part of an anti-Argive policy, sought permission from Delphi to remove the shrine of the Argive Adrastus. When he was rebuffed by the oracle, he decided to drive out Adrastus by introducing the cult of Melanippus, a mythical enemy of Adrastus (5.67). This attitude is similar to that which Evans-Pritchard noted: 'an Azande does not readily accept an oracular verdict which conflicts seriously with his interests' (*Witchcraft, Oracles and Magic* 163). The Azande were able to evade an inconvenient oracle by assuming that it was in error on this particular occasion. The Greeks, however, could not assume that Apollo was wrong; they had to reinterpret the oracle or find some alternative plan. The failure of the Therans to obey the oracle to Battus was, after all, followed by their seven-year drought. In other words, the rare cases when oracles were seemingly disobeyed illustrate not doubt but acceptance of the value of oracles.

We might wonder, however, whether this acceptance of the value of oracles was based on empirical experiments. Did the Greeks test their oracles either in advance or by noting cases when the oracle failed to predict the future accurately? Certainly Herodotus recounts the story of how Croesus put six Greek oracles to the test (1.46–9). He sent envoys to these oracles asking what he was doing at the time of consultation. Only Delphi, and the oracle of Amphiaraus, knew the truth, that Croesus had cut up a tortoise and a lamb and was boiling them together in a bronze cauldron with a bronze lid. We might imagine that such testing of the oracle was standard Greek practice, but the other cases of testing which Herodotus recounts were also by 'barbarians' (8.133–6 – Mardonius; 2.174 – Amasis; cf. Plutarch, *Moralia* 434 D–F), and Xenophon (*Cyropaedia* 7.2.17) piously makes Croesus attribute his misfortune to his distrust of the god: 'neglecting to ask the god for what I needed, I tested him to see if he could speak the truth'. For a Greek such testing was both unnecessary and impious. From this it follows that the attitude of a Greek to his lack of success did not cast doubt upon the validity of the oracle. The barbarian Croesus, after his defeat by Cyrus, king of Persia, reproached Apollo for deceiving one who had made rich offerings to Delphi (1.90–9).[21] By contrast Cleomenes, king of Sparta, had been told by the Delphic oracle that he would capture Argos (6.76–82). He therefore led an army, which succeeded in routing the Argives and pinning the survivors in a wood where they were killed. When Cleomenes learned that the wood was sacred to the god Argos, he groaned on realizing what happened: 'Apollo, god of prophecy, you did indeed deceive me greatly by saying that I would capture Argos. I infer that your oracle to me has been fulfilled.' In contrast to Croesus, he did not question the oracle. In fact he led his army home again rather than lead an assault on the town of Argos itself. For this he was tried in Sparta for having been bought off, but defended himself by adducing the oracle and another subsequent confirmation of his interpretation by the goddess Hera. 'The Spartans judged that this defence was plausible and reasonable and Cleomenes was fully acquitted.' The truth of oracles was maintained even when they were followed by misfortune. As Herodotus said (8.77), oracles did contain truth and one should not attempt to discredit them when they were expressed with clarity.

But it is often argued that this acceptance of oracles was considerably weakened in the course of the fifth century, firstly by the failure of Delphi in the Persian Wars and secondly by the critique of the Sophists. It is true that the role of Delphi changed in the course of time, but I want to suggest that this was not because of intellectual doubts. The traditional view is that Delphi had counselled submission to Persia, that her escape from Persian troops was not the miracle that was alleged, and that in consequence Delphi lost her place of respect in the Greek world. In fact Delphi had given Athens a counsel of despair, not of submission, and the plan was not as bizarre as it might seem to us. Other Greeks had already fled to the West from the advance of Persia (1.164–7; 6.22; cf. 1.168). But the Athenians did decide to resist Persia, and the Greek league against Persia, founded in 481, included a provision that a tithe of the property of those who sided with Persia should be dedicated to the god at Delphi (7.132); there is no sign that the Greeks ceased to consult the oracle when possible during the Persian invasion (e.g. 8.114). The victories over the Persians at Salamis and Plataea were followed immediately by the promised dedication of a tithe of the spoils to Apollo at Delphi, as well as other offerings to Zeus at Olympia and to Poseidon at the Isthmus.[22] The selection of Apollo at Delphi to receive the tithe was not done by people who felt that he had betrayed them. Indeed Apollo's oracles had shown the way to victory.

The second part of the traditional case is that Delphi was undermined by the Sophists; indeed it is commonly held that much of the authority of the traditional cults disappeared under the keen scrutiny of late-fifth-century intellectuals. In fact the evidence for any Sophistic criticism of Delphi is very slight, and it is in general a misreading of the Sophists to depict them as single-mindedly anti-religious. They should rather be seen as a continuation of the long-established tradition of the reinterpretation of religion by poets and philosophers.[23] It would in any case be a misjudgement of the power of intellectuals to imagine that they could alone transform religious attitudes. The power of Delphi was not something rooted primarily in belief, in an intellectual attitude which could be overthrown by intellectual argument, but in the structure of Greek society.

The change in the position of Delphi can therefore be ascribed not to the rise of doubt and scepticism but to changes in Greek society. In the fifth century Delphi continued to be a prestigious international sanctuary, much as it was before the Persian War. Rich dedications were made throughout the fifth century and the oracle continued to be consulted by states on political problems. The absence of a source comparable to Herodotus makes this difficult to document for the central part of the fifth century, but Thucydides reveals that the Epidaurians, torn by civil strife, appealed to Delphi for permission to hand over the city to Corinth, the mother city of their mother city (1.25), part of the sequence of events which led to the outbreak of the Peloponnesian War. Thucydides also informs us that the Spartans consulted Delphi before the start of the war 'whether it would be better for them to fight' (1.118).

In the fourth century, however, the structure of the Greek world began to be transformed with the emergence of the monarchies of Alexander the Great, of his successors in the Hellenistic age and finally of the Roman emperor. These dominant political powers generally took decisions autocratically without consultation of Delphi, while the Greek cities themselves found their freedom of action increasingly restricted. By the time of the Roman empire, as Plutarch noted (*Moralia* 408 BC; 805A), they could no longer make treaties or fight wars. But they continued to consult oracles on matters of pressing concern, such as how to deal with the assaults of brigands.[24] In addition to these civic enquiries, private individuals continued to have recourse to Delphi for advice on personal matters. Through these changing patterns of Greek history, the Delphic oracle continued, when human intelligence failed, to mediate to mortals the knowledge and advice of the gods.

7

Greek art and religion

MARTIN ROBERTSON

In 438/7 B.C. a statue of Athena, some forty feet high and veneered in gold and ivory, the work of the sculptor Pheidias, was dedicated in the Parthenon, the goddess' still unfinished temple on the Acropolis of Athens. Some two and a half centuries later Eumenes II of Pergamum (197–160 B.C.) raised a new building in his city to house the great library which he was creating to rival that of the Ptolemies at Alexandria. The principal room was dominated by a statue of Athena in marble, on a marble base adorned with reliefs, the whole copied, at about one third the size, from Pheidias' masterpiece [33]. The library formed part of a precinct of Athena, and one should not underestimate the religious intention of putting it under the protection of the goddess of wisdom. Nevertheless it is safe to say that the readers who used the library will have looked up at the statue in a different spirit from that in which Pheidias' contemporaries entered the temple and looked at his work: much more surely as we look at a 'work of art'. Yet we can certainly also assert that Pheidias was already a conscious, sophisticated artist who knowingly created works of art for a public, however limited, which appreciated them as such, although the prime overt motive for their creation was undoubtedly not aesthetic but religious. Motives other than aesthetic – religious and propagandist – seem to have determined almost exclusively the production of art in the great Near-Eastern civilizations from which the Greeks learnt so much. 'Works of art' those products are to us, and we cannot but feel that they must have been so also, at some level, to the artists and their patrons; but there are pointers to the Greeks having been, almost from the

155

33 Free copy of Pheidias' Parthenos from Pergamum.

start, more aware of this aspect. Through the archaic and classical periods and into the Hellenistic, one can watch this aesthetic approach strengthening, though art never becomes the independent, self-sufficient pursuit that it is today. The works are always produced to serve some other end, and that end is very often a religious one. Indeed one can probably say that most major Greek art is produced in the service of religion; only both 'art' and 'religion' need some further definition.

The Greeks had no word to distinguish art from technical skill, craft; nor had the Romans. In the tag *ars longa, vita brevis* (art is long, life short) *ars* translates the Greek *technē*, and the phrase in its original use applies to the art of healing. The difference first begins to be expressed in the Renaissance. Dürer in the early sixteenth century distinguishes between *Kunst* (art) and *Brauch* (what an apprentice was taught in the Guild). A stress on artistic personality is one of the things which sets the Renaissance off from the Middle Ages; and we can see the same thing happening as Greek art makes itself free of the Near-Eastern traditions from which it starts. In Greek, however, the distinction between craftsmanship and fine art was never so clearly expressed; probably therefore not quite so clearly felt.

Religion too meant to the Greeks something different from what it means to us; or rather perhaps for them it had a wider range of meaning. One generalization which may help us here can I think be made about Greek religion and Greek art: both are inseparable from the basic unit of Greek life, the City. The Greeks were intensely conscious of their Greekness, their difference from other peoples, but politically they were fragmented. Each city, controlling an area of greater or less extent, was totally and jealously independent, unless subdued by the imperialism of another. Different cities, and the same city at different times, had very various kinds of government, but a basic part of the machinery by which these rather small units ran themselves was always religion. At the same time their common religion, with their common tongue and their common heritage of legend, was one of the unifying elements in Greek culture. As such it found expression in certain great sanctuaries, notably those of Zeus at Olympia and of Apollo at Delphi, which held four-yearly religious festivals with athletic and musical competitions attended by Greeks from all cities. Anyone attending the Games at Olympia in time of war between cities was granted safe-conduct. Religion in Greece had of course other manifestations (personal, ecstatic, mystic) and to some we shall return, but it was in the service of religion in its public, civic character that Greek artists were primarily employed; even at the great sanctuaries, since there was rivalry among cities in the dedication at these centres of rich and elaborate buildings and monuments.

In speaking of art in this context we must make distinctions between different crafts and arts. Two in particular, architecture and sculpture, are almost confined, at first and for long, to this civic-religious public sphere. Painting seems less closely bound to it; and the 'minor arts' (vase-painting, small statuettes in bronze or terracotta, decorative metal-work, jewellery, seal-stones) though all sometimes employed for religious purposes have also a wide-spread private and domestic use. Coins are of course a strictly public, civic issue, and well illustrate, in the choice of emblems found on them, the inseparability of the civic from the religious.

It may seem odd to speak of architecture as limited to the public sphere. People must have houses; but it does seem clear that domestic architecture in Greece was for a long time of the simplest kind, that architecture as an art, architectural *style*, is confined to temples and civic buildings. This was not the case in the Minoan and Mycenaean civilizations of Bronze-Age Greece. There domestic architecture is developed into palaces and castles of elaborate design, and the same is true of most Near-Eastern cultures. The Egyptians, however, do seem to have kept grand, permanent building for temples and tombs. Architectural tombs in Greece after the Bronze Age are a late and special development (though tomb-sculpture is an important line which we shall be considering). It is of interest, though, that a building which seems to combine the characters of temple and tomb appears at the very beginning of the revival which leads on to the historical Greece of the archaic and classical ages. The civilization of the Bronze Age had collapsed under obscure conditions into a state of poverty, illiteracy and the reduction of art to the most basic crafts. An improvement begins to be perceptible late in the eleventh century, and probably to the tenth belongs a building at Lefkandi on the big island of Euboea, very recently excavated and not yet published. It was built above two very richly furnished graves, was some forty-five metres long, and was surrounded, like a later temple, by a kind of colonnade. After a very short time it was deliberately dismantled and rendered unusable; and we know nothing that seems to carry on its tradition. Like primitive little temples which begin to appear during these centuries (and which are not associated with graves) this building was of mud-brick on a stone foundation, and the surround was of wooden posts rather than columns, but in scale and concept it does look forward to the monumental temple-architecture which begins in Greece towards the end of the seventh century, when sculpture in marble and limestone was also beginning, likewise in a religious context.

The form of the first sculptures is quite clearly derived from Egyptian models. The new temple-architecture shows no such direct borrowing, though it is possible that the idea of monumental building in stone did come to the Greeks from the same source. Some of the little early buildings have as their centre a hearth or pit where some kind of sacrifice can be seen to have taken place. The evidence for this is clearest in Crete, and it is possible that it is a local and not a chronological feature, and that on the mainland in this time worship was conducted round open-air altars. Certainly when monumental temple-architecture develops, the altar for sacrifice and public ritual, itself a more or less elaborate stone structure, lies outside, in the *temenos* (enclosed sacred area), often opposite the east end of the temple where the entrance normally was. The central feature of the temple-interior is now a statue of the deity, and the building seems primarily conceived as a more or less richly adorned casket to hold that treasure. The temple of Hera on Samos, built about 800 B.C., stands apart from other early temples and anticipates the later development. It is unusually large, has a central line of columns and no central hearth (the altar being outside) but a base for a cult-statue near the back; and later in the eighth century it was given a surrounding colonnade in wood.

The form of monumental temple created in the later seventh century retains its basic character right through Greek history [8 ch. 4]: a long, narrow building, a surrounding colonnade, a low-pitched roof with gables at either end (the pediments); no use of arch or vault, so no curves. The vertical walls and columns, rising from a stepped platform, support the straight horizontals of the entablature, above which is the straight slope of the low roof and gables. The statue of the deity (the 'cult-statue') stood at the end of the long room which formed the interior, facing the east door through which one entered after passing through the outer colonnade and a columned porch within it. On the outside the area above the column-capitals and below the roof often included relief-sculpture among its adornments; and free-standing statues (*akrōtēria*) were often placed above the angles of the gables. Thus the beginnings of architecture and of sculpture are intimately linked in a strictly religious setting [34].

Sculpture is of two main kinds: statues, figures carved or modelled completely in the round, standing free; and reliefs, slabs adorned with more or less flattened figures grouped together. Statues in early Greece are used for three purposes, to which they are for a long time confined: the cult-figure within the temple; figures dedicated as offerings to a deity, sometimes within a temple, but more commonly in the open air of the *temenos*; and figures to stand on graves. From early on reliefs are likewise employed both for dedications and as grave-stones, but perhaps their most important use is in the decoration of temples.

Few early temples stand anything like complete; but substantial

34 The Parthenon.

remains of many and the general correspondence of what is there to better preserved buildings of the fifth century justify the generalizations made above, though there are many variations, early and later, on the scheme described. Sculpture too takes at the start certain distinctive forms, and adheres to these throughout the archaic period. At the beginning of the fifth century, however, profound changes take place in this art, and in painting, as they do not in architecture. This was a time when Greece was under great pressure. The king of Persia, already in control of Asia Minor with its Greek cities and of many of the Aegean islands, attempted to annex the whole country to his empire; and the Greek cities briefly and incompletely sank their differences and united to repel the threat under the leadership of Sparta and Athens. This crisis, which in Athens followed close on a revolution which established a democratic constitution, seems to have induced a sense of liberation in Greek thought. It inaugurates a great new period in literature: Attic drama, Greek prose (history and philosophy) had already begun to develop, but their flowering follows the crisis. In the representational arts it is marked by what we describe as the change from archaic to classical: the sloughing of old conventions taken over from the arts of the East, and the establishment by Greek artists of new ideals and conventions of their own. Nevertheless, though there *is* a sharp break, the seeds of the change were there before and we can trace their growth through the sixth century as Greek art in its archaic phase develops. Part of the character of this change seems to be a growing awareness in Greek artists that artists is what they are; that what they produce is valuable for its own sake and not simply for the generally religious purpose which dictated its production.

The most significant type of archaic statue (at least for us, as we try to trace the development of Greek art) is the beardless male figure standing naked, known to modern scholars though not to the Greeks by the Greek word *kouros* (youth). He stands upright, left foot forward, arms at sides, with no turn, bend or twist, so that on a picture of the front view lines drawn through eyes, shoulders, elbows, hips, knees, ankles are all parallel with each other and the ground, and a line dividing the figure vertically down the centre gives (apart from the advanced leg) a mirror-image on either side [35]. A closely similar type, obeying the same rules of 'frontality' and likewise with the left leg forward, had been in use for many centuries in Egypt, and it is fair to assume that Egyptian practice inspired the Greek; only the Egyptian figure is almost invariably skirted, the Greek almost invariably naked. Little statuettes in bronze, made in Greece for generations before large-scale sculpture starts there in the later seventh century, similarly represent naked males; and nudity for male figures in any and every context remains a feature of Greek art throughout its history. The reason for this practice, which is not found in any other art except under Greek influence but which has had a profound effect on art in the West, I do not know; but in its singularity it may be seen as one of the pointers towards the wayward new course Greek art was to

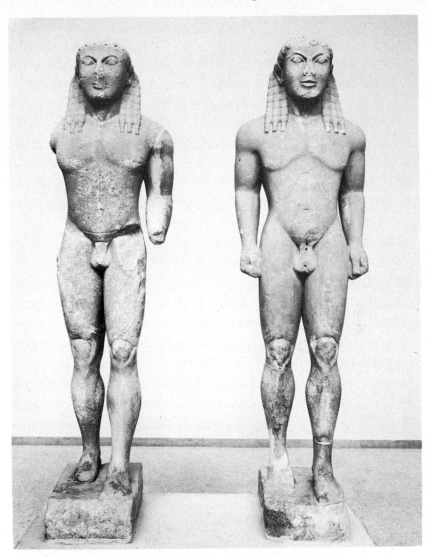

35 *Kouroi*, Kleobis and Biton.

take, away from that bondage to other causes, especially religion, which prevailed in earlier and contemporary cultures, in the direction of a relative independence. Archaic figures of women are rarely nude, and when they are it is in an appropriate context; and even when, in the fourth century and later, women are commonly shown naked, their nudity is regularly given some motivation. Archaic statues of clothed women follow the same strict rules of frontality as those of men, but at first they stand with the feet together. Later in the archaic period the left foot is advanced, evidently in imitation of the *kouros*, and this is used to make more play with the drapery, leading eventually to the very complex fold-patterns of the late archaic *korē* (girl), a type of statue as distinctive and almost as regular as the *kouros*. The drapery of early standing figures is very simple. There are also from the beginning seated figures of both sexes, always clad; clothed recliners too; and later the male figure in *kouros*-pose is sometimes given garments.

This digression on types was necessary before we consider further the relation of early sculpture to religion; and a word must also be said on materials. Almost all the large-scale sculpture we have from the archaic period is in stone (marble, or the more workaday limestone). In the course of the sixth century bronze statuary was developed, and became of the first importance in the fifth; but bronze is fatally re-usable and very few such figures survive. Wood was also used for sculpture from the beginning, as we know from remarks in ancient writers, but that too has perished, as has most work in precious materials, ivory and gold, generally in veneer on wood. Some of the earliest canonical temples were not in stone but in timber and mud-brick with terracotta adornments, but there is no clear evidence that either in architecture or in sculpture there was a phase of work in wood *preceding* that in stone.

The cult-statue in the temple was the most centrally religious use of sculpture; but these, being both specially revered and safely set within a temple, were often of wood adorned with precious materials, and very few survive. We shall come back to a few possible examples in bronze or marble. We do, however, have Roman copies of some classical pieces, and descriptions of archaic ones which can be related to marble figures of other use which have come down to us. No need seems to have been felt to distinguish different types of statue as suitable for the two different purposes of dedication to a deity or monument on a tomb; at least the unmodified *kouros*-type was used for both, though, for dedications at least, modifications of the type were also employed. In scale the dedications vary greatly, from truly colossal to quite small, whereas there does seem to be a tendency to keep tomb-figures not very far above or below life-size; but even here there is a considerable range, and the distinction may not be valid. We know that for cult-statues of Apollo a modification of the *kouros*-type was used. Several archaic examples are described, and all held the forearms forward, a bow grasped in one fist, the other palm extended with something on it; a deer in a bronze by Kanachos at Miletus and probably in the cedarwood replica by the same artist at Thebes; a group of the three Graces in the 'golden' statue by Tektaios and Angelion on Delos. The last had a belt round the naked waist, as do a few of the earliest marble *kouroi*; and fragments of a colossal marble *kouros* dedicated to Apollo on Delos show that it too had a belt and that the left fist was closed on something, no doubt a bow. The earliest of the few bronze statues which have survived is such a modified *kouros* [36]: no belt, but the forearms forward, the left hand holding what was certainly a bow, the extended right palm supporting something in thin bronze, perhaps a bowl. We do not know where this over-life-size figure, which dates from the third quarter of the sixth century, stood originally. It was found with other later bronzes in Piraeus, the port of Athens, where they were probably awaiting shipment to Italy when they were accidentally buried, perhaps in the savage sack by the Roman Sulla in 80 B.C., after the Athenians had joined Mithridates of Pontus in his bid to drive the Roman power out of the eastern Mediterranean. The bronze, which exceptionally has the right foot forward instead of the left, was quite possibly a cult-statue in a temple of Apollo. The colossal marble in Delos, however, which must equally represent the god, was not a cult-statue but an offering. It stood outside the temple on a marble base

36 Piraeus Apollo.

inscribed with a formula of dedication by the people of Naxos; but the question 'Whom do these dedicated figures represent?' has no simple, single answer.

There are two obvious possibilities: the deity to whom the figure is offered; and the person who is making the offering. There are certain examples of both categories. To the first, besides the Apollo on Delos, belong standing and seated figures in marble from the Acropolis of Athens which bear the accoutrements of Athena and can be meant for nobody else. To the second must be attributed some figures from Samos. On a long limestone base found in the *temenos* of Hera stood six marble statues some of which are partly preserved [37]. At one end was a seated figure, at the other one reclining, and between them four standing. The seated one bears, besides the signature of a sculptor Geneleos, the

37 Geneleos group.

name Phileia; two standing girls are named Philippē and (a smaller and younger-seeming figure) Ornithē; and the recliner has a damaged name with the formula of dedication. The sex of this figure, and the gender of its name, are uncertain. If a man, then this is probably a family group; if a woman, perhaps a group of priestesses and temple-servants. In any case this is unequivocal evidence for mortal dedicators having themselves represented in the gift. Surely the same is true of a famous marble from the Acropolis, the *Moschophoros* or calf-bearer. The figure stands like a *kouros*, but he has a beard and a minimal garment and his hands are lifted to hold a calf across his shoulders. He stood on a limestone base inscribed 'Rhombos dedicated, son of Palos' (the first letters of both names uncertain); and this is surely a 'portrait' of the dedicator, making an eternal offering to the goddess.

Slightly different is the case of a pair of colossal marble *kouroi* from the *temenos* at Delphi. Remains of an inscription running across the two plinths show that it was the source of a story Herodotus told about these statues a hundred years later: that they were dedicated to Apollo by the people of Argos in honour of two youths, Kleobis and Biton. When no draught-animals were available and their mother, a priestess of Hera, needed to go to the temple in the country outside Argos, they drew her there themselves; and on the mother's prayer they were rewarded, as they slept in the *temenos*, by the gods' best gift, a quiet death. These then are mortals, like the dedicators of Geneleos' group or Rhombos, but mortals in a special category, being given a civic-religious honour. All these figures 'represent' individual people, but only in the sense of standing for them; the notion of likeness does not enter Greek art until after the archaic period. Rhombos is set off from the ideal *kouros* by his beard and garment; Kleobis and Biton only by boots, perhaps in allusion to their trudge with their mother's cart.

What is perhaps the earliest marble statue we possess, an over-life-size figure of a woman of simple, even primitive, design and execution, bears a long verse inscription. It begins 'Nikandrē dedicated me to the mark-hitting arrow-pourer' (Artemis, who shared the sanctuary with her brother Apollo) and goes on to give the names of Nikandrē's father, described as a Naxian, her brother and her husband. The left hand is pierced, so she could have held a bow and so represent the goddess; or she might represent Nikandrē. One may notice, however, that whereas the inscription on the base of the calf-bearer says 'Rhombos dedicated', that on the Delos figure says 'Nikandrē dedicated *me*', the statue being deemed to speak and seeming to distinguish itself from deity and dedicator alike. This is not conclusive: it might *represent* one of them without being identified with the person represented; but there are other cases where it is impossible to see the offered statue as representing either. The great majority of the many late archaic *korai* dedicated to Athena on the Acropolis of Athens are simply girls, without helmet or aegis, shield or spear, and cannot represent the goddess. The right forearm was generally extended forward, always now lost, but the hand will have held an offering (fruit or bird) such as earlier, simpler figures from the same and other sites often clasp against the breast. So, a mortal worshipper; but by far the greater number of the inscribed bases which survive, several of them definitely associable with existing statues of girls, were offered by *men*. Thus there are three alternatives: the gift-statue may represent the deity, the dedicator,

or neither – be simply itself, a companion or servant for the goddess or god.

This fact perhaps throws some light on the religious approach.
The recipient must be thought to take equal pleasure in the gift, be
it such a companion-image, an image of the worshipper per-
petually adoring, or an image of himself or herself. From this we
might deduce that these representations of deities, being
bracketed with the other offered images, are thought of more as
simply images, objects of pleasure to the deity, 'works of art'
even, less fully embodiments of the godhead than the cult-statues
worshipped within the temples.

A statue which stands on a grave must 'represent' the dead person, but again there is a question as to what precisely that means.
Rhombos in his dedication has, we saw, a beard and a cloak. All
certainly identifiable male grave-statues (and there are quite a
number, especially from Athens and the Athenian countryside,
Attica) are beardless naked youths, undifferentiated *kouroi*. This is
the more striking since on another form of grave-monument even
more popular in sixth-century Attica, the marble tombstone carved
in relief, the figure of the dead man is clearly distinguished by
beard or lack of it, costume and gear, as young or mature, an
athlete, a warrior, a priest. Monuments on women's graves in
archaic Attica are so much rarer that one cannot generalize about
them, but one beautiful fragment shows a woman particularized as
a mother with a child [38], while two statues of girls wear a *polos*, a
little round hat more often given to goddesses or sphinxes than to
mortals. Some tomb-reliefs are topped by a figure of a sphinx, and
these may wear a *polos*. It does look as though perhaps a *statue* on a
grave in sixth-century Attica was felt to have a special meaning, a
more clearly religious character, than a relief.

It is hard to generalize about the Greek attitude to the dead. A
sphinx on a tombstone is certainly some kind of death-spirit, but
its precise character can hardly be determined. A funeral was a
religious ceremony, and other ceremonies took place later at the
grave. Offerings too were placed there, presumably for the dead;

38 Archaic Attic grave-relief.

but they were not in general worshipped as divine. Dead heroes of the past were given worship as *daimones*, a kind of intermediate level between divine and human, and this status might be bestowed on individuals in historical times: the Athenian dead at Marathon in 490 B.C., the Spartan Brasidas at Amphipolis in 422, Timoleon of Corinth at Syracuse in 334. Kleobis and Biton, honoured by statues offered to Apollo in his sanctuary at Delphi are perhaps an analogous case; and one may wonder if the placing of a *kouros* or a *korē* rather than a relief on an Attic grave in the sixth century may imply such a distinction.

Practice, and perhaps by implication belief, varies greatly between different areas of Greece, different times and different classes. Attica has yielded a far larger number of grave-monuments of one sort or another than any other region, but in the archaic period they seem there to be the exclusive preserve of the aristocracy. They cease abruptly with the establishment of democracy at the end of the sixth century, and are only revived two or three generations later with a vastly extended social range. The only other district which has produced a substantial number of archaic carved monuments apparently from graves is Laconia, the countryside of Sparta, and these are strikingly different from the Attic. They are reliefs, rather crudely carved in limestone, mostly to one pattern: an enthroned couple, approached by figures on a much smaller scale carrying offerings, a snake (another death-spirit) often prominently shown. The distinction in scale between worshipped and worshipper is found commonly in reliefs dedicated to deities; indeed one Laconian relief, indistinguishable in character from the others, was found in a sanctuary. Plainly these are religious works in a fuller and more precise sense than the reliefs from Attic graves.

The revival of tomb-reliefs in Athens and Attica begins in the 430s, when work was coming to an end on the Parthenon and the Peloponnesian War was about to break out, and they go on till 317, when they were forbidden by a law restricting expenditure. Some of these classical stones show a single figure, like the majority of the archaic ones, but they differ in that women are shown as often as men, and they are not confined to the aristocratic or the rich. There are big, careful, evidently expensive pieces, but also many much smaller and slighter, and inscriptions show that the dead may be an artisan and need not be a citizen. Some commemorate metics (resident aliens), as Sosinos of Gortyn in Crete, a bronze-worker; others slaves. Many stones show pairs or groups, and it is not always possible to be sure which is the dead [39]. Indeed they were probably often meant for family plots, where the first to die and be buried would be joined later by others, and no sharp distinction may be intended. The gestures could often be equally of farewell or greeting. There is seldom anything to suggest worship of the dead or a strongly religious ele-

39 Classical Attic grave-relief.

ment such as we saw in the archaic reliefs from Laconia. There is a strongly marked religious content in the funerary art of the fourth century in another region: Taras (Tarentum, Taranto) in South Italy. This art includes grave-reliefs in limestone (the Attic are marble) in a provincial style, but the religious element is clearest in the painted pottery designed for tombs, and we will come back to this later.

The democratization of the marble grave-relief in Attica is accompanied by a similar spread in the dedication of marble reliefs to deities. There are many more of these in the later fifth and fourth centuries than before, often small and not careful, and often given not to the Olympians but to more popular deities: the country gods (Pan, the Nymphs and the river-god Achelous); and the gods of healing: Asclepius and his family (especially his daughter Hygieia, Health) and certain heroes who were believed to be healers [40]. Pan, the Nymphs, Asclepius had long been

40 Attic votive relief, fourth century: Amphiaraus as healer.

revered, but it is only now that this stratum of belief is recorded
for us in enduring works of art. Pan had been given honour in
Athens from the time of his help at the battle of Marathon in 490,
but there is little to show for it in the early years. The worship of
Asclepius was only officially brought to the city towards the end
of the fifth century (the dramatist Sophocles played a part in this
move), and the old centre of his cult, at Epidaurus in the north-
east Peloponnese, received its first great temple and image early in
the fourth.

The most strictly and consistently religious use of relief is in the
adornment of buildings, where it is almost confined to temples
and other structures set up within a *temenos*, in particular the little
treasuries erected by many Greek cities at the great inter-state
sanctuaries of Delphi and Olympia. The only other types of building

verted by Athens into a subject-empire; and Sparta's jealousy of Athens' growing wealth and power led, in the second half of the fifth century, to the long, disastrous Peloponnesian War, in which all Greece was involved and, to a degree, ruined. The subject-matter of the sculptures on the temple of Zeus at Olympia, built while the League was still driving the Persians out of the Greek cities of Asia Minor, does seem chosen to illustrate Greek unity, though the building was paid for from booty taken by one Greek city from another; that of the Parthenon seems designed to emphasize Athenian imperialism. The pediments, we have seen glorify the city-goddess. Of the metopes, those on the east front have the old theme of the Gigantomachy, but the other three sides illustrate narratives in which Attic heroes play important parts. The continuous frieze, unusually inserted round all four sides of the building within the colonnade, is equally unexpected in its theme: a procession at Athena's greatest Athenian festival; not a divine or heroic narrative but a scene from contemporary religious ritual.

I have dwelt at length on sculpture, especially in the archaic period, since this is where art is most clearly in the service of religion; and in spite of the loosening bonds evident in the fifth and fourth centuries the religious affiliation remains. The statues of the Tyrant-slayers, Harmodios and Aristogeiton, as harbingers of the Democracy, which the Athenians set up in the Agora at the end of the archaic period, have the same special character as Kleobis and Biton at the beginning, but through the following centuries it becomes increasingly common to raise statues to public figures without any such heroic implications, and these were often dedications in sanctuaries. A special character attaches to bronze statues of athletic victors dedicated in the *temenos* where the victory took place (athletics too, like drama, were in the service of religion, the competitions taking place at religious festivals). Roman marbles identified as copies of such figures show that they were highly idealized, no more true likenesses than the archaic Rhombos; but an interest in individual features and character, portraiture as we understand it, is evidenced from at latest the end of the fifth century. Such true portrait-statues were often dedicated in sanctuaries, and for a variety of reasons. We hear of statues of priests and priestesses, and from the *temenos* of Artemis at Brauron in eastern Attica we have fourth-century marble figures of little girls who, as part of the civic-religious life of Athens, served a term there as so-called 'bears' (*arktoi*). In an interesting aside Pausanias remarks how the Ionians, in a proverbial phrase of their own, 'plastered both sides of the wall' (kept a foot in both camps) in the later stages of the Peloponnesian War and its aftermath. The Samians dedicated a bronze statue of the Athenian general Alcibiades in the famous *temenos* of Hera on their island while the Athenians were doing well, but after their fatal defeat by the Spartans at Aigospotamoi the same people put up a statue of the Spartan victor Lysander at Olympia, and the Ephesians statues of him and two of his aides in their great sanctuary of Artemis. Then, when Athens a few years later began to revive her power, statues of the Athenian admirals Konon and Timotheos appeared in both the Samian and Ephesian sanctuaries. In the fourth century Praxiteles made statues of his model and mistress, the celebrated courtesan Phrynē. One, in marble, was placed in the sanctuary of Eros (Love) at Thespiai. A second, in gilded bronze, dedicated by Phrynē herself to Apollo, stood at Delphi between portraits of the kings Archidamus of Sparta and Philip of Macedon, where the finger of moral disapproval was pointed at it not only by later Christian apologists but by the contemporary philosopher Krates, Diogenes' disciple. Dedicatory inscriptions, of the archaic period and later, often speak of the gift to the god as first-fruits or a tithe, and Phrynē's statue too was no doubt a gift from her earnings. All these are cases of art still linked to religion but hardly in its service and certainly not what we think of as religious art.

The most famous sculptor of athlete-statues, Polyclitus of Argos or Sicyon, was known to later ages as 'maker of men', opposed to Pheidias 'maker of gods'. Many of Pheidias' gods were cult-statues for temples, and these, judging from copies of the Athena in the Parthenon, kept something of a formal, hieratic character inherited from the archaic tradition. Others were dedications in sanctuaries, and these were certainly more relaxed; but evidently a difference was felt between them and the Polyclitan athletes, idealized as those were, a distinction which, as we saw, can hardly be detected in archaic work. The most famous of Pheidias' cult-figures, the seated Zeus he made for the temple at Olympia, was said to have 'added something to established religion'. It was perhaps their increasingly conscious artistry (Polyclitus wrote on ideal proportions) that encouraged these artists to make these new distinctions.

Another thing which distinguishes Greek art from the arts of earlier and contemporary civilizations is the prevalence of artists' signatures; and this too is an example of their emancipation, their consciousness of their work as existing in and for itself, apart from the cause its creation serves. From very early times signatures were appended to tomb-sculptures and dedications. We do not know if the cult-statues ascribed in later writings to archaic artists (Kanachos, or Tektaios and Angelion) were signed or if the tradition were preserved in some other way; but the doubt over the authorship of many classical cult-statues, between Pheidias and his pupils for instance, suggests that these were not signed. The only certain case of a signature on a piece of sculpture adorning a building (before the great altar of Pergamum in the third century) is not on a temple but on a little treasury set up at Delphi by the islanders of Siphnos about 525 B.C., and even that was carefully defaced in antiquity. Names of architects are recorded, often in association with particular temples, sometimes on contemporary inscriptions authorizing the work, and sculptors engaged in its adornment are similarly listed; but it does look as though some inhibition were felt about actually signing such centrally religious monuments as temples and cult-statues.

Painting was as important in Greece as architecture or sculpture, but very little survives though we can learn a good deal about it from ancient writers. There are traces of plaster painted with figure-scenes from the outside of a primitive temple of Poseidon on the isthmus of Corinth, and two early Doric temples, of canonical form but built in mud-brick and timber, had terracotta metopes painted with mythological figures. Painting, however, is naturally an indoor art, and we hear of several temples which had painted decoration within: Dionysus at Athens, for instance, Athena at Plataea. The Greek temple, however, was designed primarily for its external effect, the interior a shadowy setting for the holy image. Many famous paintings were in stoas, along the back wall, under shelter but lit through the columns; and indeed the two paintings in the temple at Plataea were not right within but in the porch, which had something of the same physical character as a stoa. Such painted stoas might be in sanctuaries, but two of the most famous were in the Agora at Athens. That of Zeus, which we noticed for its marble Nikē-*akrōtēria*, may have been given paintings when it was first built in the late fifth century, and three were certainly painted there in the mid-fourth by the sculptor-painter Euphranor, whose marble statue for the little temple of Apollo, likewise in the Agora, survives in a noble fragment. One showed the Twelve Gods, whose altar stood nearby; another the Athenian hero Theseus with Dēmos (the people of Athens) and Democracy; the third a contemporary historical event, the battle of Mantinea. On the other side of the ancient Stoa Basileios another, the Stoa Poikilē (Painted Stoa) had been put up before the middle of the fifth century and given four paintings: Troy Taken by Polygnotus; a battle of Greeks and Amazons by Mikon; the battle of Marathon (the most famous of all but of disputed authorship); and a battle of Oinoē (unascribed and of uncertain significance).

It is striking that in both these stoas divine and heroic scenes are combined with contemporary histories. The struggles of Gods against Giants, and Greek against barbarian (Amazons, Centaurs, Trojans), shown in sculpture on fifth-century temples were no doubt meant to recall the defeat of the Persians. The parallel is made explicit in the Hellenistic age, when a king of Pergamum dedicated on the Acropolis of Athens bronze groups of Gods against Giants, Greeks against Amazons, Athenians against Persians and Pergamenes against Gauls; but on the Parthenon and earlier temples it is only implied. It is in the secular context of paintings in a stoa that Marathon is first admitted to heroic company. Later in the fifth century one frieze of the temple of Athena Nikē on the Acropolis shows Greeks against Persians, almost certainly at Marathon. It has been suggested that the battle-scenes on its other friezes show contemporary fights of Greek against Greek in the Peloponnesian War. Rather, I suppose, they are battles of ancient Athenians under their legendary kings against their neighbours, and Marathon has been taken up into this heroic context.

Not that contemporary victories of Greek over Greek were not boastfully celebrated in another, though still religious, setting; only I should need clearer evidence to convince me that they might actually be shown on a temple. A tall pillar at Olympia which supported an over-life-size marble Victory was inscribed with the sculptor's name, Paionios, with the additional information that he supplied *akrōtēria* for the temple; and with a dedication by the Messenians tactfully asserting that it was a 'tithe from their enemies', no doubt meaning, as Pausanias says, the Spartans (the Messenians were allied to the Athenians in the Peloponnesian War); but an avenue of victory-monuments which greeted the visitor to Delphi immediately within the entry to the *temenos* was much more grimly explicit. Immediately after the expulsion of the Persians in 479/8 a monument had been set up by all the Greek cities involved, opposite the east end of the temple. Much later, when Athens was already turning the League into her empire, Athens raised, just inside the entrance, a monument to her private defeat of the first Persian attack at Marathon in 490. This piece of propaganda was a long base supporting fourteen bronze statues: gods, heroes and the general Miltiades. Shortly after followed two more such bases, supporting dedications by the Argives out of spoil taken from the Spartans in 456, when Argos and Athens were allied. In 405 it was Sparta's turn, celebrating the crushing defeat of the Athenian navy at Aigospotamoi by a huge base opposite the others, supporting thirty-seven statues: gods, heroes, Lysander the admiral and his captains. Thirty-five years later again the Arcadians, having beaten the Spartans, raised a monument in front of this and partly masking it, and among the sculptors they employed was one, an Argive, who had worked in his youth on the Spartan dedication. There were more such monuments to see as one went on up, and one would like to think that there were Greeks who found them more shocking than Phrynē's statue higher up the sanctuary.

The painter Polygnotus repeated the theme of the Troy Taken from the stoa at Athens in a *leschē* (club-house) dedicated by the people of Knidos in the *temenos* at Delphi. It seems to have been a kind of closed stoa, a rectangular building entered through a door in the middle of one long wall, verandahs opening on a central unroofed space; two paintings occupying the long wall opposite the entrance. This was a secular building, but like the treasuries at the same site and Olympia a dedication to the god within his *temenos*, so of a more sacred character than the Agora stoa. The picture paired with the Troy was not here a battle but a clearly religious scene: the Underworld. Near the building was shown the tomb of Achilles' son Neoptolemus, who figured prominently in the Troy, and Pausanias suggests that the building was conceived as a shrine to the hero. Other famous paintings adorned hero-shrines at Athens, apparently not of temple-form; and it seems possible that sculpture, like the canonical temple, was thought more suitable for gods, painting for the less than divine though more than human status of *daimones*.

The Underworld picture was linked to the tradition of legendary narrative by the presence of Odysseus and two companions, as the story of his visit to Hades is told by Homer. The rest of the scene, however, described in detail by Pausanias, was not mainly an illustration to the *Odyssey* but a survey of the Underworld as conceived by a fifth-century artist. There is much emphasis on a side of religious thought in Greece we have hardly touched on: the mystic and redemptive, associated variously with Orpheus (whom Polygnotus showed), Pythagoras, or the great goddesses of Eleusis and other shrines, Demeter and Persephone under their many names. I said that the form of religion which Greek art mainly serves is the official religion of the city, but there are times and places where it is harnessed to the mystical. Eleusis partook of both characters. The Hall of the Mysteries was not a conventional temple but designed primarily for its pillared interior; nor did it have conventional sculptural decoration. The big relief, from the mid- or later fifth century, with the goddesses and a mortal protégé, is unlike any other monument [41]. The Mysteries were an important part of Attic religious life, but no doubt because of the aura of secrecy, the exclusion of the uninitiated, they do not seem to have made much use of the visual arts. Some fourth-century Attic vase-paintings (and a few earlier) do illustrate the great goddesses and their worship, while those of South Italy often have Orphic implications, and this is perhaps the place to speak of vase-painting.

In the loss of most major painting the fine drawing on Greek vases is important for our understanding of Greek art; and it is at its best of far higher artistic quality than is usually associated with pottery decoration. This seems to arise from historical circumstances. After the collapse of the Bronze-Age culture, impoverished Greece was for some centuries without monumental art. Everyday crafts continued in an unbroken if reduced tradition; and when, in the ninth and eighth centuries, reviving prosperity kindled desire for some grander expression, this first took the form of monumentalizing bronze cooking-pots (tripod-cauldrons) as prizes at festival-games and for dedication, and in Athens of domestic pottery vessels, enlarged to four or five feet high, to stand on graves as markers. Thus at the start of the historical period in Athens painted pottery acquired the status of a monumental art with religious associations. As a grave-monument it was

41 Large relief from Eleusis.

replaced by marble statues and reliefs, and its religious connections became confined to a few special forms, but it retained a high place among the arts.

One special case is the 'Panathenaic amphora', the jar full of oil given as a prize at the four-yearly games in honour of Athena. These were first made in the mid-sixth century, when Pisistratus reorganized the festival, and retained their technique and basic design through all changes of style and fashion into the Hellenistic age; a rare case in Greek art of religious conservatism. The coins of Athens likewise retain their late-archaic form (Athena's head on the front, her owl and the first letters of her and the city's name on the back) and style through the centuries, but there the motivation seems to have been commercial: they were a universally recognized medium of exchange over the Greek world and beyond. The prize-vases might be kept and put in graves or sold on the second-hand market, but many were dedicated. Other dedicated vases were the gift of the potters and vase-painters, first-fruits or tithes; but most seem to be just beautiful objects offered for their own sake.

There are vases which have pictures of religious ritual: sacrifice or procession (some in the later fifth century evidently influenced by the frieze of the Parthenon). A special class shows women preparing for a festival of Dionysus; but much more often these mortal maenads are represented as transfigured, swept by the mystic ecstasy of the cult out of their common selves into the very presence of the god and his company of half-animal *daimones*, satyrs and silens.

There are cases of pots made for special ritual use. At Brauron, where we noticed the statues of the little 'bears', there were also dedicated many vases of peculiar shape and style, probably made locally and certainly illustrating races and other ritual in which the 'bears' took part. A class of little jug (*chous*) was made and decorated to be given to children in their third year at the festival of Anthesteria, one day of which was called the Day of Jugs. The largest body of vases made for ritual use comprise those designed for Attic weddings and funerals: especially the *lebēs gamikos*, a bowl on a high stand used at weddings; the *loutrophoros*, an elongated vessel in which water was brought from a sacred spring for weddings and for the funerals of those who died unwed; and the *lēkythos*, a flask for oil used at funerals. *Lebēs* and wedding *loutrophoros* are regularly adorned with bridal scenes; the funeral *loutrophoros* with rituals of death or a battle; the *lēkythos* often, but by no means invariably, with a scene at the tomb or some other reference to death [42].

Customs change; and *lēkythos* and *loutrophoros* cease to be made around the end of the fifth century. The use of special pots for funerals in Athens seems to come to an end with them, though their forms are imitated in marble tombstones. The *lebēs* and the *lekanis* (another wedding-vessel) continue to be made and decorated with bridal scenes far down into the fourth century; and the connection of painted pottery with the grave is maintained and developed in a different way in another Greek city, Taras. Up to the mid-sixth century fine painted pottery had been produced in many centres, but from then on Attic black-figure, and later red-figure, drove out all rivals. During the Peloponnesian War, however, imitations of Attic red-figure begin in several places, especially in South Italy, and during the fourth some of these western fabrics are as important as Attic, in particular Apulian, made mainly at Taras.

This area was also very susceptible to mystery religions. In the late sixth century the mathematician and mystic Pythagoras had left Samos for the West and established a politico-religious government at Kroton. That had not lasted, but the area remained addicted to this kind of religion. Orphism, supposedly based on the teachings of a legendary Thracian bard Orpheus, promised its initiates an after-life where they would be happy and free from the pains that would beset the rest; and the funerary art of fourth-century Taras is impregnated with these ideas. We noticed grave-reliefs, but more informative are vases made for funeral use. Some are huge vessels, five feet high or more, such as had not been seen

42 Attic funeral *lēkythos*: Hermes and dead woman.

since the grave-markers of early Athens. There are pictures of the Underworld: Hades (Pluto) and Persephone enthroned in their palace, suffering sinners (such as Polygnotus had shown at Delphi) grouped around, and Orpheus with his lyre leading a happy family of initiates. Many other scenes are shown, often taken from Attic tragedy, but always with symbolic allusion to the mysteries of life and death. The same is true of the pictures on the many rather smaller vases made to be placed in graves, even when they are not, as they often are, drawn from the Underworld itself.

Taras at this time had close cultural connections with the rising power of Macedonia in north Greece, and there too these ideas flourished. Orpheus himself was said to be from Macedon's north-eastern neighbour, Thrace. In one grave of a fourth-century cemetery at Derveni near Thessaloniki was found an Orphic papyrus, and in another a huge bronze vessel of precisely the form of many of the clay ones from Taras splendidly decorated with a very strange Dionysiac scene which certainly has mystic allusions [43]. In Macedon at this time there is a fashion among the aristocracy for large built tombs decorated with paintings. On the façade of one, the dead man, in armour, is led by Hermes into the presence of two of the Judges of the Dead, Aiakos and Rhadamanthys (their names written beside them, though the dead man's is not). Within another, one wall has Hades carrying off Persephone while on a second her mother Demeter sits grieving and the three Fates stand on a third. The architecture of these tombs is closely related to that of contemporary palaces and great houses (serious architecture is developing in new directions), themselves adorned with painted walls and mosaic floors; but these secular fashions are adapted in the tombs to a religious end.

The character of public, state religion and its expression in art change too in this time and area. Apelles painted Alexander of Macedon holding the thunderbolt of Zeus, and that king, and those who divided his empire after him, demanded and received divine honours from their Greek as well as from their eastern subjects. Archaic and classical coins often bore the head of a deity or

43 Bronze krater from Derveni: Dionysus and Ariadne.

daimon (nymph or hero), but Alexander's successors, when they declared themselves kings of his fragmented empire, put their own heads (a real likeness now) and superscription on their coinage. When in 300 B.C. Seleucus founded a new capital on the Orontes for his kingdom of Syria, Antiocheia (Antioch), though it contained temples and statues to the old gods, he commissioned to dominate and protect it a colossal bronze of the city's own *Tychē* (Fortune), which became a model for countless others in the new age [44]. Tychē was a goddess, but a goddess with a difference. The figure, cunningly designed for many satisfying viewpoints, sat in the open air on a rock by the river, and must have been looked at very differently from the traditional cult-statue, facing the worshippers as they entered the long, dark temple-room. We noticed at the beginning such a classical temple-statue adapted in

44 Bronze statuette copying Tychē of Antioch.

the second century to adorn and guard a library; and we may turn back to that now and look at it alongside the Tychē to illustrate the changing, loosening but indissoluble relation of Greek art to religion.

8

Religion and the new education: the challenge of the Sophists

J. V. MUIR

'We are reaping what was sown in the Sixties. The fashionable theories and permissive claptrap set the scene for a society in which the old virtues of discipline and self-restraint were denigrated. Parents, teachers and other adults need to set clear, consistent limits to the behaviour of children and young people. Children need, respond to and too often lack clear rules.'

Mrs Margaret Thatcher reported in
the *Sunday Times*, 28 March 1982

'How sweet it is to be a part of novel and intelligent developments, and to despise the established rules!'

Pheidippides in Aristophanes, *Clouds* 1399–400

The feeling that some of the most important things which bind society together are being mocked or abandoned by the young is a symptom of an older generation which has begun to lose its self-confidence. There is the fear that young people are being seduced from the enclosure into forbidden and highly dangerous territory and must be brought back within the limits – a panic nostalgia for a more controllable, safe and stable world. Such sentiments would have been intelligible to many Athenians in the last quarter of the fifth century B.C.; their city had emerged proudly victorious from the Persian Wars and had seen the rapid expansion of artistic, intellectual, political and economic horizons. Great works of art

191

and literature, increased prosperity, an empire, a participatory democracy, the records of an heroic past, all contributed to the feeling that Athens was at the centre of the world, there to teach others – the school of Hellas. Pericles' Funeral Speech in Thucydides' history recreates this idealized vision of an open society in which toughness and sensibility, adventure and steady calculation, the acknowledgement of excellence and a regard for every individual are held in even balance, and for a few years it was even possible to glimpse the idea of continuous human progress.[1] The war with Sparta which dragged on from 431 to 404 B.C. with intervals of unsatisfactory peace changed this mood for good and spoilt the vision. There were of course ups and downs, but a series of disasters like the two plagues at the start of the war which reduced the population by as much as a third, the systematic destruction of the farms of Attica year by year, and eventually the failure and annihilation of the great task-force sent to Sicily in 415 B.C. introduced strident notes of war-weariness and recrimination. Something had gone badly wrong – the standards which had fortified the troops at Marathon and made Athens glorious were no longer upheld. Technical mistakes made by politicians or soldiers were a question of competence, but, when it came to other matters which could be taken as root causes of the trouble, something else was felt to be involved.

At such times it is not uncommon for a decline in religious belief amongst young people together with lapses in moral standards to be taken as both symptoms and prime causes of a more general failure. Two results often follow: first, an accentuation of the 'generation-gap', and, second, a determined and sometimes vindictive hunt for the culprit or culprits. Such a mood was clearly detectable in the latter part of the fifth century in Athens and it is the purpose of this chapter to follow its progress. Well-to-do young men appeared to be embracing dangerous ideas which set them apart from their parents and led them to disregard the beliefs and practices of traditional religion – in extreme cases they even toyed with outright atheism. Traditional moral and social standards were likewise at risk when the new, ambitious generation seemed willing to accept and practise outrageous extremes of ruthless selfishness. Who was responsible? The answer seemed ready to hand, for this phenomenon had an obvious connection with a new and influential development in education (teachers are favourite scapegoats at such moments) – the appearance of the Sophists, those itinerant educators and lecturers who came from various parts of the Greek world to excite, to teach and (in the view of many) to corrupt young men on the verge of manhood. They taught a variety of subjects, the stock-in-trade of most of them being rhetoric, the art of speaking, but it was in the area of morals and religion that their teaching was felt to have the most serious results, and it was for this that some of them were persecuted and condemned.[2] Socrates, who was a part of this same intellectual and educational movement, though at variance with the Sophists in several important ways, died precisely because he had been prosecuted on the twin charges of corrupting the young and maintaining an unacceptable attitude towards religion.

It is first necessary to ask why religion especially was felt to be such a fundamental part of Greek life that the questioning and undermining of it could be seen as posing serious dangers to the whole fabric of society.[3] The reason lies in a curious paradox. Many of the great religions of the modern world have a system of organization which (allowing for wide national variations) is centralized and remarkably uniform. They have a professional priesthood, a central core of sacred writings, common forms of worship and a common stock of dogma and belief. Religion in the Greek world had little or none of this centralism. Priesthood was usually not a full-time occupation – many priesthoods were tenable for only one year and could be variously obtained through birth, election, lot or even purchase; no special qualifications were needed and the priest was not the servant or the representative of some larger corporate body. As might be expected, in earlier times hereditary priesthoods had often been the preserve of aristocratic families like the Eumolpidai at Eleusis or the

Asklepiadai on Kos but, by the early fourth century, Isocrates could confidently say 'Any man is thought qualified to be a priest.'[4] Likewise there was very little that could be described as holy scripture or sacred writings. Homer is sometimes cast in this role by modern critics,[5] but though the social functions of the *Iliad* and the *Odyssey* may bear some loose resemblances to the functions of the Bible at some periods of history, they were never read out to the faithful in a temple or commended by priests for private study and meditation. Certain cults like that of the followers of Orpheus did have collections of writings said to derive from their founder, and the pronouncements of Apollo or Zeus through their oracles were sometimes widely remembered, but there was nothing in Greek religion really like the Bible or the Koran. There was a certain similarity in forms and places of worship – the rituals of sacrifice and libation, for instance, were part of everyone's experience and Greek temples shared many similar features – but there were still important differences. The temple itself was not a place built so that a congregation could join in worship but was primarily the house of the god.[6] As for personal belief, there were of course countless stories about the gods in Homer and the poets, but no Greek worshipper was required to subscribe to a body of dogma or to accept a number of common doctrines as a precondition of practising religion.

The paradox is that, although Greek religion seems to lack so many of the things which characterize modern religions and which require degrees of personal commitment and faith from their followers, Greeks were involved with religion to a degree which is very hard nowadays to understand. Some form of religion seems to have penetrated all aspects of life. The Greek household had its shrine to Hestia or to Zeus Ktesios, either of whom could give special protection to hearth and home, and the head of the house normally took his duties at the shrine seriously. At a meal the libation or drink-offering to the gods was an automatic custom, and it would have been very odd to eat and drink without offering the gods a small share of what was being consumed. The great landmarks of human life – birth, coming of age, marriage and death – were all marked by rituals with religious significance. Occupations were under the protection of particular gods whose favour had to be maintained, e.g. Castor and Pollux for sailors, Hephaestus for smiths, Prometheus for potters, etc. The literary arts and sport, too, were linked to the gods' favour; the *gymnasium* had its shrine to Hermes, and some god or muse lay behind every sign of poetic inspiration. Both found their highest expression in competition at great religious gatherings like the festival of Zeus at Olympia or the Great Dionysia. Above the level of the individual family, each deme, phratry and tribe had its own cult and each city-state its divine guardian: Athens had Athena, Corinth Poseidon and so on. The maintenance of these city-cults was essential for success and no great enterprise was undertaken without proper prayers and offerings. The year was marked by a series of religious festivals and the countryside itself was alive with divine presences; springs, rivers and mountains were all liable to have an in-dwelling god or nymph or hero. Nor was the situation static; the last part of the fifth century and the early part of the fourth saw the introduction of a number of new gods like the Kabeiroi from Samothrace, Ammon from Libya or Bendis from Thrace.

It is against this background of a way of life interpenetrated by an enormous variety of religious ritual, practice and belief – what Gilbert Murray called the Inherited Conglomerate – that the questioning of religion was seen as a dangerous threat. It was not a matter of criticizing a well-defined, separate set of people with clear beliefs and formal institutions – the welfare of every individual, every family and the state itself could be at risk. And who knew whether the disasters and disappointments which Athens suffered in the latter part of the fifth century were not some kind of divine retribution? To understand the threat which some of the Sophists seemed to represent to religion it is necessary to go a little further back in time towards the origins of some of the ideas which they and their pupils discussed.

The essential background is to be found in the work of a small number of remarkable men who lived in Ionia (now Western Turkey) and Magna Graecia (Greek Sicily and South Italy) in the sixth and early fifth centuries B.C. and who asked and tried to answer fundamental questions about the nature of the physical world and the nature of human knowledge – the Pre-Socratic philosophers.[7] Two aspects of their work are particularly relevant. Three citizens of the Ionian city of Miletus in Asia Minor, Thales, Anaximander and Anaximenes, were credited with the first attempts to give a systematic explanation of the nature of the physical world. However naive these first steps now seem – Thales, for instance, took water to be the origin of all things – these men are rightly remembered with honour in the history of science; all three faced the universe and sought rational answers to the question 'Why are things as they are?' Their enquiries did not lead them in the direction of either agnosticism or atheism – quite the reverse, for the question just posed was, for them, part of a much larger enquiry. Both Anaximander and Anaximenes (and probably Thales too) believed in a single, immortal divinity which was all-powerful and all-embracing – and not human in form; what was the relationship between this supreme power and the way things were? Much of what we know about the beliefs of the Milesian thinkers comes through the mediation of Xenophanes, who lived in the second half of the sixth century B.C., a poet and travelling rhapsode from Kolophon, a city near Ephesus. He was probably not a very original thinker but he had understood and adopted many of the ideas of his fellow-countrymen and preserves them for us. The idea of a single omnipotent divinity not in human form is explained clearly and unambiguously:

One god there is . . . in no way like mortal creatures either in bodily form or in the thought of his mind. (fr. 23 trs. Hussey)[8]

But effortlessly he (= the divinity) agitates all things by the thought of his mind. (fr. 25 trs. Hussey)

This uncompromising monotheism was quite at odds with the varied world of anthropomorphic gods, heroes, nymphs and satyrs with which ordinary Greeks were familiar and it posed a new problem. What could have been the origin of all the accepted and familiar gods and demi-gods? The answer – man made god in his own image – was simple and perceptive:

But mortal men imagine that gods are begotten, and that they have human dress and speech and shape. (fr. 14 trs. Hussey)

If oxen or horses or lions had hands to draw with and to make works of art as men do, then horses would draw the forms of gods like horses, oxen like oxen, and they would make their gods' bodies similar to the bodily shape that they themselves each had. (fr. 15 trs. Hussey)

The Ethiopians say their gods are snub-nosed and black-skinned, the Thracians that they are blue-eyed and red-headed. (fr. 16 trs. Hussey)

If all this was true, what about the poets and especially Homer who regularly depicted the gods as all too human? The answer was that the poets were simply and sometimes maliciously wrong, taken in like everyone else:

Homer and Hesiod have attributed to the gods everything which brings shame and reproach among men: theft, adultery and fraud. (fr. 11 trs. Hussey)

If divinity could not have a human form, what then could it be like? Xenophanes' contemporary, Heraclitus, the darkly obscure philosopher from Ephesus, had a vision of God as the unifier of opposites, remaining essentially the same though appearing to be different:

God is day night, winter summer, war peace, surfeit famine; but he is modified just as fire, when incense is added to it, takes its name from the particular scent of each different spice. (fr. 67 trs. Hussey)

He also had challenging things to say about the place of images in worship, a subject which has always been important in Greek popular religion through Byzantine times down to the present day. Praying to a statue seemed to Heraclitus to miss the point; if you wished to communicate with someone, you did not go and talk to his house:

. . . and men pray to these statues – it is as if someone were addressing remarks to houses – not realizing what gods and heroes really are. (fr. 5 trs. Hussey)

A tendency to scepticism was even more marked in two great thinkers from the Greek West who were born just before and just after the turn of the sixth century: Parmenides (born *c.* 515 B.C.) and Zeno (born *c.* 490 B.C.) both from Elea in South Italy. Their enquiries were not directed towards the investigation of the physical world, but at the nature of knowledge and at the question of how far humans could trust the knowledge they thought they had. They identified for the first time in European history some of the deepest and most troublesome issues in the theory of existence and the theory of knowledge – ontology and epistemology – and Zeno's paradoxes are still, for many contemporary mathematicians who know nothing of Eleatic philosophy, a convenient shorthand way of referring to certain well-known problems. Their arguments are for the most part highly technical, but they put a question-mark over the foundations of human knowledge and at the same time instituted a search for some kind of logical certainty on which true knowledge could be based. They are not reported as being particularly interested in the phenomena of religion, though Parmenides, in the poem in which his philosophy is described, makes the goddess Justice his guide and teacher in a picturesque and rather old-fashioned way. However, thoroughgoing scepticism is hardly consistent with unquestioned religious attitudes and the doubts these thinkers provoked were certainly transferred to the field of religion by some of those who were influenced by them.

From this background two strands can be followed which are of great importance in the later fifth century. First, there is serious debate about the nature of the gods and some clear dissatisfaction with traditional views. Along with this goes the criticism of Homer and the poets – traditional sources of wisdom and the staples of elementary education – and a clear-sighted, almost anthropological account of how men had arrived at the traditional picture of gods in human form. Second, there is the nagging suspicion that nothing in the world, whether it be observable facts or human values or information about the gods, can be firmly and certainly established – everything may be liable to doubt and possible refutation.

These ideas did not, of course, touch most ordinary Greek citizens; they occupied the minds of a handful of remarkable intellectuals and, however disturbing and revolutionary their theories might be, theories without interpreters and an effective means of diffusion remain relatively harmless. Such a means of diffusion was lacking. Books, in the shape of papyrus rolls, were produced in very small numbers and had a tiny circulation in the sixth and early fifth centuries.[9] Greek society at this time was still largely an oral culture[10] and the only reliable way of spreading information or ideas was by word of mouth – by teaching sympathetic followers who would in their turn go elsewhere and teach others. None of the Pre-Socratics were professional teachers who took regular students and gave courses of instruction in order to earn a living.

The Sophists, however, were teachers first and foremost, making their living by fees received from pupils who made contracts for periods of instruction, and from public lectures and performances for which admission fees were charged. They travelled from city to city, sometimes settling for a time in an area which seemed particularly appreciative, but for the most part on the move, taking with them an ever-changing group of keen students. This was a new phenomenon in Greek education. In the heroic days of the early fifth century when the Greeks were defeating the Persians, professional teachers occupied an essential but lowly place in the scheme of things.[11] There were three types. First was the *paidotribēs* or physical trainer who plied his trade in the *palaistra,* an exercise-ground with sanded floor, and who coached boys and young men in all the regular skills of athletic competition. The *palaistra* and its larger counterpart, the *gymnasium,* together with the Greek custom of exercise in the nude were one of the hallmarks of Greek culture. Second came the *kitharistēs* or teacher of the lyre who taught both instrumental technique and that repertory of songs (and especially Homer) which were thought to be a necessary part of every man's equipment for social life. Third was the *grammatistēs* who, with the aid of slates and waxed tablets, taught boys to read and form their letters. By the second half of the fifth century the gaps left by this modest provision of education were becoming obvious. Young men who wished to take part in a democracy which was beginning to work in practice as well as in theory could not but be aware that speaking in public and persuading others were skills that some people were better at than others. Could these skills not be acquired or improved? Likewise, Athens, with no professional police force, was notorious for the number of cases which citizens brought against each other in the law-courts. Any citizen might find himself involved, and an appearance in court meant pleading one's case in person before 501 mature male fellow-citizens – public speaking and persuasion again at a premium. Beyond such technical skills, an expanding world and a growth in prosperity and leisure were bringing other doubts and dilemmas about, for instance, morality, the use of power, the rule of law and, of course, religion. Some of these dilemmas were articulated by poets and dramatists – Sophocles' *Antigone* is an obvious example – but poets spoke from a distance under the influence of inspiration. Democracy was bringing things down to earth. It was in this context and to fill such gaps as these that the Sophists came on the scene – both part of a changing world and themselves agents of change. They represented no organized, systematic movement and nearly all of them spent their lives travelling, demonstrating and teaching as rather colourful, much admired, but often slightly suspect figures. Most of them taught the art of public speaking – rhetoric – and with it founded a hugely influential tradition in European education. Gorgias is especially remembered here – what Aeschylus had done for tragedy, Gorgias did for rhetoric. They also taught the skills of argument, both the technique of winning arguments – eristic – and the method of so-called anti-logical argument, that is, the art of arguing with equal cogency both for and against a proposition. However, it was not so much their teaching of techniques that provoked fear and opposition, nor even the fact that they offered to teach the art of success to anyone who could pay, but rather the views they proclaimed and taught when debating topics like morals, politics and religion which were of central importance to everyone, and the fact that the diffusion of their teaching put these dangerous novelties into wider circulation.

In the field of religion the first challenge came from one of the first and most remarkable figures of the Sophistic movement, Protagoras. He was born in Thrace at Abdera about 490 B.C. and probably spent most of his life as a travelling teacher and lecturer, paying several visits to Athens and living for a while in Sicily. He was a friend of Pericles and so highly respected that although he was not an Athenian citizen, he was employed as legal consultant to a new colony sent to found Thourioi near the site of the ancient city of Sybaris in South Italy. Very few indeed of Protagoras' own words survive and much of what we know of him comes through the words of Plato. However, he wrote a famous work *On the Gods* and, according to one source, gave a celebrated reading of it in Euripides' house in Athens.[12] Undoubtedly he will have lectured and taught on the subject as well. We have one statement in Protagoras' own words, probably from the opening of this book, and though short, it sets out a point of view which to many ordinary Greeks must have sounded dangerous in the extreme:

Concerning the gods I am unable to discover whether they exist or not, or what they are like in form; for there are many hindrances to knowledge, the obscurity of the subject and the brevity of human life. (fr. 2 trs. Guthrie)

This was not a statement of atheism but of agnosticism, of suspension of judgement. But even that was a radical departure, for if
Protagoras was prepared to suspend judgement on the existence of
the gods, it also meant that he was prepared to suspend judgement
on them as the guardians or guarantors of much of human life and
its standards. If the gods were not responsible, how could life
make sense? The answer is partly given in the opening sentence of
one of his books which has become almost a slogan of the
Sophistic movement:

Man is the measure of all things, of things that are that they are, and of
things that are not that they are not. (fr. 1 trs. Guthrie)

The precise significance of this is still the subject of much debate
and Protagoras himself may not have been entirely consistent in its
application. The general drift is however abundantly clear – it
points to a position of relativism. What seems to me to be the case
is the case so far as I am concerned. Whatever modifications are
made to such a position to avoid the logical conclusion of total
anarchy (and Protagoras does seem to have made such modifications), there is little room in it for a stable code of morals
depending upon the relations of god to man. Right and wrong, or
good and bad, become not a matter of reference to absolute
religious standards but a function of the human beings who use
them. Shocking inversions are then possible such as Plato puts into
the mouth of the sophist Thrasymachus in the *Republic* when he
makes him say that Justice consists in the interest of the stronger,
or such as Thucydides puts into the mouths of the Athenian
negotiators on the island of Melos:

. . . since you know as well as we do that, when these matters are discussed by practical people, the standard of justice depends on the
equality of power to compel and that in fact the strong do what they
have the power to do and the weak accept what they have to accept.
(Thuc. 5.88 trs. Warner)

Even more thorough-going scepticism was preached by other
Sophists. Gorgias, a Sicilian Greek, who was a contemporary of

Protagoras, has already been mentioned as one of the first teachers of rhetoric. He was also the author of a treatise 'On that which is not or on Nature' in which the argument proceeded in three stages:

(a) nothing is
(b) even if it is, it cannot be known to human beings
(c) even if it is and can be known, it cannot be indicated and made meaningful to another.

The interpretation of this is again difficult but its effect was plainly to loosen still further a belief in firm, unchangeable certainty.

Doubt about the validity of traditional conceptions of the gods showed in other ways. Some who would not go so far as the open suspension of judgement nevertheless put a distance between gods and men. The notion of a self-sufficient god in need of nothing and the conviction that the gods did not care about men's deeds were both views held by other sophists (Antiphon and Thrasymachus). The quotation is probably not *verbatim* but Thrasymachus is said to have written something like this in one of his speeches:

The gods do not see what goes on among men. If they did, they would not neglect the greatest of human goods, namely justice ... (fr. 8 trs. Guthrie)

Even Pericles, who was too experienced a politician to make dangerous statements on great public occasions, is reported as having said that we do not see the gods but are assured of their immortality by the honours paid to them and the good things they provide.[13] This is a cautious step away from a simple anthropomorphic view and it is hardly surprising to find one of the leading sophists opening up much the same territory as Xenophanes, that is, trying to explain the origin of older conceptions of the gods. Prodicus was a younger man than Protagoras, born on the island of Keos *c.* 470–460 B.C., and was said to have been Protagoras' pupil. He too spent his life as an itinerant teacher, occasionally employed by his native island as an official representative, but mostly lecturing, discussing and teaching. His views on the subject of religion have to be recovered from many fragmentary sources[14] but the outline is clear enough and of the greatest interest. He said that men considered as gods those elements of the world which were basic to human life, e.g. the sun and moon, rivers, springs, bread, wine, water and fire. In this way bread became called Demeter, wine Dionysus, fire Hephaestus and so on. He also said that men honoured and deified those people who made the first vital discoveries like the basics of food-growing or the earliest practical arts. The association of Greek religion with agriculture was a penetrating and persuasive observation, for the pattern of the farmer's year with its alternations of anxiety and relief was at the heart of the Greek calendar of festivals and embedded in the practice of untold local cults. In Attica, for example, the sowing of the seed in October (Greeks sow in the autumn and harvest in early summer) was associated with the festival of the Thesmophoria whose rituals ensured the fertility of the earth, while the spring saw the festival of the Anthesteria, when amongst other things the new wine was opened and tried for the first time, and there were of course the universal celebrations of the harvest. Likewise the idea of a river or a spring having or actually being a kind of god was entirely familiar. In Homer such gods could be aggressively active as when the river-gods Simois and Scamander attack Achilles with lethal waves after he has dared to defy one of them.[15]

Prodicus' idea of god representing a phenomenon was familiar too. Especially in any form of heightened language, there was an easy association in Greek between the deity and the feeling, quality or substance associated with him or her:

What is life, what is joy without golden Aphrodite? (Mimnermus 1.1 (West)

So wrote the lyric poet Mimnermus in the seventh century. In Aeschylus' *Agamemnon* the chorus ask Clytemnestra how the news of the fall of Troy has come so quickly and she begins her great speech:

> Firegod Hephaistos flashed out from Mount Ida
> flame after flame bore the beacon's despatches.
> (Agamemnon 281–2 trs. Tony Harrison)

God and what the god represented have become interchangeable. In later antiquity Prodicus was branded as an atheist for his views but there is no evidence for this and there is a vital difference between explaining the origins of man's conception of the gods and denying the existence of divinity altogether.

Although Prodicus was interested in cosmology, the chief figure in this field in the period between the end of the Persian Wars in 480 B.C. and the start of the Peloponnesian War was Anaxagoras, who was born in Klazomenai, a small city across the Aegean in Ionia. He was not a travelling teacher or lecturer and cannot be called a sophist, but, like Protagoras, he was one of the group of intellectuals and artists known to be friends of Pericles, and his cosmological theories undoubtedly had an influence on current discussions and beliefs about religion. In one respect he was a successor of the Milesian philosophers for he too appeared to redefine deity in terms of one thing – mind:

All living things, both great and small, are controlled by Mind (*Nous*) . . . and the kinds of things that were to be and that once were but now are not, and all that now is and the kinds of things that will be – all these are determined by Mind . . . (fr. 12 trs. Hussey)

This was a no more daring theory than the Milesians had proposed but it was put forward at Athens rather than Ionia, and in an atmosphere increasingly sensitive to radical changes in religious views. According to one persuasive interpretation, the sophist Antiphon held a view very similar to this and doubtless debated it with his pupils.

There were other stirrings, too, in more technical fields.[16] One of the interesting documents in the early history of Greek medicine is a treatise on epilepsy, probably written at the end of the fifth century B.C. or early in the fourth. It is entitled *On the Sacred Disease*, and part of its interest comes from the author's firm resolve not to accept divine or magical accounts of epilepsy but to insist that the disease has a natural cause, divine and magical explanations being attributed to human ignorance:

I do not believe that the sacred disease is any more divine or sacred than any other disease but, on the contrary, just as other diseases have a nature from which they arise, so this one has a nature and a definite cause. Nevertheless, because it is completely different from other diseases, it has been regarded as a divine visitation by those who, being only human, view it with ignorance and astonishment. (ch. 1 paras. 2ff. trs. Lloyd)

The author was even more fiercely explicit about how 'sacred' explanations came about:

It is my opinion that those who first called this disease 'sacred' were the sort of people we now call magi, purifiers, vagabonds and charlatans. These are exactly the people who pretend to be very pious and to be particularly wise. By invoking a divine element they were able to screen their own failures to give suitable treatment and so called this a 'sacred' malady to conceal their ignorance of its nature. (ch. 1 paras. 10ff. trs. Lloyd)

The determination to search for certain causes only in nature – to establish a category of events to which only natural explanations are appropriate – is a procedure which throws into serious question the credentials of a religion in which a god or divine presence may be held responsible for everything that happens; divine intervention must henceforth be put in a special, *un*natural category. It might be thought that doctors and their writings would have had little influence on general opinion, and it would be wise not to exaggerate the effect of such ideas, but it should equally be remembered that the doctor in the fifth century was not a fully-fledged professional with an established round of patients. Custom and confidence had to be won from the public by persuasion as well as by results, and demonstrations and defences had to be mounted to maintain a reputation; the practices of sophists and doctors were closer to each other than might be thought.[17]

There was of course in Athens at this time someone whose activities are often sharply distinguished from those of the Sophists but who belonged, as Aristophanes well knew, to the same movement of thought – Socrates.[18] He was born in Athens in 470 or 469 B.C. and spent most of his life there, taking part in public affairs and, on at least three occasions, serving in the armed forces. He did not, like the Sophists, make a profession of teaching and lecturing and never offered courses of instruction for money; he never gave public exhibitions of his learning at any of the great festivals and never toured other Greek cities. Indeed he insisted that his reputation for wisdom rested largely on the honesty with which he recognized his ignorance, and claimed to be an intellectual midwife, helping others to give birth to ideas without necessarily having original thoughts of his own. Above all, he had an unshakeable faith in knowledge as the only firm basis for action. He remained at Athens as a familiar citizen and his 'teaching' consisted of conversations with friends and acquaintances, some of which Plato has recreated in the Dialogues. He left no written works. In all this he was unlike the Sophists, and Plato constantly and vehemently emphasizes the difference. However, Socrates is rightly revered as an outstanding teacher, and in both the subjects and the mode of his teaching he can be seen to have clear affinities with the Sophists and their activities. He shared many of their intellectual interests – morals, politics, education, epistemology, the status of rhetoric – and he too was surrounded by groups of young men who often came to him regularly in the conviction that they would get something of lasting value from their association with him. He died in 399 B.C., condemned to death by a jury of 501 fellow-citizens on two counts: first, that he refused to recognize the gods recognized by the state and introduced new divinities, and second, that he corrupted the youth.

Socrates' views on religion remain something of a puzzle.

Someone who made such an enormous contribution to our
capacity to understand ourselves and our world might be thought
to have had something very challenging and penetrating to say on
the subject of religion, especially as his views on religion were one
of the reasons for his prosecution. In fact he seems to have held to
a dignified, sincere and cautious belief in a single divine power in
whom there is supreme wisdom and intelligence and who is responsible for the order of the world. In Plato's Dialogues Socrates
uses 'the god' or 'gods' indiscriminately but the underlying idea is
very like that of Anaxagoras' idea of Mind as the controlling
power in the universe. As to notions of immortality, the same
word is used in both the *Apology* and the *Phaedo* to describe what
happens immediately after this life – a *metoikēsis* or 'change of
home'.[19] Socrates seems to have believed that the nature of our
new home is beyond knowledge and in the *Apology* speculates with
gentle humour that it may either be like an eternal dreamless
sleep, or a real opportunity to meet our predecessors in a different
life (in which case he looks forward with enthusiasm to new
opportunities for fresh and stimulating conversation – who would
not wish to meet Orpheus, Hesiod or Homer?).[20] One aspect of
Socrates' experience was inexplicable and incommunicable, and
that was what he called the *daimonion* – 'divine presence' or 'divine
sign' – which on several occasions turned him away from a certain
course of action (e.g. from taking up a political career) and which
he seems to have taken quite seriously. Some of his friends
believed that this was behind the phrase in his formal accusation
which referred to introducing new divinities. So far as traditional
religious belief and practice were concerned, it seems in the
highest degree unlikely that Socrates ever made deliberate
attempts to denigrate or decry them. His respect for the Delphic
oracle was genuine and in none of the Dialogues are there traces
of deliberate iconoclasm or of that cheap humour at the expense
of religion which is the sure sign of an unhappy agnostic. His
belief in a single divine power was certainly a part of the new

thinking and was doubtless one of the ideas which rubbed shoulders with more daring and provocative challenges to orthodox belief and practice, but he himself seems to have maintained a scrupulous tact and reticence in such matters.

The one obvious omission in the attitudes examined so far is outright atheism. In fact none of the major sophists about whom there is any information can certainly be said to have been an atheist or to have taught atheistic views. One notorious atheist who was alleged to have written a book describing his personal path to unbelief is mentioned, Diagoras from the island of Melos. He was not a sophist but a poet who lived most of his life at Mantinea and Athens, and became converted to atheism, possibly under the influence of Democritus, but it is interesting that he is *so* notorious that Aristophanes, when he called Socrates 'the Melian' in the *Clouds*, expected that the audience would immediately take the reference.[21] Diagoras-stories were common. He was said to have been at a friend's house for dinner when his host was called away. He noticed that the lentil soup was not cooking because the fire had burnt too low and there was no wood. Looking round he caught sight of a wooden statue of Heracles, smashed it and threw it on the fire saying that the divine Heracles had just added a thirteenth labour to the other twelve.[22]

Although the major sophists cannot be called atheists, it is clear that views very close to atheism were much in the air in the later fifth century and, even if they were too shocking for any but rebels to embrace publicly, they were put into the mouths of characters on the stage. There are two remarkable examples of mythological characters railing against their fate in language which seems almost self-consciously shocking. Both speeches are fragments – we do not know the context – and one is certainly and the other probably by Euripides, a playwright who was greatly influenced by the Sophists and in whose works clear signs of sophistic terminology and thought have been identified.[23] The first fragment is a speech by Bellerophon:

Does any man say then that there are gods in heaven? No there are none. If any man says so, let him not be fool enough to believe the old story. Let not my words guide your judgment, look at matters for yourselves. I say that tyranny kills thousands and strips them of their goods, and men who break their oaths cause cities to be sacked. And in doing so they are happier than men who remain pious day after day. I know of small cities that honour the gods, and they are overwhelmed in battle by numbers and are the subjects of greater cities that are more impious than they. (Eur. fr. 286 trs. Kerferd)

The unjust are happier and more successful than the just and this is taken as proof, not of divine injustice, but of the fact that there are no gods. Even more uncompromising is a speech by Sisyphus in a play of that name, which in its form – 'There was a time . . .' – unmistakably recalls Protagoras' myth of the birth of society in Plato's dialogue:

There was a time when the life of men was disorderly and beastlike, the slave of brute force, when the good had no reward and the bad no punishment. Then, as I believe, men laid down laws to chastise, that justice might be ruler and make insolence its slave, and whoever sinned was punished. Then when the laws prevented men from open deeds of violence, but they continued to commit them in secret, I believe that a man of shrewd and subtle mind invented for men the fear of the gods, so that there might be something to frighten the wicked even if they acted, spoke or thought in secret. From this motive he introduced the conception of divinity. There is, he said a spirit enjoying endless life, hearing and seeing with his mind, exceedingly wise and all-observing, bearer of a divine nature. He will hear everything spoken among men and can see everything that is done. If you are silently plotting evil, it will not be hidden from the gods, so clever are they. With this story he presented the most seductive of teachings, concealing the truth with lying words. For a dwelling he gave them the place whose mention would most powerfully strike the hearts of men, whence, as he knew, fears come to mortals and help for their wretched lives; that is, the vault above, where he perceived the lightnings and the dread roars of thunder, and the starry face and form of heaven fair-wrought by the cunning craftmanship of time; whence too the burning meteor makes its way, and the liquid rain descends on the earth. With such fears did he surround mankind, and so by his story give the godhead a fair home in a fitting place, and extinguished lawlessness by his ordinance ... So, I think, first of all, did someone persuade men to believe that there exists a race of gods. (fr. 25 [Critias] trs. Guthrie)

This explains away the gods as the cunning invention of a brilliant individual, an invention made for social and moral purposes and so disguised by the majesty of nature as to deceive the majority of men. It is a clear statement of atheism – an extreme view – and the kind of thing that made Euripides one of the cult figures of the new movement.

The considered positions of prominent and influential teachers are, however, one thing; the public image of them which unsympathetic critics project is usually rather different – more simplified and more extreme. Plato put into the mouth of Anytus, later one of Socrates' accusers, what many of the older generation must have thought about the Sophists:

I hope no relative of mine or any of my friends, Athenian or foreign, would be so mad as to go and let himself be ruined by those people. That's what they are, the manifest ruin and corruption of anyone who comes into contact with them. (Plato, *Meno* 91c trs. Guthrie)

A reflection of many critical conservative attitudes and some important clues to the results of the Sophists' work in the field of religion can be found in Aristophanes' play, *The Clouds*, first produced in 432 B.C. and later partly revised. This essentially concerns the encounter of a not-very-bright, conservative father, Strepsiades, and his fast-living, 'modern' son, Pheidippides, with the teaching of the new thinkers typified rather unfairly by Socrates. The father is looking for a way out of his economic problems, caused by a spend-thrift son and an expensive wife (Strepsiades had married 'above his station'). Having heard that the new learning solves all problems and re-arranges values to order, he enrols himself as a pupil in the Thinking-Factory of the Sophists presided over by Socrates. There he encounters in carica-

ture most of the subjects which the Sophists discussed and taught.
One of the first is the new view of religion:

Str.   . . . I'll swear by the gods that I'll deposit whatever fee you
        ask of me.
Soc.   What kind of gods will you swear by? To start with, gods just
        aren't in circulation with us . . .

(*Clouds* 245–8)

Strepsiades finds this hard to grasp. He no longer swears by the
gods, but what of Zeus?

Str.   Come now, by Earth, don't you believe that Olympian Zeus
        is a god?
Soc.   What Zeus? Don't talk rubbish. Zeus doesn't exist.

(*Clouds* 366–7)

Later in the play, Strepsiades has become thoroughly indoc-
trinated and talks to his son as if Zeus were a kind of Father
Christmas:

Pheid. My god, what's happened to you, father? By Olympian Zeus,
        you're not in your right mind.
Str.   There you are, there you are – Olympian Zeus! How stupid! To
        believe in that Zeus of yours at your age.

(*Clouds* 816–19)

And later still, when Strepsiades has come to his senses, he has no
doubt who was responsible for his flirtation with atheism:

Str.   How mad I was when, because of Socrates, I rejected Zeus.

(*Clouds* 1476–7)

There are echoes, too, of rationalist arguments about the actions
of the gods. Strepsiades asks Socrates about the thunderbolt,
Zeus's weapon against perjurers. Socrates mentions three notable
contemporaries who should be prime targets but who have got
away with it, and points out by contrast that Zeus strikes his own
temple, Sunium and great oak trees with the thunderbolt. To what
purpose? Socrates then goes on to give a meteorological, scientific

explanation of the noise of thunder. Explaining the gods away in scientific terms, accounting for the universe by one basic physical principle, and replacing the old pantheon by one new-style deity are cleverly combined in another comic exchange:

Str. But who is it who makes the clouds move? Isn't it Zeus?
Soc. Not at all; it's the celestial vortex.
Str. Vortex? I'd missed this altogether – that Zeus no longer exists but in his place Vortex now is king.

(Clouds 379–81)

All this leaves no doubt that the abandonment of religion was felt to be one of the obvious consequences of sophistic education. Aristophanes makes fun of it, but the fun contains a note of warning; this is not the kind of thing which made Athens great. The new thinkers including Socrates are represented as the prophets of amorality and atheism, lazy, unwholesome, unwashed, ineffective logic-choppers. They are lampooned to the point of not seeming to be worth serious attention, but embedded in the comedy are signs of some revealing trends. One of the most important is the extent to which the new movement had evidently acquired a certain solidarity. The pupils in the Thinking-Factory are represented as an almost religious community and indeed Socrates refers to new pupils as initiates and takes Strepsiades through a little initiation-ceremony before entry; he even makes him subscribe to a mini-creed:

Soc. Will you then believe in no other gods but ours – Chaos, the Clouds and the Tongue, these three?
Str. I simply wouldn't talk to the others, not even if I met them; I wouldn't sacrifice or pour libation or make an incense-offering.

(Clouds 423–6)

Then the teacher is accorded exaggerated respect and an almost guru-like status. Strepsiades' first encounter with Socrates is intended to inspire awe; shortly after he has entered the Thinking-

Factory he catches sight of a figure hanging aloft in a basket and questions one of the students:

Str.   Say, who is this, the man in the basket?
Stud. It's himself.
Str.   Who's himself?
Stud. Socrates.

(*Clouds* 218–19)

There is an interesting parallel in the wry humour with which Plato describes Protagoras walking to and fro with his band of pupils in Kallias' house:

Those who followed behind listening to their conversation seemed to be for the most part foreigners – Protagoras draws them from every city that he passes through, charming them with his voice like Orpheus, and they followed spellbound – but there were some Athenians in the band as well. As I looked at the party I was delighted to notice what special care they took never to get in front or to be in Protagoras's way. When he and those with him turned round, the listeners divided this way and that in perfect order, and executing a circular movement took their places each time in the rear. It was beautiful. (Plato, *Protagoras* 315a–b trs. Guthrie)

It would be an exaggeration and an anachronism to talk of a youth-movement or a youth-cult, but there are clear signs that the Sophists helped to widen the 'generation-gap'. Old customs of everyday social life like songs at the *symposium* are despised, and great, respected authors from the past whom parents had been brought up to revere, like Simonides and Aeschylus, are treated with contempt. Parents belong to the old world and do not understand.

Most intellectual movements have their deliberately shocking extremes which provoke and crystallize opposition and, so far as religion is concerned, the last quarter of the fifth century supplies several examples. There was the notorious club of the *kakodaimonistai* – three aristocratic young men who chose to meet together for dinner on unlucky days to cock a snook at popular superstition.[24] More seriously there were two acts of wanton sacrilege which preceded the departure of the great task-force to Sicily in 415 B.C., both rightly or wrongly associated with Alcibiades and his circle. It was said that the holy mysteries of Eleusis had been profaned and mocked in private houses at Athens and – a more obvious and public act of vandalism – the statues of Hermes which stood at the entrance to houses and temples all over the city were discovered one morning to have had their sexual organs removed.[25] This concerted and planned sacrilege on the eve of a great (and finally disastrous) state enterprise made a serious impression; nothing like it occurred again.

The questioning of traditional religious belief and practice, the rise of a new and increasingly self-conscious intellectual movement amongst the young which seemed commonly to lead to scepticism, amorality or even atheism, the diffusion of dangerous ideas by teachers who were not part of the city and who took away some of its promising young men, a growing lack of respect for traditions, customs and the rights of parents – all these might reasonably be expected to have provoked more opposition than the appearance of a satirical play at a dramatic festival. There were doubtless many collisions about which no evidence has survived, but one of the most serious lines of attack by conservatives was a series of prosecutions in the courts for *asebeia* or impiety.[26] *Asebeia* was a conveniently vague term with no set legal definition; injustice – *adikia* was a matter of wrong-doing in man's relationship with man, *asebeia* involved wrong-doing in his relationship with the gods – a much trickier concept. The prosecutions began in the 430s (the exact date is not known) after a decree was introduced by a soothsayer who was also involved in politics, Diopeithes, the terms of which are very revealing. The decree allowed for the public prosecution of two categories of offender: first, those who did not admit the practice of religion (the Greek word *nomizein* is the same one used by Aristophanes for believing in the gods), and second, those who taught rational theories (*logoi*) about the heavens. The motives behind the prosecutions were not always simple; in some cases political considerations, such as opposition to the policies of Pericles, probably played a part, but the significant fact is that anyone who was even loosely associated with the intellectual revolution and the 'new thinking' on religion was thought to be vulnerable.

Of the Sophists, Protagoras was the most prominent victim. According to the tradition he was condemned on a charge of *asebeia* probably soon after 421 B.C. and was drowned at sea while escaping from Athens on his way to Sicily. As Diogenes Laertius wryly observed, he escaped the judges but not Pluto. Prodicus is also said to have been condemned to death and, though this is probably the result of the sources transferring Socrates' experience to Prodicus, there is evidence that he too ran into opposition and was expelled from a *gymnasium* for 'unsuitable' teaching. Another minor sophist, Damon, was ostracized for ten years. Diagoras was prosecuted and was already in exile by 414 B.C. The great playwright Euripides, in whose house Protagoras was said to have read his book 'On the Gods', was attacked in the courts although in his case the prosecution was unsuccessful. Anaxagoras was prosecuted successfully and either had to leave Athens or was imprisoned there. Finally just after the turn of the century Socrates himself was prosecuted and condemned in a trial which has become a legend.[27]

Freedom of thought in education has always been a risky business and it is no wonder that Aristotle in the fourth century said that being a sophist was one of the dangerous occupations, if not quite as dangerous as that of being a general.[28] The Sophists and Socrates can be regarded as the founding fathers of higher education and they have an honourable record. They dared to face some of the most basic questions of personal and social life and to centre some of their discussion and teaching upon them, and this should be set in the balance against the work-a-day uses to which the skills of the Sophists were also directed. In the field of religion they may not have been the originators of ideas, but they helped to stimulate two lines of speculation which are still eagerly and hotly debated. The first is the study of religion as a social and anthropological phenomenon; this has since taken many forms and modern structuralism is only one of them. The second is the attempt to understand the universe and its apparently miraculous order in terms of one controlling power or principle, and to get behind the absurdities of anthropomorphic deities and too literal an interpretation of 'picture-language'. They also opened the way to a divorce between religion and morals, and to debates about the relativity of moral standards which are still very much with us. These lines of enquiry invited criticism and repression, and, as isolated individuals, the Sophists and Socrates were all too vulnerable. Their successors founded institutions – Plato had his Academy, Aristotle his Lyceum, Isocrates his school – and institutions are notoriously more cautious than committed individuals.[29] The professional teachers of following generations learnt their lesson and not many of them appeared in the courts or dared the displeasure of local rulers. The issues had not changed, but educators had learnt to back off to a safe distance. *Gymnasia* continued to keep their shrines to Hermes and the Muses, success in educational or sporting competition was a regular occasion for thanking the gods, and the 'school calendars' of the Hellenistic world were largely based upon religious celebrations and festivals. Already in the fourth century some of the trials for *asebeia* seem to show an even tighter control over the technicalities and proprieties of religion. Archias, a priest at Eleusis, made a mistake in the ritual by himself sacrificing on a day when a priestess should have offered a basket of fruit. He was a member of a well-known local family but was accused and condemned to death. Another man who got drunk and attacked someone with a whip during a sacred procession suffered the same fate. Even someone who came to blows with another man over a reserved seat at the Great Dionysia found himself accused of impiety. These were, perhaps, unusual and extreme cases but they represented a sharp warning.[30]

It is one of the most remarkable features of the age of the

Sophists and Socrates that, for a few years and at considerable risk to themselves, a number of gifted teachers dared to bring education face to face with some of the basic problems of religion, morals and politics, in short, with what Plato said philosophy ought to be about – how one ought to live.

Notes

1 On making sense of Greek religion

*It is entirely right that a present for John Sharwood-Smith should have had its first airing as a lecture to the JACT Greek Summer School at Cheltenham (in July 1981), and its second to the undergraduate Classical Society of Oxford University (in February 1982). In its present form it has benefited very considerably from discussions on both occasions, as also from valuable suggestions from John Muir (twice over!) and from my wife, Gill. It is offered here as a token of more than thirty years of affectionate friendship and admiration.

1 E.E. Evans-Pritchard, *Witchcraft, Oracles and Magic among the Azande* (Oxford 1937) 12. Evans-Pritchard's later works, *Nuer Religion* (Oxford 1956), and *Theories of Primitive Religion* (Oxford 1965) do not materially alter his stance on the 'unscientific' nature of 'mystical' notions, though the latter in particular has a great deal to offer students of ancient Greek religion.

2 Evans-Pritchard, *Witchcraft, Oracles and Magic* 63.

3 Leszek Kolakowski, *Religion* (Oxford 1982) 14. I should add that Kolakowski's brilliant and lucid book starts from a *rejection* of such assumptions.

4 See Peter Winch's essay 'Understanding a primitive society' in D.Z. Phillips (ed.), *Religion and Understanding* (Oxford 1967) 9–42 and S.J. Tambiah, 'Form and meaning of magical acts: a point of view' in R. Horton and R. Finnegan (edds.), *Modes of Thought: Essays on Thinking in Western and non-Western Societies* (London 1973) 199–229.

5 Evans-Pritchard, *Witchcraft, Oracles and Magic* 99.

6 A self-justifying system of ideas is one which imposes its own assumptions on the discussion of any data which might seem to call them into question; for example, Christian theology in its treatment of the problem of evil face-to-face with an omnipotent god, or modern science in its treatment of paranormal experience.

7 Quoted by George Steiner, *On Difficulty and other Essays* (Oxford 1978) 143. In an extreme form this thesis is vulnerable to *reductio ad absurdum* arguments, to the effect that it makes impossible communication between members of different cultures (see S. Lukes, 'On the social determination of truth', in Horton and Finnegan (edds.), *Modes of Thought* 230–48), but, in the weaker form in which I assume it here, it is fundamental to any understanding of how cultures differ from one another.

8 C. Geertz, 'Religion as a culture system', in M. Banton (ed.), *Anthropological Approaches to the Study of Religion* (London 1966) 14.

9 G.E.R. Lloyd (ed.), *Hippocratic Writings* (Harmondsworth 1978) 87–138.

10 Herodotus 7.219.1; 221; 228.3–4; 8.27.2–3; 9.33–5; 37.1; 38.2; Xenophon, *Anabasis* 1.7.18; 5.6.16ff.; 6.4.9 ff.; Thucydides 6.69.2; 7.50.4; cf. 3.20.1.

11 G. Lienhardt, *Divinity and Experience: the Religion of the Dinka* (Oxford, 1961) 57–64.

12 Herodotus 6.75–84. A more disinterested example of uncertain interpretation arises from the two storms that wreck the Persian fleet off the coast of Magnesia and off Euboea: Herodotus is sure that the second case is a sign of divine activity, but uncertain of the first, though the Athenians are sure that this is the result of their sacrifice to Boreas, and even build a new shrine to him on the Ilissos as a thank-offering (Hdt. 7.188–9; 8.12–13).

13 See especially, Walter Burkert, 'Greek tragedy and sacrificial ritual', *Greek, Roman and Byzantine Studies* 7 (1966), esp. 102–13; also the essays by J.-P. Vernant in R.L. Gordon (ed.), *Myth, Religion and Society* (Cambridge 1981) 43–79. Original sources include *Iliad* 1.447–74; 2.402–31; *Odyssey* 3.418–72; 14.412–56; Aristophanes, *Peace* 937–1126; Euripides, *Electra* 774–843; *Heracles* 922–41.

14 Burkert, 'Greek tragedy and sacrificial ritual' (cit. n.13); *Homo Necans* (Berkeley 1983) 1–12; *Structure and History in Greek Mythology and Ritual* (Berkeley 1979) 52–6.

15 See, for example, Edmund Leach's essay 'Virgin Birth', in *Genesis as Myth and other Essays* (London 1969) 85–112, 117–22.

16 For this interpretation of supplication ritual, see my essay 'Hiketeia',

Journal of Hellenic Studies 93 (1973) 74–103, esp. 94–6. For another interpretation, Burkert, *Structure and History* 43–5.

17 J. Fontenrose, *The Delphic Oracle* (Berkeley 1978), argues against the historical truth of this account of the oracle's pronouncements. There is not space here to review his arguments, but his treatment of some of the evidence for how fifth-century Greeks *perceived* the workings of the oracle is palpably special pleading. It needs to be stressed that, for the purposes of the present discussion, it is the perceived image of the oracle that is crucial (all the more so if it is historically inaccurate), and for that the evidence of Herodotus, for example, is decisive for the fifth century.

18 Heraclitus fr. 93 DK; compare Aeschylus, *Agamemnon* 1251–5 (both misinterpreted by Fontenrose, *Delphic Oracle* 236 n.3; 238).

19 Louis Macneice, 'Snow'. On the incident which led to the poem's writing, see E.R. Dodds, *Missing Persons* (Oxford 1977) 117.

20 In this, I agree with the view of divinity in Homer put forward by Jasper Griffin, *Homer on Life and Death* (Oxford 1980) 144ff.

21 'As if' is important: Sophocles' felt inevitability is irretrievably coarsened if, as in Cocteau's *La Machine Infernale*, it is made explicit.

22 Richard Buxton, 'Blindness and limits: Sophocles and the logic of myth', *Journal of Hellenic Studies* 100 (1980) 22–37.

23 Oliver Taplin, *Greek Tragedy in Action* (London 1978) 43–4, 152–3.

24 And of modern Greek society: see George Seferis' poem, 'Spring A.D.' – the view of the displaced old.

2   Greek poetry and Greek religion

1 Cf. above, pp. 68, 78–81.

2 For details of the festival see A.W. Pickard-Cambridge, *The Dramatic Festivals of Athens* 2nd edn, rev. J. Gould and D.M. Lewis (Oxford 1968) 57–63. Cf. also above, pp. 118–27.

3 *Aristophanic Comedy* (London 1972) 33.

4 Cf. (on tragedy) B. Vickers, *Towards Greek Tragedy* (London 1973) 41.

5 An oboe-like instrument, often inaccurately translated 'flute'.

6 For Dionysus' Eleusinian role as Iacchus cf. Sophocles, *Ant.* 1115–52. On the Mysteries cf. above, pp. 57–8 and 87–91.

7 See E.R. Dodds on Euripides, *Bacchae* 64–169 (2nd edn, Oxford 1960).

8 For the prayer for victory cf., e.g., *Knights* 581–94; *Thesmophoriazusae* 972–3.

9 Cf., e.g., Plato, *Symposium* 176a; Aeschylus, *Agamemnon* 246–7, with G. Thomson's note (Cambridge 1938, repr. 1966). Three libations were normally made: to Zeus Olympios (or Zeus Olympios and the Olympian gods), the heroes, and Zeus the Saviour.

10 'The Greek gods formed a constant background and, we may say, consecration of conviviality . . .: their blessing rested on wine and food', A.D. Nock, 'The cult of heroes', *Harvard Theological Review* 37 (1944) 155, repr. in his *Essays on Religion and the Ancient World* (Oxford 1972) 587–8. Nock cites a passage from Athenaeus (192B), which illustrates what the Greeks liked to believe about their traditions, even if the reality was much less solemn: 'Every gathering among the ancients to celebrate a symposium acknowledged a god as the occasion for it, and they made use of chaplets appropriate to the gods as well as hymns and songs.'

11 Cf. especially J. Defradas, 'Le banquet de Xénophane', *Revue des Études Grecques* 75 (1962) 344–65. Of course, Xenophanes' views in this passage accord with his well-known critique of Homer's treatment of the gods and to that extent have a 'philosophical' tinge.

12 Wreaths, perfumes and incense were natural concomitants (cf. Athenaeus 641F); the mention of an altar is more unusual (D.A. Campbell, *Greek Lyric Poetry* (London 1967, repr. 1982) 335, suggests that what is intended is a small terracotta altar for burning incense, but this one is big enough to be 'decorated all around with flowers'. Professor Martin Robertson has more plausibly suggested that what is meant is the altar of Zeus Herkeios in the courtyard of the house). C.M. Bowra, *Problems in Greek Poetry* (Oxford 1953) 1–15, emphasizes the literary tradition to which this poem belongs, though Xenophanes' tone is more solemn than that of most other poets (Anacreon 11 (*PMG* 356) and elegiac fr. 2 (West); Critias 6 (West); Ion of Chios 26 and 27 (von Blumenthal); Theognis 467–

96). Pindar makes similar remarks on the impropriety of songs about divine battles (*Ol.* 9.35–9).

13 Some examples: *Ol.* 3 was performed at a festival (*theoxenia*) at Acragas, *Ol.* 14 accompanied a procession to the temple of the Graces at Orchomenus, *Pyth.* 11 was designed for a ceremony at the shrine of Ismenian Apollo near Thebes.

14 *Pyth.* 8.95–6.

15 For example, C.M. Bowra's comment on Pindar's religion oddly introduces the idea of 'orthodoxy': 'He was clearly determined to present his gods and goddesses in a familiar and orthodox guise and to leave no doubt about his acceptance of them as they were known to other men', *Pindar* (Oxford 1964) 43.

16 See N.J. Richardson, *The Homeric Hymn to Demeter* (Oxford 1974) 252.

17 E.g. Homer, *Iliad* 16.384–92; Solon 13.16–25 (West).

18 See R. Parker, *Miasma* (Oxford 1983).

3   Early Greek views about life after death

1 J. Griffin, 'The Epic Cycle and the uniqueness of Homer', *Journal of Hellenic Studies* 97 (1977) 42–3.

2 J.N. Coldstream, *Geometric Greece* (London 1977) 346–8; also 'Hero-cults in the age of Homer', *Journal of Hellenic Studies* 96 (1976) 8–17.

3 E. Rohde, *Psyche* trs. W.B. Hillis (London 1925, repr. 1950) 346–7; E.R. Dodds, *The Greeks and the Irrational* (Berkeley 1951) 135ff.

4 Dodds, *Greeks and the Irrational* 155–6.

5   The Greek religious festivals

1 M.I. Finley (ed.), *The Legacy of Greece: a New Appraisal* (Oxford 1981) 4.

2 The standard work on religious festivals outside Athens is still M.P. Nilsson, *Griechische Feste von religiöser Bedeutung mit Ausschluss der Attischen* (1906, repr. Stuttgart 1957); even those who cannot read German will find useful the indices listing (i) the places where fes-

tivals are attested, (ii) the names of the festivals, and (iii) the gods and heroes in whose honour the festivals were celebrated. For Athens see H.W. Parke, *Festivals of the Athenians* (London 1977); but this is not always reliable. J.D. Mikalson, *The Sacred and Civil Calendar of the Athenian Year* (Princeton 1975) is highly technical and establishes the days of the month on which festivals are known for certain to have been held.

3 Herodotus 8.144.2 (in the dated but dependable Everyman translation of George Rawlinson).

4 Aristotle, *Nicomachean Ethics* 8.9, 1160a25–8 (trs. J.A.K. Thomson).

5 W.K. Pritchett, *The Greek State at War* III (Berkeley, Los Angeles, London 1979) 165, in a section of a chapter on war festivals discussing the Greek festival calendar.

6 Aristophanes, *Clouds* 615–19 (CA 219 in LACTOR 12 'The Culture of Athens').

7 M.P. Nilsson, *Greek Popular Religion* (New York 1940) 40. See also J.D. Mikalson, 'The Heorte of Heortology', *Greek, Roman and Byzantine Studies* 23 (1982) 213–22.

8 On all aspects of Olympia and the Olympic Games see M.I. Finley and H.W. Pleket, *The Olympic Games: the First Thousand Years* (London 1976), published to coincide with the Montreal Olympics. An Olympiad earlier the Munich Games prompted H.V. Herrmann, *Olympia, Heiligtum und Wettkampfstätte* (Munich 1972); A. Mallwitz, *Olympia und seine Bauten* (Munich 1972); and the exhibition catalogue *100 Jahre deutsche Ausgrabung in Olympia*, ed. B. Fellmann and H. Scheyhing (Munich 1972); all are excellently illustrated and contain many suggestions for further reading. A more modest but useful booklet is the catalogue of an exhibition held in the year of the Moscow Olympics: Judith Swaddling, *The Ancient Olympic Games* (British Museum 1980). A selection of sources in English translation: S.G. Miller, *Arete* (Chicago 1979).

9 This expression is borrowed from A. Snodgrass, *Archaic Greece: The Age of Experiment* (London 1980), in my view the best study of the period from about 800 to 500 B.C.

10 For the athletic technicalities see H.A. Harris, *Greek Athletes and Athletics* (London 1964); *Sport in Greece and Rome* (London 1972) chs. 1, 7, 8; copious colour illustrations of athletes in training and com-

petition in N. Yalouris, *The Eternal Olympics: the Art and History of Sport* (New York 1979).

11 Peter Brown, *New York Review of Books*, 25 November 1976, 23–4, reviewing Finley and Pleket, *Olympic Games*.

12 *emporikon ti pragma*: Strabo 10.5.4, p. 486.

13 J.J. MacAloon, *The Great Symbol. Pierre de Coubertin and the Origins of the Modern Olympic Games* (Chicago 1981).

14 Pleket, 'Games, prizes, athletes and ideology', *Stadion* 1 (1976) 49–89.

15 'The Sporting Spirit' (1945), repr. in *The Collected Essays, Journalism and Letters of George Orwell* IV. *In Front of Your Nose 1945–1950* (Harmondsworth 1971) 63.

16 Xenophon, *Hellenica* 7.4.28–32.

17 Thucydides 5.50. An extraordinary number of Spartans, including a princess, won this event: G.E.M. de Ste Croix, *The Origins of the Peloponnesian War* (London 1972) App. XXVIII.

18 The coin issued to commemorate his victory in the mule-cart race is illustrated in Finley and Pleket, *Olympic Games* pl.23b.

19 Three bronze spear-butts carry the following inscription of a date soon after 440 B.C.: 'Booty from Thourioi, (this) the men of Taras dedicated to Zeus Olympios as a tithe.' One of the spear-butts is illustrated in *100 Jahre deutsche Ausgrabung* no. 74.

20 Diodorus 13.34.1.

21 Plutarch, *Life of Lycurgus* 22.8.

22 Thucydides 6.16.

23 H.H. Scullard, *Festivals and Ceremonies of the Roman Republic* (London 1981).

24 See Parke, *Festivals* and Mikalson, *Sacred and Civil Calendar*.

25 'Old Oligarch' = Pseudo-Xenophon, *Constitution of the Athenians* 3.2, 8.

26 Thucydides 2.38 (trs. Rex Warner).

27 Penguin Classics translation under the title *A History of My Times*.

28 J.M. Moore, *Aristotle and Xenophon on Democracy and Oligarchy* (London 1975, 2nd edn 1983) 39–40.

29 For the Panathenaia see Parke, *Festivals* 33–50. On the Great Dionysia some ancient sources are translated in LACTOR 12

(above, n.6) CA 304–38; the standard modern works are: A.W. Pickard-Cambridge, *Dithyramb, Tragedy and Comedy*, 2nd edn (Oxford 1962); *The Dramatic Festivals of Athens*, 2nd edn (Oxford 1968) ch. 2. Simpler accounts will be found in H.C. Baldry, *The Greek Tragic Theatre* (London 1971) and F.H. Sandbach, *The Comic Theatre of Greece and Rome* (London 1977) chs. 1–3. See also T.B.L. Webster, *Monuments Illustrating Tragedy and Satyr Play*, 2nd edn (London 1967); *Monuments Illustrating Old and Middle Comedy*, 3rd edn (London 1978).

30 O. Taplin, *Greek Tragedy in Action* (London 1978) 23.

31 One talent, it has been estimated, would keep alive some fifteen families of four for one year at Athenian subsistence level. Looked at in other ways, it might purchase about thirty slaves or pay the crew of a trireme for one month. It would be misleading to try and translate it into an equivalent sum in a modern currency.

32 R.E. Wycherley, *The Stones of Athens* (Princeton 1978) 216.

33 M.I. Finley, *The Idea of a Theatre* (British Museum 1980).

34 Lysias, *Oration* 21 translated in N.R.E. Fisher, *Social Values in Classical Athens* (London 1976).

35 The parallel is noticed in P. Walcot, *Greek Tragedy in its Theatrical and Social Context* (Cardiff 1976) 26.

36 L. Gernet in Gernet and A. Boulanger, *Le génie grec dans la religion* (1933, repr. Paris 1970) 46; this book contains an excellent chapter on peasant festivals.

37 Nilsson, *Greek Popular Religion* 101.

6   Delphi and divination

1 I offer my thanks to Mary Beard and Lucia Nixon who have greatly improved this piece.

2 The best book on Delphi in English is H.W. Parke and D.E.W. Wormell, *The Delphic Oracle* (Oxford 1956). See also Parke's shorter and more general *Greek Oracles* (London 1967); E.R. Dodds, *The Greeks and the Irrational* (Berkeley 1951) 70–5 on the Pythia; and an interesting, if difficult essay by A.D. Nock, 'Religious attitudes of the Ancient Greeks', *Proceedings of the American Philological Society* 85 (1942) 472–82 = *Essays on Religion and the Ancient World* II (Oxford 1972) 534–50. J. Fontenrose, *The Delphic Oracle* (Berkeley 1978)

240–416 translates the oracular responses. G. Roux, *Delphes. Son oracle et ses dieux* (Paris 1976) is the best account of the site and the procedures of consultation, to which I am indebted.

3 *Blue Guide* (4th edn, London 1981) 402.

4 All references are to Herodotus, unless otherwise stated; the translations I have adapted from the Penguin by A. de Selincourt (Harmondsworth 1954). Unfortunately oracles inscribed on stone survive only from the 430s onwards.

5 Plutarch, *The Oracles at Delphi no longer given in Verse* and *The Obsolescence of Oracles*, both in the *Moralia* (Loeb ed. vol. V, London 1936). These works, together with the early-sixth-century *Homeric Hymn to Apollo*, are the most important extended ancient texts about Delphi. The actual procedures in Plutarch's day were, so far as we can tell, the same as in the classical period, but it would be wrong, as we shall see, to project back Plutarch's specific philosophical explanations of the procedures.

6 Fontenrose, *Delphic Oracle*.

7 Tampering by the envoys to the oracle was also a danger: Herodotus 1.158; Theognis 805–10.

8 E.E. Evans-Pritchard, *Witchcraft, Oracles and Magic among the Azande* (Oxford 1937). I cite this from the abridged paperback (Oxford 1976), of which chapters 8–9 are especially pertinent. C.R. Whittaker, 'The Delphic Oracle. Belief and behaviour in Ancient Greece – and Africa', *Harvard Theological Review* 58 (1965) 21–47 poses good questions and illustrates another African oracle.

9 Evans-Pritchard, *Witchcraft, Oracles and Magic* 121–2; also 141–4. 141–4.

10 Fontenrose, *Delphic Oracle* 211.

11 Roux, *Delphes* 69. Unfortunately the details of her appointment and life are obscure.

12 T.K. Oesterreich, *Possession, Demoniacal and other* . . . (London 1930) 319 n.3.

13 W.K.C. Guthrie in *The Oxford Classical Dictionary* (2nd edn, Oxford 1970) 323.

14 Cf. Herodotus 8.133–5 on the oracle of Apollo near Thebes.

15 6.66 and 75. Cf. the bribery by the Alcmeonidae, 5.63, 90–1; 6.122.

16 W.G. Forrest, 'Colonisation and the rise of Delphi', *Historia* 6

(1957) 160–75; *Cambridge Ancient History* 2nd edn, III.3 (Cambridge 1982) 305–20.

17 Cf. the consultations of Lemnos (6.139) and the people of Apollonia (9.93).

18 See the stimulating piece by J.-P. Vernant, 'Parole et signes muets', in ed. Vernant, and *Divination et rationalité* (Paris 1974) 9–25.

19 Cf. the Theban debate, 5.79.

20 R. Meiggs and D. Lewis, *A Selection of Greek Historical Inscriptions* (Oxford 1969) no. 5, lines 24–5; cf. Pindar, *Pythian* 4.60.

21 Cf. 2.133 (Mycerinus).

22 8.121; 9.81 and Meiggs and Lewis no. 27.

23 G.B. Kerferd, *The Sophistic Movement* (Cambridge 1981) ch. 13.

24 M.N. Tod, *A Selection of Greek Historical Inscriptions* II (Oxford 1948) no. 158; *Inscriptiones Graecae* XII Supp. no. 200 with L. Robert, *Hellenica* 11–12 (Paris 1960) 505–6 and *Revue des Études Grecques* 76 (1963) 142 no. 129. Cf. other oracles: Didyma – W. Dittenberger, *Sylloge* 3rd edn, 633, 15–17; Dodona – H.W. Parke, *The Oracles of Zeus* (Oxford 1967) 262 no. 8; Claros – L. Robert, *Documents de l'Asie Mineure méridionale* (Geneva & Paris 1966) 91–100.

8   Religion and the new education

1 Thucydides 2.35–46; E.R. Dodds, *The Ancient Concept of Progress* (Oxford 1973) 1–13.

2 The best modern accounts are W.K.C. Guthrie, *The Sophists* (Cambridge 1971) = *A History of Greek Philosophy* III part 1 (Cambridge 1969), and G.B. Kerferd, *The Sophistic Movement* (Cambridge 1981).

3 See especially ch. 1; also M.P. Nilsson, *Greek Popular Religion* (New York 1940), and E.R. Dodds, 'The religion of the ordinary man in classical Greece', *The Ancient Concept of Progress* 140–55.

4 Isocrates, *Nemean Oration* 7.23.

5 E.g. P. D. Arnott, *An Introduction to the Greek World* (London 1967) 96.

6 See ch. 1; also J.E. Sharwood Smith, *Temples, Priests and Worship* (London 1975).

7 The best short account is E. Hussey, *The Pre-Socratics* (London 1972).

See also G.S. Kirk, J.E. Raven and M. Schofield, *The Pre-Socratic Philosophers* (2nd edn Cambridge 1983), and J. Barnes, *Pre-Socratic Philosophers* I and II (London 1978).

8 All quotations of fragments (fr.) are from the standard collected edition by H. Diels and W. Kranz, *Die Fragmente der Vorsokratiker* (Berlin 1952), usually referred to as DK. In their collection, passages are sorted into two categories: category-B passages are the actual words of the person concerned, category-A passages contain information about the person and his work. In this chapter all references are to category B. A translation – to be used with caution – of category-B passages can be found in K. Freeman, *Ancilla to the Pre-Socratic Philosophers* (Oxford 1971).

9 E.G. Turner, *Athenian Books in the Fifth and Fourth Centuries B.C.* (London 1952); J.P. Kenyon, *Books and Readers in Ancient Greece and Rome* (Oxford 1932).

10 J. Goody and I. Watt in *Literacy in Traditional Societies* (Cambridge 1968) 27–68; E.A. Havelock, *The Literate Revolution in Greece and its Cultural Consequences* (Princeton 1982); R. Finnegan in R. Horton and Finnegan edd. *Modes of Thought* (London 1973) 112–45.

11 H.-I. Marrou, *A History of Education in Antiquity* trs. G. Lamb (London 1956) 36–45. For useful evidence from vase-painting, see F.A.G. Beck, *Album of Greek Education* (Sydney 1975).

12 Diogenes Laertius 9.54.

13 Plutarch, *Pericles* 8.

14 Guthrie, *Sophists* 238–9 gives them in translation.

15 *Iliad* 21.211ff.

16 See G.E.R. Lloyd, *Magic, Reason and Experience* (Cambridge 1979) 1–58.

17 Lloyd, *Magic, Reason and Experience* 96.

18 Writing a 'neutral' account of Socrates' life and works has always proved to be impossible. For a full, courteous, sympathetic and balanced account, see W.K.C. Guthrie, *Socrates* (Cambridge 1971) = *A History of Greek Philosophy* III part 2.

19 *Apology* 40c; *Phaedo* 117c.

20 *Apology* 40c.

21 *Clouds* 830.

22 For a collection of all the sources on Diagoras, see F. Jacoby,

Diagoras ὁ ἄθεος (Berlin 1960) 3–8.

23 Kerferd, *Sophistic Movement* 170–1.

24 Lysias fr. 53.2 (Thalheim).

25 Thucydides 6.27–8.

26 E. Derenne, *Les procès d'impiété intentés aux philosophes à Athènes au Vme et au IVme siècles avant J-C* (Liège 1930; repr. New York 1956). Sir Moses Finley has kindly pointed out to me the need for extreme caution in using some of the late sources quoted by Derenne.

27 M.I. Finley, 'Socrates and Athens' in *Aspects of Antiquity* (London 1972) 60–73. It is a sad irony that Socrates' execution was delayed by an age-old *religious* observance – the despatch of a ship to the island of Delos as a thanksgiving for Theseus' success in Crete against the Minotaur. The city could not be polluted by executions during the voyage out and back. Plato, *Phaedo* 58a–c; Xenophon, *Memorabilia* 4.8.2.

28 *Rhetoric* 1397b24.

29 Both the Academy and the Lyceum had *Mouseia* or shrines to the Muses and a conscious sense of a dedicated community. It is, however, doubtful whether they were legally registered as *thiasoi* or religious communities proper as most modern books say. See J.P. Lynch, *Aristotle's School* (Berkeley 1972) 112–27.

30 For the reaction in general, see E.R. Dodds, *The Greeks and the Irrational* (Berkeley 1951) ch. 6.

Notes for further reading

1. General

Walter Burkert, *Greek Religion* (Oxford 1985) is both a helpful introduction and a comprehensive work of reference. E.R. Dodds, *The Greeks and the Irrational* (Berkeley 1951) is still stimulating, but it overstresses the irrational and emotional aspects of religion. More recent work, particularly that of the French school centred on J.-P. Vernant, has studied Greek religion as a way of conceptualizing the world. Some key works by this group, including important pieces by P. Vidal-Naquet on sacrifices and on festivals, are available in R.I. Gordon (ed.), *Myth, Religion and Society* (Cambridge 1981); note also J.-P. Vernant, *Myth and Society in Ancient Greece* (Brighton 1980) ch. 9 on approaches to mythology.

For other interesting discussions of Greek religious thought and practice see: L.J. Alderink, *Creation and Salvation in Ancient Orphism* (California 1981); W. Burkert, 'Jason, Hypsipyle, and New Fire at Lemnos', *Classical Quarterly* 20 (1970) 1–16, which reopens the old issue of the relationship of myth to ritual, and 'Greek tragedy and sacrificial ritual' in *Greek, Roman and Byzantine Studies* 7 (1966) 87–121, esp. 102–13; P. Friedrich, *The Meaning of Aphrodite* (Chicago & London 1978): an analysis of a deity normally seen as simply frivolous; A. Henrichs, 'Greek maenadism from Olympias to Messalina', *Harvard Studies in Classical Philology* 82 (1978) 121–60; R. Parker, *Miasma: Pollution and Purification in Early Greek Religion* (Oxford 1983); F. Zeitlin, 'Cultic models of the female: rites of Dionysus and Demeter', *Arethusa* 15 (1982) 129–57.

It is helpful to think about general approaches to the study of religion. Here there is much of interest in anthropological works. R. Towler, *Homo Religiosus* (London 1974) is a useful introduction; E.E. Evans-Pritchard, *Theories of Primitive Religion* (Oxford 1965) discusses

231

theoretical issues in anthropology first outlined at the beginning of the century; *Anthropological Approaches to the Study of Religion* (ed. M. Banton, London 1966) includes interesting papers by M. Spiro and C. Geertz.

2. Particular cults and sites

Athens

For the organization of the cults in the demes see J.D. Mikalson, 'Religion in the Attic demes', *American Journal of Philology* 98 (1977) 424–35, *Athenian Popular Religion* (Chapel Hill & London 1983), and for the cults of the *genos* of the Salaminioi see W.S. Ferguson, 'The Salaminioi of Heptaphylai and Sounion', *Hesperia* 7 (1938) 1–74.

On the civic festivals: H.W. Parke's *Festivals of the Athenians* (London 1977) is comprehensive but rather old-fashioned and inaccurate. E. Simon, *Festivals of Attica* (Wisconsin 1983) discusses and illustrates a selection of Athenian festivals.

Individual festivals: on the Dionysia, A.W. Pickard-Cambridge, *The Dramatic Festivals of Athens* 2nd edn, rev. J. Gould and D.M. Lewis (Oxford 1968) sections 1–2; on the Diasia, M. Jameson, 'Notes on the sacrificial calendar from Erchia', *Bulletin de Correspondance Hellénique* 89 (1965) 159–72; on the Genesia, F. Jacoby 'ΓΕΝΕΣΙΑ, a forgotten festival of the dead', *Classical Quarterly* 38 (1944) 65–75.

On the cults on the Acropolis: C.J. Herington, *Athena Parthenos and Athena Polias* (Manchester 1955); (ed.) G.T.W. Hooker, *Parthenos and Parthenon* (Oxford 1963).

Delphi

H.W. Parke and D.E.W. Wormell, *The Delphic Oracle* (Oxford 1956).

Eleusis

G.E. Mylonas, *Eleusis and the Eleusinian Mysteries* (Princeton 1961); N.J. Richardson, *The Homeric Hymn to Demeter* (Oxford 1974, repr. 1979): the Introduction includes a brief discussion of the Mysteries.

3.   Architecture and art

Architecture

H. Berve and G. Gruben, *Greek Temples, Theatres and Shrines* (London 1963): excellent photographs by M. Hirmer; J.N. Coldstream, *Geometric Greece* (London 1977) ch. 13: 'Sanctuaries, Gods and Votives'; P.E. Corbett, 'Greek temples and Greek worshippers: the literary and archaeological evidence', *Bulletin of the Institute of Classical Studies* 17 (1970) 149–58; J.J. Coulton, *Greek Architects at Work* (London 1977); A.W. Lawrence, *Greek Architecture* (3rd edn London 1973; new edn 1984); R.E. Wycherley, *How the Greeks built cities* (2nd edn London 1967); N. Yalouris, 'Problems relating to the temple of Apollo Epikourios at Bassai' in *Acta of the XI International Congress of Classical Archaeology* (London 1979) 89–104.

Art

Martin Robertson, *A Shorter History of Greek Art* (Cambridge 1981) is a general introduction and account of the subject. Most of the things mentioned in chapter 7 are discussed there and many illustrated. *A History of Greek Art* (Cambridge 1975) is a much fuller treatment and gives references to illustration and detailed discussions elsewhere.

4.   Death and the afterlife

For a preliminary orientation see S.R.F. Price, *Journal of Hellenic Studies* 103 (1983) 195–7.

The rituals of death

M. Alexiou, *The Ritual Lament in Greek Tradition* (Cambridge 1974) discusses laments for the dead in Greece from Homer to the present day. D.C. Kurtz and J. Boardman, *Greek Burial Customs* (London 1971): a full discussion with many illustrations.

See also: S. Humphreys, *The Family, Women and Death* (London 1982).

Death in literature and art

R. Lattimore, *Themes in Greek and Latin Epitaphs* (Urbana Illinois 1962). E. Vermeule, *Aspects of Death in Early Greek Art and Poetry* (Berkeley

1979) is mainly concerned with imagery and mythology; fully illustrated.

The afterlife

The classic account of ancient Greek views about life after death is Erwin Rohde's *Psyche* (English trans. by W.B. Hillis, London 1925, repr. New York 1966).

Hero cults

L.R. Farnell, *Greek Hero Cults and Ideas of Immortality* (Oxford 1921, repr. 1970): a valuable collection of evidence for hero cults despite its outdated theoretical framework. A.D. Nock, 'The cult of heroes', *Harvard Theological Review* 37 (1944) 141–76 repr. in his *Essays on Religion and the Ancient World* (Oxford 1972) 575–602.

Orphic poetry

M.L. West, *The Orphic Poems* (Oxford 1983) is the most up-to-date discussion. See also W.K.C. Guthrie, *Orpheus and Greek Religion* (London 1935) and I.M. Linforth, *The Arts of Orpheus* (Berkeley & Los Angeles 1941).

Index

Abdera, 201
Academy, 217
Achelous, river-god, 172
Achilles, 26, 27, 51, 106, 181, 204
Acropolis, Athens, 48, 69, 119, 121–2, 147, 148, 155, 166, 167, 168, 180
Adonia festival, 22
Adrastus, 17, 151
adynaton, 23
Aeacus (Aiakos), 60, 145, 151, 187
Aegean islands, 161
Aegeus, 138 fig. 31
Aegina, 112, 145–6, 151, 175
Aeschylus, xix, 10, 27–8, 29, 36, 47, 49, 60, 123, 124, 126, 127, 201, 204–5, 214
Aetolia, 73
Africa, religions of, xiv; *see also* Azande, North Africa
after-life, 50–66, 185, 208; *see also* Hades, Underworld
Agamemnon, in *Iliad*, 14
Agelastos Petra, 88
Ages of Mankind, 55
agora, 76, 174; at Athens, 174, 176, 179, 181
Agrigentum (Akragas), xvii, 114, 223 n. 13
Aigospotamoi, 177, 181
Ajak, 9–11
Alcibiades, 115, 177, 215
Alexander of Macedon (the Great), 154, 187–8, 189
Alexandria, 54, 155
Alpheios R., 45, 105 & fig. 22, 106; valley of, 81
altars, xvii, 41, 42, 68, 69, 72, 88, 92, 99, 134, 159, 160, 174, 179
Altis, 78, 105, 110, 113
Amasis, 152
Amathus, 14
Amazons, 82, 179, 180

Ammon, 195
Amphiaraus, 151, 173
Amphictyonic League, 131, 141
Amphipolis, battle of, 170
Anaktoron, 87 fig. 14, 90, 91 & fig. 16
Anaxagoras, xv, 205, 208, 216
Anaximander, 196
Anaximenes, 196
Anchises, 47
Angelion, 165, 178
Anthesteria festival, 19–21, 184, 204
anthropomorphism, 24, 46, 84, 197, 203, 217
Antioch, 189 & fig. 44
Antiphon, 203, 205
Anytus, 211
Apelles, painter, 187
Aphaia, 175
Aphrodite, 26, 28, 46, 47, 204
Apollo: *Archēgētes*, 95; and Asclepius, 91; and battle of Lapiths and Centaurs, 78; and Chryses, 14–15, 26, 44–5; dedications to, 165, 166, 167, 170, 177; Delphinios, Crete, 69; Epikourios, 81; Hymns to, 46, 96; and Iamidai, 42, 45; Jocasta's prayer to, 30; and Muses, 101; *prophētis* of, 28; as sender of plague, 45; shrines, sanctuaries, temples and oracles of; (Delphi), xviii, 7, 16, 31, 48, 95–7, 128–54 *passim*, 158, 170, 194; (with Artemis), 168; (Athens), 179; (Delos), 48, 165, 166; (Didyma), 93–5; (Eretria), 175; (near Thebes), 223 n.13, 228 n.14; and slaughter of Patroclus, 26–7; statues of, 165; (Delos), 165, 166; (Dreros), 69; (Olympia), 26; (Piraeus), 165, 166 fig. 36; and Teiresias, 31
apotropaic reliefs, 175
Apulia, 185
Arcadia, Arcadians, 81, 82, 84, 149, 181

235

Archias, 217
Archidamus of Sparta, 177
architecture, 67–97 *passim*, 158–60
Archon, 124–5
Ares, 46
Argeiphontes (Hermes), 46
Argos, Argives, 12–13, 70, 136, 151, 152, 167–8, 180–1
Ariadne, 188 fig. 43
Ariston, King, 12
Aristophanes, 35–9, 123, 124, 207; *Acharnians*, 20; *Birds*, 18, 36; *Clouds*, xx, 102, 191, 209, 211–15; *Frogs*, 36–9, 59, 60; *Peace*, 36
Aristotle; on festivals, 100; and Lyceum, 217; on *Oedipus Tyrannus*, 30; on sophists, 216; on soul, 63–4, 66
Arrephoria festival, 22
Arrian, 81
Artemis: and Aphaia, 175; cult statue of, Dreros, 69; dedication of statue to, 168; Elaphēbolos, 119; at Ephesus, 177; in Euripides' *Hippolytus*, 28; in *Homeric Hymn to Apollo*, 46; temple, Brauron, 177; temple, Kerkyra, 73–4, 75 fig. 4
Artemisium, bronze god from, 26
Asclepius, xiii, xvi, 8, 91–2, 172–3, 175; *see also* Asklepiadai
asebeia (impiety), 215–16, 217
Asia Minor, 74, 161, 176, 196
Asklepiadai, 194
atheism, 192, 196, 202, 205, 209, 211, 212, 215; *see also* scepticism
Athena, 18, 26, 28, 62, 147; and Athens (Parthenos), 48, 69, 81, 99, 155, 166, 175–6, 178, 184, 195; on coins, 184; *korai* dedicated to, 168; Marmaria sanctuary of, 95; Nike, 99, 180; in Pergamum library, 155, 156 fig. 33; Pheidias' statue, 155; Polias, Priene, 74–7, 98, 118; temple, Plataea, 179; temple, Tegea, 175; on temples, 175
Athenaeus, 222 n.10
Athens, 191–218 *passim*; and Aeginetans, 145–6, 151; Alcibiades and, 115; Arcadians serve, 82; and Argos, 181; *arktoi*, 177; and bones of Theseus, 56; calendar of, 101–2, 115–16; and Cleomenes, 12; coins, 184; and Delphic oracle, 134, 153; and Demeter, 59; democracy, 115, 116–17, 118, 121, 123, 124, 126, 127, 161, 176, 179, 200; early

temples, 69; and Eleusis, 37, 58, 90; epigram for dead at Potidaea, 63; festivals, xviii, xix, 19–22, 35, 99, 101–3, 115–17, 176, 177, 184; funerals and graves, 51, 52, 169, 171–2, 185, 187; hero-shrines, 181; Herodotus on, 99; league and empire, 121, 176, 180; new gods in, 8; and Pan, 173; and Pelasgians, 23; in Peloponnesian War, 116, 176, 177, 181, 192; and Persia, 12, 146–9, 150, 153, 170, 179–80, 191; plague, 11, 82, 192; pottery, 182; *Pythochrestoi*, 144; revival in fourth century, 177; and Samos, 177; Sicilian expedition, 84–5; stoas, 174, 179, 181; and Sulla, 165; temple on Delos, 174; temple of Dionysus, 179; theatre of Dionysus, 111, 120–7, 122 fig. 25; Treasury, Delphi, 96; worship of heroes, 55; *see also* Acropolis, Agora, Attica, drama, Parthenon
athletics, xviii, 176, 177, 200; *see also* games
Attica: Aeginetans and, 145; Athenians abandon, 147; Brauron, 177; Cape Sunium, xvii; destruction of farms, 192; Eleutherai, 119; farming and peasantry, 2, 6, 192, 204; grave statues, 169, 170, 171–2; heroes of, on Parthenon, 176; religious life, 182; rural Dionysia, 118; strife between gods for, 175; vases for funerals, 185; votive reliefs, 172–3
Azande, xiv, 3–4, 12, 133, 143, 146, 151

Bacchoi, 62
Bacchus, *see* Dionysus
Bacchylides, 41
Bassae, 81–4
Battus of Thera, 150, 151
Bendis, 8, 195
blasphemy, xvi; *see also asebeia*
books, holy, *see* sacred writings
Brasidas, 170
Brauron, 177, 184
Bronze Age, 55, 67, 69, 84, 158, 159, 182
burial, 50–1, 56; *see also* funerals, graves, tombs
Burkert, Walter, 18–19, 21
Buto, Leto's oracle at, 16

Cadmus, 47
Calypso, 54

Caria, 76
Carthaginians, 86, 114
Cassandra, 10
Castalian spring, 96
Castor and Pollux, 54, 195
Centaurs, 40, 78, 82, 179
Cerberus, 52
Charon, 52
Chios, 72
choregos, 124–5
Christ, body and blood of, 19
Christians, Christianity, xiii, 7, 8, 19, 34–
    5, 36, 50, 60, 68, 87, 98, 107, 136, 177,
    219 n.6
Chrysaor, 73
Chryses, 14–15, 26, 44–5
Cicero, 52
Cimon, 56, 90
Cithaeron, 31
Cleisthenes of Sicyon, 151
Cleomenes of Sparta, 12–13, 142, 152
Cnidos, *see* Knidos
coins, 184, 187–9, 225 n.18
competition, competitiveness, xviii–xix, 43,
    103, 106–7, 111, 112, 126–7, 195; *see also*
    festivals, games
'Cooking pots', 19, 20
Corcyra (Corfu), *see* Kerkyra
Corinth; and Doric order, 73; early
    temples, 69; and Epidaurus, 154; and
    Poseidon, xvii, 179, 195; Timoleon, 170
Corinthian order, 84
Cos, *see* Kos
Coubertin, Pierre, Baron de, 111, 113
cremation, 50–1
Creon, 30–1, 51
Crete, 69, 88, 159, 171
Croesus, 13, 16, 32, 131, 149, 151, 152
Cronos, *see* Kronos
Croton, 185
Cyrene, 145, 150
Cyrus, 16, 149, 152

daimones (spirits), 141, 170, 181, 184, 189
Damon, 216
dance, dancing, xviii, 35, 37, 39, 41, 46,
    100, 117, 118, 122–3
Darius, 23
Dark Ages, 68, 69, 71, 89
Dawn, 54
death, 50–66 *passim*, 169–70, 171, 185, 187,

    195, 217; *see also* funerals, graves, tombs
dedications, offerings, 81–2, 110, 131, 145
    fig. 32, 153, 158, 160, 165–9, 171, 172,
    176, 177, 178, 180, 182, 184
Delos, 35, 48, 110, 165–6, 168–9, 174, 230
    n.27
Delphi, 128–54; games, xviii, 96, 103;
    oracle, xv, 7, 12, 13, 23, 30, 48, 56, 63,
    95–7, 106, 128–54, 158, 208; Polygnotus'
    picture, 60, 187; statues, monuments,
    dedications, 167, 170, 177, 180, 181;
    treasuries, 173, 174, 178
Demaratus of Sparta, 12, 13, 142
Demeter: Homeric Hymn to, 47, 57, 58–9;
    land sacred to, 12; and Mysteries, 12,
    37–9, 57–8, 64, 87, 88, 90, 101, 182;
    and Persephone, 12, 187; Prodicus on,
    204; and Thesmophoria, 101
Demetrius of Phalerum, 52
Democracy, 179; *see also under* Athens
Democritus, 209
Demophon, 88
Demos, 179
Derveni, 187, 188 fig.43
Diagoras, 209, 216
Didyma, 93–4
Diktynna, 11
Dinka, xiv, 9–11
Diodorus Siculus, 139
Diogenes the Cynic, 59, 177
Diogenes Laertius, 216
Dionysia festival, Athens (Great Dionysia),
    19, 35–40, 102–3, 115–27, 195, 217;
    rural Dionysia, 118
Dionysus: and Anthesteria, 19–21; in
    Bacchae, 29, 64–5; Eleuthereus, 119; at
    Delphi, 135, 136 fig.29; festival shown
    on vase, 184; in *Frogs*, 36–40 *passim*; and
    Muses, 101; opposition to, 64–5; and
    Orpheus, 37; Prodicus on, 204; scene on
    Derveni krater, 187, 188 fig. 43; temple,
    Athens, 179; and Titans, 62, 64, 65; *see
    also* Dionysia, Iacchus
Dionysus, Theatre of, Athens, 111, 120,
    122 fig.25
Diopeithes, 215
dithyrambs, 35
divination, xvi, 128–54 *passim*; *see also*
    oracles, prophecy
Dodona, 48, 129
Dolonkoi, 144
Dorians of Sicily, 84–5

Doric order, 73, 74, 78, 81, 86, 92, 174–5, 179
Dorieus, 146
Dracon, 55
drama, theatres, xviii, xix, 96, 103, 118–27, 162, 187, 215; *see also* Aeschylus, Aristophanes, Dionysia, Euripides, festivals, Sophocles
dreams, 11, 22, 117
Dreros, 69
Dürer, A., 157

Earth, *see* Gē; *see also* Demeter
education, 191–218 *passim*
Egyptians: architecture, 158, 159; and reincarnation, 61; statues, 162
Elaphēbolion, 119, 120
Elea, 198
Eleusis, Eleusinian Mysteries, xvi, 7, 12, 37, 57–8, 59, 64, 87–91, 96, 101, 117, 144, 182, 183 fig. 41, 193, 215, 217
Eleutherai, 119, 120
Elis, 78, 107, 114
Elpenor, 53
Elymians, 84, 85
Elysium, Elysian plain, 54, 60
Empedocles, 62
Emporio, 72
Eos, 174
Epaminondas, 59
Epharmostos of Opus, 42
Ephesus, 177, 196, 197
Epidaurus, xvi, 92, 154, 173
epinikia (victory odes), 41–2
epiphanies, 45, 47
Erechtheus, 55
Eretria, 175
Erinyes, 51, 58; *see also* Furies
Eros, 177
Ethiopians, 197
Euboea, 159
Eumenes II of Pergamum, 155
Eumenides, 28, 48; *see also* Furies
Eumolpidai, 193
Euphranor, 179
Euripides, xiv, xix, 2, 11, 17, 28–9, 36, 37, 62, 120, 124, 201, 209–11, 216
Evans-Pritchard, E. E., xiv, 3, 133, 142–3, 151
exēgētai, xvi, 7

Fate, 28; *see also* Tychē

Fates, 187; *see also* Moirai
female gods, 25
fertility, 107, 120
festivals, xv, xviii–xix, 19–21, 34–49 *passim*, 72, 92, 98–127, 135, 158, 176, 182, 184, 195, 204, 217, 223 n.13; *see also* drama, games
Forms, theory of, 63
Fortune, *see* Fate, *Tyche*
funerals, 51–3, 64, 169–70, 185; *see also* death, graves, tombs
Furies, 25, 26, 28, 127; *see also* Erinyes, Eumenides

games, xvii, xviii, 41–3, 98, 117, 131, 182, 184; *see also* Isthmian, Nemean, Olympic and Pythian Games
Ganymede, 54
Gē (Earth), 95, 105
Geertz, Clifford, xiv, 5, 6
Geneleos, sculptor, 166, 167 fig.37, 168
Geometric style, 70
Giants, 40, 175, 179–80
Gigantomachy, 25, 175, 176, 179–80
Glaucus, Spartan, 13
Gnesippos, 124
Gobryas, 23
gods: belief in, 1–33 *passim*; epiphanies of, 45, 47; and heroes, 42; in poetry, 43–9; Pre-Socratics on, 196–9; *see also* anthropomorphism, atheism, *daimones*, Olympians, polytheism, prayer, sacrifice, scepticism, theology *and names of individual gods*
God, Xenophanes on, 197
Golden Age, 55
Gorgias, 201, 202–3
Gorgon(s), 25, 28, 73, 175
Gortyn, 171
Graces, 46, 165, 223 n.13
Graiai; 25
graves, 53, 159, 160, 169, 170–2, 182–4, 185–7; *see also* tombs

Hades, 50–1, 53, 58, 88, 181, 187; *see also* Underworld
Hagesias, 42
Halicarnassus, 92; Mausoleum, 76
Harmodios and Aristogeiton, 176
Harmonia, 46
Harpies, 28
harvest, 100

Hebe, 46
Hecate, 11
Hector, 27, 51
Hekatompedon, 70–1, 78
Helen, 8, 26
Hell, 60; *see also* Hades, Underworld
Hellenism, spread of, 85
Hellenistic Age, 54, 92, 95, 154, 157, 180, 184, 189, 217
Hephaestus, 195, 204, 205
Hera, 42, 69–70, 70–2, 73, 78, 152, 160, 166, 167, 177
Heracles, xiii, 18, 37, 41, 48, 57, 78, 96
Heraclitus, 2, 23, 197–8
heresy, xv
Hermes, 36, 46, 186, 187, 195, 215, 217
Herodotus; on bones of Orestes, 56; on Cleomenes, 12–13; on Croesus, 13; on cult of Onesilos, 14; on divine power, 9, 12, 16, 30; on dreams, 11; on Egyptians and reincarnation, 61; on foundation of Cyrene, 150; on Greek brotherhood, 99; on Homer and Hesiod and genealogy of gods, xv, xix, 25; on Kleobis and Biton, 167; on men aspiring to divinity, 23; on oracles, 13, 16, 132–3, 144–54 *passim*, 221 n.17; on Pelasgians and Athens, 23–4; on Solon, 32; on spirits and possession, xiv
heroes, hero cults, xiii, 41–2, 55–7, 60, 65, 106, 122, 145, 170, 172, 174, 175, 176, 179–80, 181, 189, 195, 197, 198
Hesiod, xv, xix, 18, 19, 25–6, 33, 40–1, 46–7, 53, 55, 65, 197, 208
Hestia, 194
hiereis, 7; *see also* priests
Hieron, 96
hierophants, Eleusinian, 7
Hippias of Elis, 105
Hippocrates, 92; Hippocratic doctor, 6
Hippodamus of Miletus, 75
Hippolytus, 29
holy writings, *see* sacred writings
Homer: Chryses in, 14–15, 26, 44–5; and competitive ideal, 106; in education, 200; gods and divine power in, xv, xix, 9, 24–6, 27, 29, 42; influence on Greek religious imagery, 26; life after death in, 54, 55, 57, 58, 64, 65; Lucian on, 53; Odysseus summons ghosts, 53–4; opening of *Odyssey*, 18; Orestes in, 8; Patroclus' death and funeral games, 26–

7, 106; on persecution of Lycurgus of Thrace, 64–5; plague in *Iliad*, 11; philosophic criticism of, 199; on Priam and body of Hector, 51; river gods in, 204; as scripture, 194; Socrates on, 208; and soul, 50–1, 53, 60, 65; as source for festivals, 101; on temple at Delphi, 130; Underworld in, 53–4, 60, 181–2; Xenophanes on, 197, 222 n.11
Homeric Hymns: to Aphrodite, 47; to Apollo, 46, 143, 148; to Demeter, 47, 57, 58–9, 88–9
Horae (Seasons), 42
Hygieia (Health), 172
Hymettus, Mt, 122
hymns, 37–9, 57, 222 n.10; *see also Homeric Hymns*, paeans, singing
Hyperboreans, 136 fig.29

Iacchus, 37–9, 90
Iamidai clan, 42
Iamos, 45
Iktinos, 81, 82, 89, fig.15, 90
images, worship of, xvi, xvii, 197–8; *see also* statues
impiety, *see asebeia*
India, 6
inhumation, 50
Ino, 54
Ionia, Ionians, 177, 196, 205
Ionic order, 74, 82, 93, 175
Islands of the Blest, 55, 60
Isocrates, 194, 217
Isthmian games, xviii, 103
Isthmus, Poseidon at, 153
Italy, Greeks of, 114, 131, 172, 182, 185, 196, 198, 201
Italy, modern, 99, 102
Itea, 128 fig. 26, 129

Jews, Sabbath, 19
Jocasta, 30
Judges of the Dead, 60, 187
Jugs, Day of, 19, 20, 184
Justice, 198

Kabeiroi, 195
kakodaimonistai, 214
Kallias, 214
Kanachos, 165, 178
Keos, 203

Kephalos, 174
Kephisos, 90
Kerameikos cemetery, 116
Kerkyra (Corfu), 73–4, 75 fig.4
Klazomenai, 205
Kleitos, 54
Kleobis and Biton, 163 fig.35, 167–8, 170, 176
Knidos, 181
Kobon, 142
Kolophon, 196
kōmos, 118
Konon, 177
Korē, 12, 37; *see also* Persephone
Korybantes, 11
Kos, 91–2, 194
kouroi, 162–70
Krates, philosopher, 177
Kronos, 25, 55; hill of, Olympia, 45

Laconia, grave monuments of, 171–2
Laius, 30–1
Lampsacus, xv
lawgivers, 59
laws: on burial, 51; on honours to heroes, 55
League, Athenian, 175–6, 180
Lefkandi, 159
Lemnos, 23
Leonidas, 145
Leto, 16, 44, 46, 69
libations, xvii, 16, 40, 120, 194, 222 n.9
Libya, 150, 195
Lienhardt, Godfrey, xiv, 9–10
liturgies (*leitourgiai*), 124–5
lottery oracle, 132–3, 148
Lucian, *On Mourning*, 52–3
Lyceum, 217
Lycurgus, King of Thrace, 64
Lydia, 131, 149
Lysander, 177, 181

Macedonians, 117, 187
Maeander, R., 74
maenads, 184
Magna Graecia, *see* Italy, Sicily
Magus, 23
manteis, 7, 11; *see also* prophets
Mantinea, 179, 209
Marathon, 170, 173, 179, 180, 192
Mardonius, 152
Marmaria, 95

Marseilles *see* Massilia
Marshes, sanctuary in, 20
Massilia (Marseilles), 99
Mausoleum, Halicarnassus, 76
Mausolus, 76
Medea, 29
Medes, 149
medicine, 6, 67, 92, 206; *see also* Asclepius, Hippocrates
Melanippus, 151
Melos, 202, 209
Menelaus, 54
Messenians, 180
Metaneira, 47
metempsychosis, 61
metics, 171
Meuli, Karl, 18–19
Mikon, 179
Miletus, 93, 165, 196, 205
Miltiades, 23, 144, 146, 180
Mimnermus, 204
Mind (*nous*), 63–4
Minoan civilization, 67, 68, 69, 158
Minos, 54
Minotaur, 230 n.27
Mithridates of Pontus, 165
Moirai (Fates), 25, 26, 187
monotheism, 197
Moschophoros, 167
Mountain Mother, 11
mourning, 50–3, 64, 120
Musaeus, 59, 61
Muses, 46, 101, 217, 230 n.30
music, xviii, 34, 37, 41, 46, 96, 158; *see also* dance, hymns, singing
Mycenaean civilization, 67, 68–9, 71, 87, 89, 90, 91, 95, 158
Mykerinos, son of Cheops, Egyptian pharaoh, 16
Mysteries, 49; Eleusinian, *see* Eleusis; Orphic, 37, 185–6
myth, xix–xx, 1, 2, 8, 9, 19, 24–33, 42, 55, 61–2, 64, 65, 88, 95, 98, 106, 122, 139, 179, 209, 210

Naxos, 166, 168
Near East: and art, 155, 157, 158, 162; and Hesiodic succession myth, 25
Nemean games, xviii, 103
Neoptolemus, 181
Nicias, xx
Night, children of, 28

Nikandrē, 168
Nikē (Victory), 174, 179, 180
North Africa, 131, 145, 146
Nymphs, 42, 172, 189, 195, 197

Odeion, 120
Odysseus, 26, 53–4, 181
Oedipus, 30–2, 45, 48
Oenomaos, King, 78
Oeta, Mt, 48
Oinoē, 179
Old Comedy, 36; *see also* Aristophanes
Old Oligarch, 116, 117–18
Oknos (Sloth), 60
Olympia; hill of Kronos, 45; Pelops'
    shoulder, 56; pillar and Victory, 180;
    sanctuary of Hera, 73, 78; sanctuary of
    Zeus, xvii, 41–2, 48, 78–81, 153, 158, 174,
    175, 176, 178; statue of Lysander,
    177; treasury, 173, 174, 181; *see also*
    Olympic games
Olympians, xvii, 16, 18, 24, 25, 26, 27, 28,
    29, 33, 62, 65, 103, 118, 172; *see also*
    under names of individual gods
Olympic games, xviii–xix, 41–2, 78, 100,
    101, 102, 103–15, 119, 123, 126, 131,
    158
Olympus, Mt, 46, 47, 103
omens, 22
omphalos, 135, 136 fig.29
Onesilos, 14
'Opening the storage jars', 19–20
oracles, 11, 14, 16, 22, 67, 98, 105, 129–
    30, 132–3, 133–4, 143, 146, 151; *see also*
    under Delphi
oracle-mongers, soothsayers, xvi; *see also*
    manteis, prophets
Orchomenus, 223 n.13
Orestes, 8, 20, 28, 56
Orpheus, Orphism, xiv, 35, 37, 59, 61–2,
    182, 185, 187, 194, 208, 214
orthodoxy, xv; *see also asebeia*
Ouranos, 25

paeans, 35, 40; *see also* hymns, singing
painting, 178–84
Paionios, sculptor, 180
Pan, 11, 172–3
Panathenaia festival, xviii, 19, 35, 118, 184
panhellenic institutions, xviii, 67, 103, 111,
    113, 114; *see also* Olympic games
Paradise, 60

Parmenides, 198
Parnassus, 96
Parthenon, 26, 81, 82, 121, 155, 161 fig.34,
    171, 175–6, 178, 180, 184
Pataikion, 59
Patroclus, 26–7, 106
Pausanias, 60, 73, 81, 177, 180, 181
Pegasus, 73
Pelasgians, 23
Peloponnese, 105, 106, 131, 173
Peloponnesian War, 82, 116, 120, 154,
    171, 177, 180, 185, 192
Pelops, 41, 45, 56, 78
Pentheus, 65
Perachora, 69, 70 fig.1
Pergamum, 155, 178, 180
Perialla the Pythia, 142
Pericles, 116, 117, 120, 192, 201, 203, 205,
    216
Persephone, 37–9, 53, 57–8, 62, 64, 87,
    88, 101, 182, 187; *see also Korē*
Persia, Persian Wars, 12–16 *passim*, 99,
    107, 132, 134, 146–54 *passim*, 161, 175–
    6, 179, 180, 191, 199
Phaedra, 11, 28
Pheidias, 78, 81, 111, 155, 156 fig. 33,
    177–8
Phaidriades, 96
Phigaleia, 81
Philip of Macedon, 177
philosophy, xiii, 7, 191–218 *passim*; *see also*
    Aristotle, Plato, Socrates
Phrynē, 177, 181
Phoibos *see* Apollo
Phorkydes, 25
Pindar, xiv, 41–2, 45, 49, 57, 62, 111–12,
    223 nn.12, 15
Piraeus, 116, 117, 165
Pisistratus, 90, 119
plague, 45, 82, 146, 192
Plataea, 153, 179
Plato, xiii, xv, xx, 2, 59, 60, 62, 63, 65,
    66, 76, 100–1, 201, 202, 207, 208, 210–
    11, 214, 217, 218
Polydeuces, 54
Polygnotus, 60, 179, 181, 182, 187
Polynices, 51
Plutarch, 63, 132–7 *passim*, 140, 152, 154
Pluto, 216; *see also* Hades
pollution, xvi, 20, 48, 51, 58, 230; *see also*
    purity, purification
Pollux, 195

Polyclitus, 177, 178
polytheism, 43, 98
Porphyry, 55
Poseidon, xvii, xviii, 18, 26, 29, 36, 42, 45, 153, 175, 179, 195
possession, xiv, 10, 11; *see also* prophets
pottery, Attic, 182–5
Praxiteles, 177
prayer, 14–16, 22, 28–9, 40, 44–5, 110, 120, 195, 198
Pre-Socratics, 196–9
Priam, 51
Priene, 74–6, 77 fig.6
priests, priesthood, xv–xvi, 7, 17, 34, 42, 69, 92, 95, 131, 134, 177, 193, 194
Proagōn, 120
processions, xvii, xviii, 35, 37, 42, 53, 71, 90, 98, 99, 103, 120, 176, 184, 223 n.13
Prodicus, 203–5, 216
Prometheus, 18, 33, 195
prophets, prophecy, 28, 129, 134, 135, 137–9, 141–2, 147, 149; *see also* Delphi, oracles, possession, Teiresias
Protagoras, xx, 201–3, 205, 210, 214, 216
Ptolemies, 155
punishment after death, 54, 57–64 *passim*
purity, purification, xvi, 41, 48, 59, 61, 90, 96, 144, 145, fig.32
Pythagoras of Samos, 61, 182, 185
Pythia, 7, 12, 97, 129, 131, 132–54 *passim*
Pythian games, xviii, 96, 103; *see also* Delphi
Pythian Odes, Pindar, 112
Pythios, architect, 76
Pythochrestoi, 144
Pythomantis Hestia, 97

Quintilian, 81

reincarnation, 61, 62, 63, 64
Rhadamanthys, 54, 60, 187
Rhegion, 114
Rhombos, 167, 168, 169, 176
ritual, 1, 2, 7, 8, 14, 16–24 *passim*, 25, 35–8 *passim*, 43, 50, 52, 57, 58, 59, 62, 69, 87, 98, 99, 100, 106, 121, 122, 141, 159, 184, 185, 194, 195, 217
Rome, xvi, 115, 154, 157, 164, 165, 176

Sabbath, 19
Sacred Disease, On the, 206
Sacred Way, 96, 128 fig.26, 130 fig.27

sacred writings, xiv, 35, 193–4
sacrifice, xv, xvii–xviii, 14, 16–19, 21, 27, 35, 36, 55, 68, 69, 72, 90, 96, 98, 99, 100, 101, 102, 103, 106, 110, 111, 116, 117, 134, 137, 159, 184, 194, 217
Salamis, 147, 148, 153
Samos, 70–2, 78, 160, 166, 177
Samothrace, 195
sanctuaries, 48, 67, 87, 91, 92, 95, 96, 129, 130–1, 151, 154, 158, 171, 173, 176, 177, 178, 179; *see also* shrines, temples
Saracens, 84
Scamander, 204
scepticism, xx, 132, 150–4, 191–218 *passim*; *see also* atheism
sculpture, 158–78, 179, 180, 181; *see also* statues
Scythians, 12–13, 23, 61
Seasons *see* Horae
secularization, 102, 103, 175
Segesta, 84–5
Seleucus, 189
Selinus, 84, 85–7
Semele, 47
shrines, xvii, xix, 111, 114, 174, 181, 194, 217, 220 n.12, 223 n.13, 230 n.29; *see also* oracles, sanctuaries, temples
Sibylline books, xiv
Sicily, 74, 84–7, 102, 114, 192, 196, 201, 202, 215, 216
Sicyon, 151
Silver Age, 55
Simois, 204
Simonides, 214
singing, 41, 46, 117, 119, 122–3; *see also* hymns, music, paeans
Siphnians, 149, 178
Sisyphus, 60, 210
Skira festival, 22, 101
Skiron, 174
Socrates, xiii, xv, xx, 62–3, 65, 193, 207–9, 211–14, 216, 217, 230 n.27
Solon, 32, 52, 90
soothsayers, xvi; *see also* oracles, prophets
Sophists, 152–3, 193–218
Sophocles, 11, 28, 30–2, 45, 48, 49, 51, 120, 123, 124, 173, 200
Sosinos of Gortyn, 171
Sōteira (Persephone), 39
soul, spirit, 50–1, 60–5, 141
Sparta, Spartans, 12–13, 56, 99, 114, 115, 116, 134, 136, 142, 144, 146, 148–9,

152, 154, 161, 170, 171
181, 192, 225 n.17
Sphinx, 31
spirit *see* soul
spirits, xiv; *see also* daimon
statues, 35, 69, 71, 78–81,
120, 135, 155, 159–60,
stoas, 72, 92, 174, 179–80, 181
Stoa Basileios, 174
Stoa Poikilē, 179
Stoa of Zeus, 174, 179
Strabo, 81
Styx, 52
Sudan, 133–4; *see also* Azande, Dinka
Sulla, 165
Sunium, Cape, xvii, 212
supplication, 21; *see also* prayer
Sybaris, 201
Syracuse, 170
Syria, 189

Talthybius, patron hero of heralds, 12
Tantalus, 60
Taras (Tarentum, Taranto), 114, 172, 185,
187, 229 n.19
technology, 6
Tegea, 149, 175
Teiresias, 30–1, 53
Tektaios, 165, 178
Telemachus, 8
Telesterion, Eleusis, xvi, 87–9 figs. 14, 15;
see also Eleusis
temenos, 160, 167, 170, 173, 174, 176, 177,
181
temples, xv, xvi–xvii, 67–97, 173–9 *passim*,
194; *see also* sanctuaries, shrines, *and
names of individual deities and places*
Testaments, Old and New, 8
Thales, 196
Thasos, 174
Theagenes of Thasos, 111
theatre, theatres *see* drama, festivals
Thebes, 31, 55, 165, 223 n.13, 228 n.14
Themis, 138 fig.31
Themistocles, 147–8
theology, 7, 8, 36, 43–4, 61, 143, 219 n.6
Thera, 146, 150, 151
Thermon, 73
Thermopylae, 144
Theseus, 28–9, 56, 96, 138 fig. 31, 174,
179, 230 n.27
Thesmophoria, 101, 204

144, 185, 187,
195, 197, 201
Thrasymachus, 202, 203
Thucydides, xvi, xx, 2, 6, 84, 116, 154,
192, 202
Timoleon, 170
Timotheus, 177
tombs, tombstones, 53, 55, 57, 68, 158–9,
165, 169, 171, 172, 178, 185, 187; *see
also* graves
Tiryns, 68
Titans, 33, 40–1, 62, 64, 65
Tithonus, 54
Tityus, 60
Trapezous (Trebizond, Trabzon), 99
Triptolemus, 59, 60
Troy, Trojans, Trojan War, 8, 55, 179, 181
Twelve Gods, 179
Tychē, 189, 190; *see also* Fate
Tyrant-slayers, 176

Underworld, 37, 57, 58, 59, 60, 88, 181–2,
187; *see also* after-life, Hades

vase-painting, 182–5
Victory *see* Nikē
victory odes *see* epinikia
votive offerings, 81–2

Xanthias, in *Frogs*, 39
Xenophanes, xx, 2, 32, 40–1, 61, 196–7,
203, 222 nn.11, 12
Xenophon, xx, 63, 117, 152
Xerxes, 12, 144

Zeno of Elea, 198
Zeus: Alexander as, 187; arbitrates in race
of Pelops and Oenomaos, 78; in *Clouds*,
21–3; and Delphic oracle, 147, 148; at
Dodona, 48; god of thunder and lightning, 47–8; as head of Olympians, 24,
26, 62; Herkeios, 222 n.12; in Hesiodic
succession myth, 25; in *Homeric Hymn to
Apollo*, 46; Ktesios, 194; mind of, 47;
Oeta sacred to, 48; at Olympia, xvii,

xviii, 4   Dionysus, 62; the
109, fig   and Semele, 47; sons
176, 19   , 26, 78, 80 fig.9, 111,
n.9, 22   ens, 174, 179
Persephc